The Best of the Frontier Guardian

Documents in Latter-day Saint History

An imprint of BYU Studies

Brigham Young University
Provo, Utah

The Best of the Frontier Guardian

Susan Easton Black

BYU Studies
Provo, Utah
and
University of Utah Press
Salt Lake City

Distributed to the academic trade and libraries by University of Utah Press,
www.UofUpress.com

This volume is part of the BYU Studies series
Documents in Latter-day Saint History

Other volumes in this series:
Opening the Heavens: Accounts of Divine Manifestations, 1820–1844
Exemplary Elder: The Life and Missionary Diaries of Perrigrine Sessions, 1814–1893
The Personal Writings of Joseph Smith, rev. ed.
Eliza R. Snow: The Complete Poems
Mountain Meadows Massacre: The Andrew Jenson and David H. Morris Collections

Cover design by Robert E. M. Spencer and Bruce Patrick
Steel engraving of Kanesville, Iowa, by Frederick Piercy c. 1850s and photograph of Orson Hyde, both courtesy Church History Library

Library of Congress Cataloging-in-Publication Data

The best of The frontier guardian / [edited by] Susan Easton Black.
p. cm. — (Documents in Latter-day Saint history)
ISBN 978-0-8425-2740-8 (pbk. : alk. paper)
1. Church of Jesus Christ of Latter-day Saints—Missouri River Valley—History--19th century. 2. Mormons—Missouri River Valley--History—19th century. 3. Missouri River Valley—Church history—19th century. I. Black, Susan Easton. II. Frontier guardian. III. Series: Documents in Latter-day Saint history.

BX8611.B37 2009
289.3'7809034--dc22

2009027878

Printed in the United States of America
10 9 8 7 6 5 4 3 2 1

Contents

Exploring the Latter-day Saint Experience at the Missouri, 1849–1851

Susan Easton Black

As the largest Mormon primary source from 1849 to 1851, the *Frontier Guardian* is crucial to understanding the Latter-day Saint experience at the Missouri River. Until now, historians have extracted only small sections of the paper, such as marriage announcements, obituaries, and advertisements,[1] because of the *Guardian*'s size. Although it is only four volumes, the newspaper contains eighty-one issues, each spanning four pages in length and divided into six columns. This translates into roughly four thousand single-spaced pages on 8.5 x 11″ paper. Fortunately, the recent publication *The Best of the Frontier Guardian* along with its searchable DVD-ROM of all eighty-one issues will help researchers explore the Mormon experience in Pottawattamie County, Iowa.

As the *Guardian*'s editor in chief, Elder Orson Hyde believed the newspaper was an essential tool to help the region's Saints remain focused on their westward trek. Although he occasionally visited Church branches, Hyde knew regular communication between ecclesiastical leaders and members was imperative. Since ecclesiastical leaders previously had used newsprint to connect with members in Missouri, Ohio, Illinois, and England, he employed the same medium in Iowa.

1. See Lyndon W. Cook, comp., *Death and Marriage Notices from the "Frontier Guardian," 1849–1852* (Orem, Utah: Center for Research of Mormon Origins, 1990).

Hyde looked to the first five Church periodicals—*The Evening and the Morning Star, Latter Day Saints' Messenger and Advocate, Elders' Journal of the Church of Latter Day Saints, Times and Seasons,* and *Millennial Star*—as examples for the *Guardian.* He utilized this newspaper foremost as a Church oracle, publishing First Presidency epistles, doctrinal treatises, and news and letters from the Salt Lake Valley before printing local news, poetry, wise sayings, or fictional stories. A brief history of Mormon newspapers places the *Guardian* in context, and an account of Hyde's appointment to preside over the Pottawattamie area, a historical overview of the *Guardian*, and an analysis of its contents introduce readers to this important source.

History of Latter-day Saint Newspapers

The first Church newspaper was *The Evening and the Morning Star* edited by William W. Phelps and published in Independence, Missouri. Religious doctrine, history, hymns, instruction, revelation, and missionary letters kept the Saints informed. From June 1832 to July 1833, this eight-page, double-columned paper was applauded by its Latter-day Saint readership as informative and inspiring. However, a mob soon destroyed the press and what it believed was the last issue of the *Star*. In some respects, the paper survived the attack. In distant Kirtland, Ohio, under the able editorship of Oliver Cowdery, issues of the *Star* were printed in 1833. Cowdery reprinted previous issues, believing they had not had a wide circulation among the eastern Saints. He also ended up adding ten issues of his own to this Ohio edition. Differences between the final issues and the preceding ones were the inclusion of a commentary describing the problems faced by the Saints in Missouri, a new sixteen-page format, and fewer grammatical errors.[2]

In 1834 the *Star* was succeeded by the *Latter Day Saints' Messenger and Advocate*, a paper whose very name suggested its purpose—a messenger of the restored gospel and an advocate of true principles. Under Cowdery's leadership, the first issues of the *Messenger and Advocate* were printed from October 1834 to May 1835. Cowdery was replaced by John Whitmer and Warren Cowdery, then in February and March 1837 by Joseph Smith and Sidney Rigdon. Although the paper had multiple editors, neither its purpose nor its tenor changed. In a sixteen page, double-column format, the paper contained selected doctrinal addresses, letters from traveling missionaries, inspirational poetry, hymns, minutes of Church conferences, and local events, such as marriages and deaths. The newspaper reported 8 births, 242 marriages, and 195 deaths. The new

2. See Ronald D. Dennis, "The Evening and the Morning Star," in *Encyclopedia of Mormonism*, ed. Daniel H. Ludlow, 4 vols. (New York: Macmillian, 1992): 2:477.

twist that did not mirror old issues of the *Star* was the inclusion of an annual index printed in the last issue of each volume.[3]

In late 1837, nearly four months after the final issue of the *Messenger and Advocate,* another Mormon newspaper came into existence. The *Elders' Journal of the Church of Latter Day Saints,* with Joseph Smith as editor and Thomas B. Marsh as publisher, began publication in Kirtland. Although the concept of an Elders' journal had merit—to keep traveling elders informed of Church business—after only two issues (October–November 1837) printing of the paper stopped. Its small run in Kirtland was repeated in Far West, Missouri, where two additional issues were printed, before the paper again ceased publication.[4]

In many respects, the next paper, the *Times and Seasons,* was much more successful than other Church periodicals. The print run of 135 issues symbolized the success. Similar to its predecessors, the sixteen page, double-column paper contained Church doctrine, history, local events, missionary letters, minutes of meetings, as well as general contemporary news. The paper was printed monthly in Nauvoo between November 1839 and October 1840. After that it became a biweekly publication, appearing on the first and fifteenth of each month through February 15, 1846. The first editors were Don Carlos Smith and Ebenezer Robinson. In 1842, Joseph Smith became the next editor. Under his editorship, documents such as the translation and facsimiles of the Book of Abraham and the Wentworth Letter were published. Between late 1842 and May 1844 John Taylor and Wilford Woodruff co-edited the paper. Then from June 1844 until mid-February 1846 Taylor worked as the sole editor.[5]

The *Latter-day Saints' Millennial Star* was the fifth newspaper to be recognized as an official organ of the Church. The *Star* began in England in 1840 with Parley P. Pratt as editor and continued publication until 1970. Pratt

---

3. See J. Leroy Caldwell, "Messenger and Advocate," in Ludlow, *Encyclopedia of Mormonism,* 2:892.

4. See Kirtland Elders' Quorum Record, 1826–1844, December 6, 1837, Church History Library, Family and Church History Department, The Church of Jesus Christ of Latter-day Saints, Salt Lake City.

5. See Reed C. Durham Jr., "Times and Seasons," in Ludlow, *Encyclopedia of Mormonism,* 4:1479–80; Robert T. Bray, "'Times and Seasons': An Archaeological Perspective on Early Latter Day Saints Printing," *Historical Archaeology* 13 (1979): 53–119; Parry D. Sorensen, "Nauvoo Times and Seasons," *Journal of the Illinois State Historical Society* 55 (1962): 117–35. The *Nauvoo (IL) Times and Seasons* should not be confused with The *Nauvoo (IL) Neighbor,* a weekly newspaper published from May 3, 1843, to October 29, 1845, and edited by John Taylor. This paper was not an official Church publication but rather was a replacement for the *Nauvoo (IL) Wasp,* which had begun in April 1842. The *Neighbor* was not altogether without Latter-day Saint news, however. Taylor printed articles about conflicts between the Saints and what he perceived as their enemies at all levels of society. See Darwin L. Hayes, "Nauvoo Neighbor," in Ludlow, *Encyclopedia of Mormonism,* 3:999.

unabashedly announced that the purpose of the *Star* was to proclaim the restoration of the gospel of Jesus Christ and to gather into one fold his sheep:

> The long night of darkness is now far spent.... It has pleased the Almighty to send forth an HOLY ANGEL, to restore the fulness of the gospel with all its attendant blessings, to bring together his wandering sheep into one fold, to restore to them "the faith which was once delivered to the saints," ... [and] to prepare all who will hearken for the Second Advent of Messiah, which is now near at hand.[6]

To accomplish this far-reaching purpose, Pratt and his many subsequent editors printed doctrinal addresses of Church leaders and excerpts of the history of the Church. The inclusion of conference minutes, missionary letters, local news, and poems mirrored the content of other Church periodicals.[7] The dramatic difference with the *Star* was the inclusion of emigration statistics, news of the Perpetual Emigrating Fund, ship departures, and so forth. By including similar information about emigration train rosters and departures, the *Frontier Guardian* mirrored the *Star* more closely than any other early Mormon periodical.

Orson Hyde and the *Frontier Guardian*

In 1848 hundreds of Mormons heeded President Brigham Young's advice to cross the Missouri River from Winter Quarters and settle in Pottawattamie County, Iowa, as they prepared to travel to the Salt Lake Valley. Young appointed Hyde to oversee the Saints residing on the eastern side of the Missouri.[8] At the time, neither man realized thousands of Saints would migrate from every state in the Union and from across the Atlantic Ocean to reach Pottawattamie County.

Hyde was baptized in October 1831 by Sidney Rigdon. Hyde served a series of missions, preaching the good news with such famed Latter-day Saint leaders as Hyrum Smith and Hyrum's brother Samuel. With Joseph Smith and many others, Hyde participated in Zion's Camp in hopes of assisting the exiled Saints to regain their lands in Jackson County, Missouri. As a member of the Quorum of the Twelve Apostles, Hyde proselyted in Great Britain and was one of the first missionaries to a European country.[9]

---

6. "Prospectus," *Latter-day Saints' Liverpool (Eng.) Millennial Star,* May 1840, 1.

7. See Stanley A. Peterson, "Millennial Star," in Ludlow, *Encyclopedia of Mormonism,* 2:906; James P. Hill, "Story of the Star," *Millennial Star* December 1970, 10–13.

8. Hyde's counselors were George A. Smith and Ezra T. Benson. "Conference Minutes," *Kanesville (IA) Frontier Guardian,* May 2, 1849, p. 1, col. 4.

9. Howard H. Barron, "Orson Hyde," in Ludlow, *Encyclopedia of Mormonism,* 2:665–67.

Steel engraving by Frederick Piercy of the Missouri River in Council Bluffs, Iowa, c. 1850s. Courtesy Church History Library.

Yet his commitment to the Church and its leaders wavered during the Missouri persecutions in 1838. A slanderous affidavit signed by him tipped the pen of Governor Lilburn W. Boggs, and in its wake severe persecution of the Saints went unchecked in Missouri. For the affidavit and the persecution that attended it, Hyde was dropped from the Quorum of the Twelve in spring 1839. Of his sorrow over his own untoward actions, he wrote, "Few men pass through life without leaving some traces which they would gladly obliterate. Happy is he whose life is free from stain and blemish.... I sinned against God and my brethren; I acted foolishly.... I seek pardon of all whom I have offended, and also of my God."[10] Joseph Smith pardoned Hyde, and on June 27, 1839, he was reinstated as a member of the Twelve.[11]

With new resolve, he followed Joseph Smith's counsel and direction. For example, over the next few years Hyde filled a mission to dedicate Jerusalem for the prophesied return of the Jews and he traveled to Washington, D.C., to present a memorial summarizing the outrages of the state of Missouri against Latter-day Saints. Although this last assignment was a difficult reminder of his role in that persecution, Hyde did as he was instructed. While on that errand,

10. Joseph Smith Jr., *The History of the Church of Jesus Christ of Latter-day Saints*, ed. B. H. Roberts, 2nd ed. rev., 7 vols. (Salt Lake City: Deseret Book, 1971), 3:167–68; Orson Hyde, "History of Orson Hyde," *Millennial Star*, December 10, 1864, 792.

11. Barron, "Orson Hyde," 2:666.

Orson Hyde served as editor in chief of the Frontier Guardian, *president of the Quorum of the Twelve, and president of the Church in Kanesville. He believed the* Guardian *was essential to helping Saints in Iowa stay focused on their westward trek to the Salt Lake Valley. Courtesy Church History Library.*

on June 27, 1844, "he felt very heavy and sorrowful in spirit, and knew not the cause.... He retired to the further end of the hall alone, and walked the floor; tears ran down his face.... He never felt so before, and knew no reason why he should feel so then."[12] Days later he learned of the Prophet's martyrdom, which he believed had caused this sorrow. Although the loss of Joseph Smith weighed heavily on Hyde for many years, he spoke optimistically of the Church's destiny: "I will prophesy that instead of the work dying, it will be like the mustard stock that was ripe, that a man undertook to throw out of his garden, and scattered seed all over it, and next year it was nothing but mustard. It will be so by shedding the blood of the Prophets—it will make ten saints where there is one now."[13]

After his return to Nauvoo, Hyde saw the fulfillment of his prophesy. New converts arrived almost daily in the community, eager to help build up the Church. The Saints needed a shepherd to assist them as they prepared to continue their journey to a westward Zion. Although he wanted to follow Brigham Young to the West, Hyde accepted a call to stay behind in Nauvoo to complete and dedicate the Nauvoo Temple and encourage even the most reluctant Saints to push westward. History repeated itself when Young asked Hyde to fulfill similar duties in Iowa two years later. Rather than lasting only a few months, as had his assignment in Nauvoo, Hyde's work in Iowa lasted roughly four years.[14] Mormon emigration, establishing temporary settlements, organizing the Church structure within those settlements, keeping peace with the Native Americans, and bolstering the faith of the Saints in this frontier setting were but a few of his main responsibilities. Such responsibilities would have been difficult for a team of people, let alone one man. But Hyde had the organizational

12. Smith, *History of the Church*, 7:132.

13. Smith, *History of the Church*, 7:198.

14. See Howard H. Barron, *Orson Hyde: Missionary, Apostle, Colonizer* (Bountiful, Utah: Horizon, 1977), 163, 178–95.

skills and the "loyalty and devotion to Brigham Young" needed to keep the Iowa Saints focused on their westward journey.[15]

Young had chosen Hyde to gather the scattered Saints of Iowa because he was familiar with the land, having named the center of the Pottawattamies, Kanesville—in honor of Thomas L. Kane in April 1848.[16] Hyde had traveled up and down the mid-Missouri Valley, speaking to Saints scattered throughout the small communities. Hyde was a father figure to many as he offered encouragement and advice to those headed west. Third, he had experience settling Church business and aiding migration. As historian Richard E. Bennett said, "With Young and most of the authorities now in Salt Lake Valley, it was once again left to Hyde, as had been done earlier in Nauvoo, to complete unfinished business, settle conflicts and defections, and facilitate migrations westward."[17] Hyde

Thomas Leiper Kane befriended the Latter-day Saints and became a confidant to Brigham Young. Orson Hyde named the Pottawattamie County Mormon settlement Kanesville in honor of Kane. In 1853, Kanesville was renamed Council Bluffs. Courtesy Church History Library.

15. Marvin S. Hill, "An Historical Study of the Life of Orson Hyde, Early Mormon Missionary and Apostle from 1805–1852" (master's thesis, Brigham Young University, 1955), 3.

16. Journal History of the Church, April 8, 1848, Church History Library, also available on *Selected Collections from the Archives of The Church of Jesus Christ of Latter-day Saints,* 2 vols. (Provo, Utah: Brigham Young University Press, 2002) vol. 2, DVD 2, microfilm copy in Harold B. Lee Library, Brigham Young University, Provo, Utah.

17. Richard E. Bennett, *Mormons at the Missouri, 1846–1852: "And Should We Die..."* (Norman: University of Oklahoma Press, 1987), 220. The *Davenport (IA) Gazette* pronounced Hyde the successor of Joseph Smith: "Orson Hyde, it is rumored, is about to become the successor of Joe Smith. Whether he claims the leadership by revelation from heaven, does not appear. But no doubt he will appeal to their superstitions." "Mormonism," *Davenport Gazette,* May 1, 1845, 2. The *Bloomington Iowa Democratic Enquirer* editorialized, "The celebrated Orson Hyde, by far the most influential man in the Mormon church." "Mormon Vote," *Iowa Democratic Enquirer,* August 26, 1846, 2. The *Keokuk (IA) Dispatch* printed, "Orson Hyde is another of the Twelve, and head of the Colony at Council Bluff." "The Mormon Bribery," *Keokuk Dispatch,* September 16, 1848, 2.

accomplished much of his work through the *Frontier Guardian.* On February 7, 1849, its first issue rolled off the press as an official Church publication.[18]

Overview of the *Frontier Guardian*

Assuming his position as editor, Hyde confessed, "It is with a trembling hand and a faltering knee that we step forward to our seat in the Editorial Chair."[19] Nevertheless, Hyde frequently used the *Guardian* to vent his frustrations and disappointments, and an overview of the paper says as much about the editor as it does about the paper itself. It reveals Hyde's need for money, his assistants' unscrupulous tactics, and his transition from printing an official Church newspaper to a secular publication.

Volume One. As the editor of a newspaper that would be distributed in most of the twenty-six states of the Union and in England, Wales, Ireland, France, Italy, and Denmark, it was Hyde's "ardent wish, and sincere prayer that the words we employ, and thoughts we record may be the dictation of that Spirit, that is destined to bless the world, make an end of sin and triumph gloriously over all things." To accomplish the ambitious goal, he wrote a prospectus that outlined the paper's objectives: (1) to conspicuously display principles of the gospel, (2) to maintain a "healthy moral atmosphere," (3) to aid the education of youth, (4) to avoid political interference, (5) to appeal to all classes of

---

18. Editors of the *Fairfield Iowa Sentinel* expressed concern over what they perceived was a "Mormon–Whig" newspaper to be published in Kanesville, Iowa: "Mr. Orson Hyde has issued a prospectus for a semi-monthly paper to be published at Kanesville, Council Bluffs, Iowa, to be called the 'Frontier Guardian.' Terms $2,00 per annum in advance. This new Mormon–Whig paper will owe its existence to Fitz Warren's letter introducing Orson Hyde to friends in the east 'who had the ability to give him aid.'" "New Paper," *Iowa Sentinel,* October 13, 1848, 2. Editors of the *Dubuque (IA) Weekly Miners' Express* claimed the press on which the *Frontier Guardian* was published was financed by the Whig party: "The Republican, of St. Louis, announces the shipping of a 'Printing Press,' and printing material, from that city, for Council Bluffs, or Kanesville, Iowa. This is the celebrated *press* obtained as the price of corruption, for giving the Mormon vote to the Whig party, in August last. A paper is to be established at one of the above places, by the notorious *Orson Hyde,* to be called the '*Frontier Guardian.*' The 'latter day saints' are now recognized as the legitimate allies of Whiggery; and thus furnished by them with the powerful assistance of a printing press may be expected to promulgate the elegant compund formed by a union of the principles of Zachary Taylor and Jo. Smith." "The Mormon Press—Their Vote," *Weekly Miners' Express,* October 17, 1848, 2. Hyde countered the claim. In fall 1848, he was offered a free printing press provided the Saints would endorse Democrat Lewis Cass in his bid for President of the United States. As a supporter of Zachery Taylor, Hyde refused to support Democrat Cass, press or no press.

19. "To Our Readers," *Frontier Guardian,* February 7, 1849, p. 2, col. 1.

citizens, and (6) to advertise businesses and prices that would help the Saints emigrate.[20]

On March 7, 1849, Hyde's counselor George A. Smith encouraged Church members to subscribe to the paper: "Every Elder should have the Guardian by him; from it he can learn the principles, which it is his duty and calling to communicate to his fellow men." He added, "Every farmer [also] should take the Guardian. Its matter will instruct the young and inexperienced, in relation to their agricultural pursuits."[21]

George A. Smith was a member of the Quorum of the Twelve and a counselor to Orson Hyde in the Kanesville presidency. Courtesy Church History Library.

Confident that Smith's directives would lead to increased subscriptions, Hyde announced on March 21 that the *Guardian* would become a weekly newspaper.[22] Yet such preparations never materialized. To help fill the *Guardian*'s pages, Hyde depended on mail carriers for newspapers from other cities. In this era, newspapers frequently reprinted stories from other publications; when carriers failed to bring the needed papers, Hyde could not publish a weekly newspaper because of lack of material.

This dilemma, exacerbated by the need of an expert printer, caused Hyde much duress until he hired printer John Gooch Jr. in May 1849.[23] With Gooch in place, Hyde was relieved from the daily work at the Guardian office to attend to ecclesiastical matters. However, when Gooch printed statements such as "The lack of Editorial matter in this number must be attributed to

20. "To Our Readers."

21. "To the Saints in Iowa," *Frontier Guardian,* March 7, 1849, p. 2, col. 5.

22. Orson Hyde, "Prospectus," *Frontier Guardian,* March 21, 1849, p. 4, col. 6.

23. John Gooch Jr. was born in Concord, Massachusetts, worked as a printer on the *Frontier Guardian*, ran a boarding house, sold building lots, and journeyed to the Salt Lake Valley in 1852. See the annotated list of people mentioned in the newspaper on the *Frontier Guardian* DVD-ROM. Gooch is first listed as the printer of the *Guardian* on page 2 of the May 30, 1849, issue.

THE FRONTIER GUARDIAN.

BY ORSON HYDE. KANESVILLE, IOWA, WEDNESDAY MORNING, FEBRUARY 7, 1849. VOLUME I.---NUMBER 1.

Original masthead of the Frontier Guardian.

the continued absence of the Editor," Hyde returned.[24] On December 12 the paper reported the hiring of Daniel MacIntosh[25] as an assistant editor to help shoulder the responsibility.[26]

Hyde hoped MacIntosh could make the *Guardian* a weekly publication, yet Hyde continued to worry about the late mail. He solicited friends, even from abroad, to send him "a few papers when you have the chance."[27] In addition, he also asked for money to help defray the expense of printing the *Guardian* because many subscribed, but few paid a full subscription rate. Hoping to resolve what had become a personal financial drain to him, on December 12 Hyde announced a change in delivery: instead of distributing the papers to subscribers through an agent, he dropped them off at the individual post offices where subscribers could retrieve them and pay their postage.[28] Then he asked that commodities be brought, without hope of compensation, to the Guardian office. Hyde specifically requested "pork, beef, … cash or California Gold Dust" and "10,000 feet good lumber at $2[.]00 per hundred.… Besides cheese, eggs, chickens."[29]

Volume Two. On February 6, 1850, Hyde boasted that one year had lapsed since the *Guardian* first came off the press and that it had never "been delayed an hour behind its regular time." He expressed gratitude to printer John Gooch, "whose long and bony fingers can pick up type as fast as a chicken can pick up corn." Then, in salesmanlike fashion, Hyde asked, "Who, among the Saints, will raise up a family of children without giving them education, the bible, and the *Guardian*?" "You who feel too poor to subscribe for the Guardian, just ask yourselves how much money you pay out for comparatively useless

24. "The lack of editorial matter…," *Frontier Guardian,* October 3, 1849, p. 2, col. 1.

25. Daniel MacIntosh served as an agent and editor of the *Frontier Guardian*. See the annotated list of agents mentioned in the newspaper on the *Frontier Guardian* DVD-ROM.

26. Daniel MacKintosh, "Response," *Frontier Guardian,* December 12, 1849, p. 2, col. 1. MacIntosh's name was spelled several different ways in the newspaper.

27. "Request," *Frontier Guardian,* November 14, 1849, p. 2, col. 4.

28. "To Our Agents," *Frontier Guardian,* December 12, 1849, p. 2, col. 3.

29. "Wanted in Exchange for the Guardian," *Frontier Guardian,* November 14, 1849, p. 3, col. 4; "Wanted on Subscription for the Guardian," *Frontier Guardian,* September 5, 1849, p. 2, col. 1.

things."[30] He also invited loyal subscribers to attend a printer's banquet, with the proceeds benefiting the *Guardian* staff. Although the banquet was profitable, the financial woes of the paper remained apparent.[31] Hyde wrote, "A failure to give notice of a wish to discontinue the paper at the expiration of the term subscribed for, will be considered as an engagement for the next year," and "Advertisements not marked on the copy for a [definite] period, or a distinct number of insertions, will be continued until ordered out, and payment exacted accordingly."[32] Believing this fiscal policy would solve the money problems, Hyde left Kanesville in June for the Salt Lake Valley at Brigham Young's request.[33]

In Hyde's absence, Gooch and MacIntosh published the *Guardian* as usual. Although neither held a Church leadership position, they continued Hyde's clarion call to repent. Using the *Guardian*, they rebuked those who entertained company on Sunday and claimed that "idleness [was] a crime next akin to stealing."[34] To James Allred, president of the Pottawattamie High Council, such unsolicited advice overstepped Gooch and MacIntosh's ecclesiastical bounds. Allred insisted that columns in the *Guardian* be made available for his advice. Gooch and MacIntosh hesitated before printing one brief statement by Allred: "It was not wisdom for the Saints to go forth in the dance" before they pray, help the poor, and pay tithing.[35]

Another peculiarity of the Gooch and MacIntosh publishing efforts was their multiple requests for remuneration. For example, they wrote in one issue: "Wanted—Flour, meal, . . . to keep the printers from going hungry. Don't forget the cash to buy clothing."[36] After Gooch and MacIntosh had used such tactics for months, some readers questioned Hyde's judgment in giving the two men responsibility for the paper. Others wondered whether Hyde would return to Kanesville and reclaim his rightful place as editor in chief.

---

30. "Punctuality," *Frontier Guardian,* February 6, 1850, p. 2, col. 3; "Question . . . ," *Frontier Guardian,* February 6, 1850, p. 2, col. 3; "Subscribe for the Guardian," *Frontier Guardian,* February 6, 1850, p. 2, col. 4.

31. "Printers Banquet," *Frontier Guardian,* February 20, 1850, p. 2, col. 6.

32. "A failure to give notice . . . ," *Frontier Guardian,* March 6, 1850, p. 2, col. 3.

33. "It is expected that Elder Hyde . . . ," *Frontier Guardian,* June 26, 1850, p. 2, col. 3.

34. "Sunday Visiting," *Frontier Guardian,* July 10, 1850, p. 2, col. 1; "Idleness," *Frontier Guardian,* July 10, 1850, p. 2, col. 5.

35. "A Word to the Saints in Pottawatamie County," *Frontier Guardian,* November 13, 1850, p. 2, col. 5.

36. "Wanted," *Frontier Guardian,* July 24, 1850, p. 2, col. 5. See also, "The man who would . . . ," *Frontier Guardian,* October 2, 1850, p. 1, col. 5; "Would you prosper . . . ," *Frontier Guardian,* October 2, 1850, p. 2, col. 2; "To Those Who Owe for the Guardian," *Frontier Guardian,* October 16, 1850, p. 2, col. 1.

When Hyde returned in November, a great celebration ensued. Following the festivities, Hyde went to the Guardian office and resumed his position. He implemented changes to the paper and reduced subscription rates to one dollar per year. More important, he announced that the paper would enter the political arena: "In politics we are decidedly [W]hig, and we intend still to maintain inviolate those principles, because we believe them to be the most productive of good to our favored country."[37] This announcement was a dramatic shift from earlier days when the Latter-day Saints were decidedly Democrats. Beginning in fall 1832, the Saints had endorsed Democrat Andrew Jackson's reelection. By November 1836, Oliver Cowdery, using the *Weekly Northern Times* in Kirtland, Ohio, had endorsed Democrat Martin Van Buren. Van Buren decidedly won in Kirtland, receiving 396 votes to only 116 for the Whig candidate. The *Northern Times*, edited by Oliver Cowdery and published by Frederick G. Williams, was referred to as the "Mormon Van Buren paper."[38]

By February 1840, the political shift from Democrat to Whig could be seen. Van Buren was no longer favored by the Latter-day Saints. Whig candidate William Henry Harrison had become a popular choice. But by 1844, the Saints again embraced a Democrat. They helped give James K. Polk of Tennessee a 54–42 percent victory over Whig candidate Henry Clay in the state of Illinois.[39]

By 1848 the political turf had once again shifted. Whig party leaders in Iowa came to Pottawattamie County to court the Mormon vote by promising "liberal collections through the whole state of Iowa" to aid the Saints.[40] Wanting to believe help possible, Orson Hyde said that if the Whigs would "swear by the Eternal Gods … that they will use all their powers to suppress mobocracy, insurrection, rebellion and violence … And that they will give to the Saints their full share in the choice of county, District, and State officers," then the Mormon vote would go to the "Whigs of Iowa at the elections" in

37. "End of the Second Volume," *Frontier Guardian*, January 22, 1851, p. 2, col. 2. Hyde's decision to favor the Whig party did not sit well with the editor of the *Keokuk Dispatch*. He reprinted a letter written by A. W. Babbitt to the editor of the *Statesman:* "Mr. Hyde announces himself a whig, (but not an ultra whig,) has no set notions, has never voted but once in his life, knows little or nothing about Federal and State policy, yet he assumes the responsibility of influencing a whole community; and lest he sh[o]uld betray ignorance as their guide, he directs them to a political knave to counsel them 'when and where to act.'" "The Mormon Bribery," *Keokuk Dispatch*, November 2, 1848, 2.

38. "Important," *Painesville (OH) Telegraph*, June 12, 1835, 3.

39. See Mark E. Byrnes, *James K. Polk: A Biographical Companion* (Santa Barbara, Calif.: ABC-CLIO, 2001), 139, as cited in Michael Kent Winder and Ron Brough, *Presidents and Prophets: The Story of America's Presidents and the LDS Church* (American Fork, Utah: Covenant Communications, 2007), 65.

40. Journal History of the Church, March 26, 1848, 1.

The Frontier Guardian.

BY ORSON HYDE. KANESVILLE, IOWA, FRIDAY MORNING, FEBRUARY 7, 1851. VOLUME III.----NUMBER 1.

The new masthead of the Frontier Guardian *debuted with the first issue of volume 3 in February 1851.*

1848.[41] Recognizing the importance of the Mormon vote to the Whigs, Hyde and Democrat Almon W. Babbitt met with Fitz Henry Warren, Chair of the Whig Executive Committee and other party leaders in Burlington, Iowa. At their meeting, Hyde expressed a willingness to support General Zachary Taylor for the presidential chair and shared his wishes to obtain a printing press. Whig leaders expressed an interest in aiding him in obtaining a press. Babbitt reacted to the Whig offer, by offering "a press on the spot" if Hyde would support the Democratic presidential candidate, Lewis Cass.[42] Hyde was not swayed by Babbitt's gesture. He wrote to the Iowa Saints, "It has seemed good to me, your Brother and companion in tribulation, and counsellor in the Church of God, to advise and request you to cast your votes at the ensuing election for the Whig candidates for office."[43] His letter led to allegations, especially those of Almon W. Babbitt, that Hyde had taken a bribe and traded the Mormon vote for a printing press.[44]

Volume Three. With these changes in place, the third volume was printed on February 7, 1851. To most subscribers, everything about this volume was new: masthead, political direction, even the publication day—Friday, which corresponded with the departure of the Kanesville mail. But the biggest change was the absence of a doctrinal treatise on page one; in its place were articles promoting temporal wealth. The content also shifted, with a three-to-one increase in the number of emigration articles.

Hyde hoped all these changes would help sell the paper prior to his permanent move west. On June 13, Hyde wrote, "This is probably the last article that we may write previous to our departure for [Salt Lake City]." He advised newspaper agents "that the vacancies occasion by those who may have left for the Valley be filled immediately. Therefore let each Township, or Branch of the Church, call a meeting, and elect by the vote of said meeting, a good man to receive and

41. Journal History of the Church, March 27, 1848, 5.
42. Journal History of the Church, April 5, 1849, 6.
43. Journal History of the Church, October 2, 1848, 7.
44. Hill, "Historical Study of the Life of Orson Hyde," 96. See note 18.

distribute the Guardian in their location."[45] However, Hyde left Kanesville on June 28, with an expected return date of October, even though he had not sold the paper. His departure this time was again in response to Brigham Young's request that he come to Salt Lake.[46]

During Hyde's absence, Gooch and MacIntosh were responsible for publishing the *Guardian*. They also were in charge of the new general store in the Guardian office. For sustenance they penned, "We are still in want of Wood to keep the Printers warm.... Our Devil [printer's assistant] says: if fuel for fire is not furnished him quickly, he will quit work." Then, unbeknown to Hyde, Gooch and MacIntosh increased the price of the yearly subscriptions by ten cents to $1.10. They also organized a contest, asking readers to bring the biggest vegetables to their office. Although subscribers may have balked at the increased rate, the contest was an immediate success. "Squash weighing sixty-four pounds" and "a Radish weighing four pounds and fourteen ounces" were brought to the office. "Who can beat these?" was the question asked in the next issue.[47] As if the contest were real, and not a trick to get food for the staff, more vegetables were brought. MacIntosh and Gooch reported this news of extraordinary vegetables while neglecting such important matters as minutes of an Church conference held in Kanesville.[48] To even the casual reader, the *Frontier Guardian* had changed again.

When Hyde returned to Kanesville, he did not express disdain at the past actions of Gooch and MacIntosh. Selling the *Guardian* and moving to the Salt Lake Valley was more important. For those who wondered if the newspaper would immediately cease publication, Hyde assured them, "We shall continue the publication of this paper until we remove" or sell.[49] With that said, Hyde announced that the portion of Pottawattamie County "owned and occupied by the Mormon population [was] for sale." To prospective buyers, he advised, "Now is the time for speculation and investment."[50] For those who called themselves Saints, a letter from the First Presidency advised them to purchase horses, mules, oxen, and wagons for the westward trek.[51]

45. "Warning," *Frontier Guardian*, June 13, 1851, p. 2, col. 1; "To Our Agents, and Others in this County," *Frontier Guardian*, June 13, 1851, p. 2, col. 3.

46. "Fifth General Epistle," *Frontier Guardian*, May 30, 1851, p. 1, col. 6.

47. "Wood! Wood!!" *Frontier Guardian*, October 17, 1851, p. 2, col. 3; "Some of the Products of Pottawatamie County," *Frontier Guardian*, October 17, 1851, p. 2, col. 3.

48. The conference was held October 6, 1851, but the minutes of the conference were not printed until the end of the month. "Conference Minutes," *Frontier Guardian*, October 31, 1851, p. 1, col. 5.

49. "Reminiscence," *Frontier Guardian*, November 14, 1851, p. 2, cols. 3–4.

50. "Pottowatamie County For Sale," *Frontier Guardian*, November 14, 1851, p. 2, col. 4.

51. "To all the Saints in Pottawatamie," *Frontier Guardian*, November 14, 1851, p. 2, col. 6.

Volume Four. The first two issues—two more than Hyde had planned—were printed as the *Frontier Guardian* before the name was changed to *Guardian and Sentinel.* These first two issues lacked articles on doctrine. Instead, articles appeared on the nation's capital, France, and England, coupled with an honorific poem extolling the past greatness of the *Frontier Guardian.*[52] The new direction of the paper and the attractive masthead succeeded in bringing an interested buyer. On February 20, 1852, Hyde announced the paper had been sold to attorney Jacob Dawson from Fremont County, Iowa.[53]

Analysis of the *Guardian*'s Content

Compared to other Mormon newspapers, the *Guardian*'s content was not unique in its approach to religious doctrine, Church news, day-to-day secular events, weather, politics, and business opportunities. However, the subject matter of the *Guardian* was unique because it was the Church's only newspaper at Kanesville that chronicled life in this way station for western emigration. And, like other nineteenth-century papers, the *Guardian* was a composite of exchanges or clippings and telegraph dispatches. Most of the national and international news, short fictional stories, pithy sayings, and humor were reprints from other publications.

The paper reflected the religious persuasion of its editor in chief and most of its readership. From the selection of newspaper agents, most of whom were also set apart as missionaries, to the lead article—a doctrinal treatise—the *Guardian* was a Mormon newspaper in Iowa. As such, Hyde believed it deserved a place in every Mormon home.[54] To help him circulate the paper among Church members, thirteen men were named in early 1849 as "missionary" newspaper agents.[55]

---

52. See North Pigeon Joe, "The Frontier Guardian," *Frontier Guardian,* February 6, 1852, p. 4, col. 1.

53. Under Dawson's leadership, the *Kanesville (IA) Guardian and Sentinel* featured "Politics, Literature, Arts, Sciences, and ... General news of the day." Politically, it remained Whig, but its columns were opened to discussion. In his final issue as editor, Hyde wrote, "We may scribble a little now and then for the Guardian and Sentinel to benefit, arrange, and order our emigration." "Prospectus for Publishing the Frontier Guardian and Iowa Sentinel Weekly," *Frontier Guardian,* February 20, 1852, p. 2, col. 5; "Valedictory," *Frontier Guardian,* February 20, 1852, p. 2, col. 3.

54. See, "Who that is a friend...," *Frontier Guardian,* February 7, 1849, p. 2, col. 5; "Suppose that every subscriber...," *Frontier Guardian,* February 21, 1849, p. 2, col. 4; "If a man...," *Frontier Guardian,* May 2, 1849, p. 2, col. 5; "Be kind...," *Frontier Guardian,* September 5, 1849, p. 1, col. 4.

55. The most renowned of the newspaper agents in Missouri was David Whitmer of Richmond. "Agents for the Guardian," *Frontier Guardian,* March 7, 1849, p. 2, col. 1.

During the first year of publication, agents were not called to labor in the Missouri Valley. This suggests first and foremost that they were expected to be proselyting missionaries, which confused the missionary/agents who failed to forward "money that is paid to [them] by subscribers for the Guardian."[56] Most missionary/agents had assumed subscription monies should offset mission expenses. Once this matter was resolved, more agents were called.[57]

It was not until January 1851 that Hyde sent agents to several former Mormon encampments in Pottawattamie County. By this time, however, these encampments were surveyed communities with a post office and an organized Church branch. Hyde assigned branch officers in these communities to select a "man to be your neighborhood Postmaster to receive the papers for you."[58] This action changed the status of missionary/agent to agent for those called to Pottawattamie County and put in place fifteen agents in the Missouri Valley by January. Almost one year later, the number of local agents had increased to twenty-eight. This brought the total number of agents, including local and those assigned throughout the United States and England, up to 109.[59]

Lead Articles. As an official Church publication and hoping to attract Latter-day Saint subscribers, Hyde printed lengthy doctrinal treatises that covered all six columns of page one. Although he was editor in chief and a member of the Quorum of the Twelve, he never featured his own doctrinal writings. Instead he often relied on Orson Pratt's writings that were first printed in the *Millennial Star*, because "a flood of testimony from the pen of Elder Pratt is poured upon the world, and if they can resist its clear and majestic current, it would really seem to us, that they possess more of a reckless opposition to the dictates of conscience, than of simple honesty of heart that is a pre-requisite to eternal life and salvation."[60]

Unfortunately, issues of the *Star* were not always available. Rather than delay publishing the *Guardian*, Hyde sometimes printed letters from prominent missionaries.[61] When such letters failed to arrive at the office, Hyde turned to

---

56. "Agency," *Frontier Guardian,* May 2, 1849, p. 2, col. 2.

57. See "Agents for the Guardian," *Frontier Guardian,* January 22, 1851, p. 1, col. 1; "Agents for the Guardian in this County," *Frontier Guardian,* January 22, 1851, p. 1, col. 1.

58. "Home Regulations," *Frontier Guardian,* June 13, 1849, p. 2, col. 5.

59. "Travel Agents," "Agents for the Guardian," "Agents for the Guardian in the County," *Frontier Guardian,* January 23, 1852, p. 1, col. 1. See the annotated list of newspaper agents mentioned in the newspaper on the *Frontier Guardian* DVD-ROM.

60. Orson Pratt, "The Question Answered, Was Joseph Smith Sent of God!" *Frontier Guardian,* February 21, 1849, p. 2, col. 1.

61. For example, on June 13, 1849, Hyde printed a letter from Elder Addison Pratt written in the Sandwich Islands. Addison Pratt, "Letter from Elder Addison Pratt," *Frontier Guardian,* June 13, 1849, p. 1, cols. 1–3. This was followed by letters from Elder Dan Jones in Wales, John Taylor in France, Lorenzo Snow in Italy, Erastus Snow

doctrinal treatises printed in earlier newspapers such as *Times and Seasons*, *Messenger and Advocate*, and *The Evening and the Morning Star*. Hyde sometimes quoted portions of the Doctrine and Covenants to fill the *Guardian*'s columns.

Joseph, Nauvoo, and Past Wrongs. Page two usually contained articles about Joseph Smith. Although the young Prophet had met a martyr's fate, his life, teachings, and struggles were never far from the thoughts of Hyde and other Church members.

Hoping to keep the memory of Joseph Smith in the forefront, Hyde informed readers of sundry events in old Nauvoo.[62] He took special interest in updates about the Nauvoo Temple[63] and in the widowed mother, Lucy Mack

---

in Denmark, and on October 31, 1849, a letter written by Hyrum Smith and Hyde in 1833. "The following letter…," *Frontier Guardian,* October 31, 1849, p. 1, cols. 5–6. Hyde explained that he would have included more letters had traveling missionaries come to the Guardian office like Elder Thomas McKenzie, who "has been on a mission to collect school books by donation for the education of our children in the Valley of the Salt Lake." "Elder Thomas McKenzie," *Frontier Guardian,* October 17, 1849, p. 2, col. 2.

62. Hyde was not the only editor reporting news from Nauvoo. For years, editors of local papers across Iowa had found any news of Nauvoo worth space in their columns. For example, the editor of the *Davenport Gazette* reported the repeal of the Nauvoo Charter and added, "We condemn the meanness which repealed the charter as much as we rejoice at its repeal." "Nauvoo Charters," *Davenport Gazette,* February 13, 1845. The *Des Moines Iowa Capital Reporter* reported disdain for the Mormons of Nauvoo: "The more we see and hear of these people the better we are convinced of the preponderance of rascality among them, in their communication with their neighbors.… Travellers now shun Nauvoo as they would a den of robbers." "The Mormons," *Iowa Capital Reporter,* November 5, 1845, 2. When rumors surfaced that Mormons were preparing to leave Nauvoo, the *Bloomington (IA) Herald* refuted the report: "Some persons apparently believe that the mass of Mormons are going to leave Nauvoo and vicinity in the spring. We have no such belief.… We will risk our judgment on this declaration." "Mormons," *Bloomington Herald,* February 21, 1846, 2. By May 1846, the *Herald* admitted, "Property of every description is sold at a great sacrifice in Nauvoo. Strangers are flocking in and locating there, and in a few weeks Nauvoo and the country around it will have an almost entire new population." "The Mormons," *Bloomington Herald,* May 8, 1846, 2. In the article "Mormon Troubles," the *Herald* printed news of the Mormon exodus and anti-Mormon sentiment: "From all accounts it is evident that the Mormons are leaving Nauvoo and vicinity with all possible haste, and yet the Anti-Mormons are not satisfied." See "Mormon Troubles," *Bloomington Herald,* June 19, 1846, 2. In "Later from Nauvoo," the *Iowa City Iowa Standard* of September 1846, reported: "The sick and invalid, it is said will be protected until means can be furnished for their removal. Thus it is hoped that the long protracted disturbances in our neighboring county, Hancock, is finally terminated." "Later from Nauvoo," *Iowa Standard,* September 23, 1846, 2.

63. See "Dreadful Tornado—Destruction of the Temple Walls," *Frontier Guardian,* July 24, 1850, p. 1, cols. 1–2.; "Night of Martyrdom," *Frontier Guardian,* June 27, 1849,

Smith, of the slain Prophet who "concluded to stay there and lay her bones with her husband and sons."[64]

News from Salt Lake Valley. News from the valley took precedence over local Church news.[65] The information came in three forms—First Presidency epistles, letters from ecclesiastical leaders, and news from traveling missionaries. To Hyde, however, the most reliable news came from epistles and letters.

Six general epistles of the First Presidency were printed verbatim in the *Guardian*. The first contained information about a city being built in the Salt Lake Valley and the return of the Mormon Battalion. The epistle also advised emigrants to be properly outfitted before heading to Zion.[66] The second epistle informed the Pottawattamie Saints of the status of the Perpetual Emigrating Fund.[67] The third contained news of settlements in Utah Valley and southern Utah. It also instructed leading elders to come quickly to the Salt Lake Valley.[68] The fourth epistle mentioned the establishment of other settlements to the north and new mission assignments,[69] while the fifth began with a brief history of the Church and encouraged emigration to Zion.[70] The final epistle assured the Pottawattamie Saints of Hyde's safe arrival in the valley and announced that the poor in Kanesville would be gathered to Zion.[71]

As for letters from Church leaders, "Some have thought it very hard and extortionate to be obliged to pay 40 cents postage on a letter from the Salt Lake [Valley] here," printed Hyde.[72] He urged payment, especially when the unclaimed letter was from a Church leader, for these letters often contained

---

p. 1, cols. 4–5; "Death of Joseph and Hyrum Smith," *Frontier Guardian*, June 27, 1849, p. 2, col. 3; "Nauvoo Temple," *Frontier Guardian*, June 27, 1849, p. 1, col. 3.

64. "Mother Smith," *Frontier Guardian*, November 14, 1849, p. 2, col. 1.

65. Statements such as "Much important matter had to be omitted, to give place to the news from the Great Salt Lake Valley" were commonplace in the *Guardian*. See, for example, "Much important matter . . . ," *Frontier Guardian*, May 30, 1849, p. 2, col. 2.

66. "First General Epistle . . . ," *Frontier Guardian*, May 30, 1849, p. 2, cols. 2–6.

67. "Important from Salt Lake City," *Frontier Guardian*, December 26, 1849, p. 1, cols. 1–4.

68. "Third General Epistle of the Presidency," *Frontier Guardian*, June 12, 1850, p. 2, col. 5–p. 3, col. 2.

69. "Fourth General Epistle of the Presidency," *Frontier Guardian*, December 11, 1850, p. 1, cols. 1–4.

70. "Fifth General Epistle," *Frontier Guardian*, May 30, 1851, p. 1, col. 2–p. 2, col. 1; "See the General Epistle on First Page," *Frontier Guardian*, May 30, 1851, p. 2, col. 3.

71. "Sixth General Epistle," *Frontier Guardian*, November 14, 1851, p. 1, col. 2–p. 2, col. 2.

72. "Salt Lake Postage," *Frontier Guardian*, March 7, 1849, p. 2, col. 2.

minutes of conferences held in Salt Lake City. Letters also contained descriptions of celebrations in the valley—July 24 being the most elaborate.[73]

Mormon Emigration to Salt Lake Valley. "Push the Saints to Zion, and pursuade all good brethren to come, who have a wheelbarrow, and faith enough to roll it over the mountains," wrote the First Presidency.[74] To those leaving Babylon, Hyde warned, "We say to all persons abroad, when you leave for this place, leave honorably, so that if you should be sent back to preach the gospel to your old neighbors, you would not be afraid or ashamed to meet them."[75] He also printed news of their departure aboard ships in Liverpool.[76]

With such a massive exodus underway, it is unsurprising that Kanesville became a major trailhead for Mormon emigrants. For some travelers, the community was more than a way station for the journey ahead. As they waited for grass to grow on the plains to sustain cattle and teams, these emigrants were schooled on commodities needed for the next leg of their journey: rifles, turkeys, geese, ducks, cows, coins, good teams, and good wagons.[77] After these trains were outfitted, the newspaper declared, "We hope to see trains starting from this point every week."[78] Hyde believed a spring launch was critical for a successful journey.[79] To facilitate migration, he printed the dates and places of expected departures.[80]

Often the size of the trains was larger than even Hyde had expected. One train, for example, consisted of 700 wagons, 4,000 sheep, and 5,000 head of cattle, plus unnumbered horses and mules.[81]

---

73. See "24th of July, at Great Salt Lake City," *Frontier Guardian,* September 19, 1849, p. 4, cols. 1–5. News of Mormon emigration was reported in the *Iowa Standard*: "The Mormons are said to be crossing in large numbers at Council Bluffs, and from 1,500 to 2,000 wagons are expected to leave in a few weeks for the Great Salt Lake." "Oregon and California Emigrants," *Iowa Standard,* May 24, 1848, 2.

74. "From the Presidency," *Frontier Guardian,* July 24, 1850, p. 2, col. 4.

75. "Zion no Refuge for the Wicked," *Frontier Guardian,* August 8, 1849, p. 2, col. 4.

76. See "The Mormons," *Frontier Guardian,* April 18, 1849, p. 1, col. 3; "The ships 'James Pennell' and . . . ," *Frontier Guardian,* October 17, 1849, p. 2, col. 6; "Emigrants from Britain," *Frontier Guardian,* June 12, 1850, p. 2, col. 2; "We learn that . . . ," *Frontier Guardian,* April 18, 1849, p. 2, col. 2; "The St. Louis Intelligencer . . . ," *Frontier Guardian,* June 12, 1850, p. 3, col. 2.

77. See "Salt Lake Emigrants," *Frontier Guardian,* February 21, 1849, p. 2, col. 3; "Take turkeys . . . ," *Frontier Guardian,* February 21, 1849, p. 3, col. 5; "Small Coin," *Frontier Guardian,* April 4, 1849, p. 2, col. 3; "How to Prosper on the Plains," *Frontier Guardian,* May 29, 1850, p. 2, col. 2.

78. "Goods for the Valley," *Frontier Guardian,* January 9, 1850, p. 2, col. 2.

79. See "Official," *Frontier Guardian,* May 29, 1850, p. 2, col. 2.

80. See "Rally! Rally!" *Frontier Guardian,* May 16, 1849, p. 2, col. 1.

81. "Emigration," *Frontier Guardian,* June 12, 1850, p. 2, col. 1.

Hyde also consistently advised the emigrants to form a "strictly military" company and have every wagon "examined to see if it contains the requisite amount of provisions, utensils and means of defence."[82] Assured that his advice would be heeded and that all were ready, Hyde urged a speedy journey to avoid unfavorable weather and instructed the emigrants to follow "the North side of the Platte, the entire distance; not even crossing it at Laramie. This route is, at least, one hundred miles shorter."[83] He also warned of marauding Indians, because "they say that the Indians were rapidly assembling for the great council at Fort Laramie.... They '*will be the white man's friendly enemy as long as they live*.'"[84] With this said, wagon trains departed from the greater Kanesville area.

It should be noted that those who headed for the gold fields in "California companies" received a different message from Hyde: "Every man engaged in hunting gold, and every one that visits the gold region, goes armed to the teeth. Scenes of violence occur; there is no security for life and property."[85] He spoke of "men loaded with gold, [who] appear like haggard vagabonds, clothed in filthy and tattered garments of the meanest kind" and that "miners were suffering from sickness and want of provisions."[86] Despite this description, California companies left Kanesville with marked regularity.

Minutes of Church Conferences in Kanesville. Minutes of the annual and semi-annual Kanesville conferences (from April 1849 to October 1851) were printed in the *Guardian*. In addition to sustaining general and local authorities—including Hyde—at these conferences, those who attended listened to sermons on a variety of topics.[87]

---

82. "Salt Lake Emigrants," *Frontier Guardian,* February 21, 1849, p. 2, col. 3.

83. "North Side of the Platte!" *Frontier Guardian,* December 11, 1850, p. 2, col. 2.

84. "Arrivals Through the Plains," *Frontier Guardian,* October 17, 1851, p. 1, col. 6 [italics in original]; see also "Western Emigrants, Take Notice," *Frontier Guardian,* May 2, 1849, p. 2, col. 4.

85. "A letter from San Francisco...," *Frontier Guardian,* February 21, 1849, p. 2, col. 1; see also "The Gold Region and Gold Fever," *Frontier Guardian,* February 7, 1849, p. 2, col. 3.

86. "Late from the Gold Regions—More Extensive Discoveries," *Frontier Guardian,* March 7, 1849, p. 1, col. 6; "California," *Frontier Guardian,* March 7, 1849, p. 3, col. 4.

87. At the different conferences Hyde was sustained as "President of Pottawatamie county," with George A. Smith and Ezra T. Benson as his counselors and as "President over the different branches of the Church, this side of the Rocky Mountains." See "Conference Minutes," *Frontier Guardian,* May 2, 1849, p. 1, col. 4; "Conference Minutes," *Frontier Guardian,* May 1, 1850, p. 1, col. 3; "Adjourned Conference," *Frontier Guardian,* May 2, 1851, p. 1, col. 6; "Conference Minutes," *Frontier Guardian,* October 31, 1851, p. 1, col. 5.

In 1849, Hyde spoke of severe weather and local affairs before calling the congregation to emigrate to Zion and to remember the Kanesville poor.[88] At the April 1850 conference, hundreds of non-Mormons in California companies attended. Seizing the missionary moment, Hyde welcomed the guests and spoke of angels visiting the earth and of his visit to Jerusalem. He went on to speak about American politics and what he perceived to be the threatening dissolution of the Union. Then, unexpectedly, he asked if the congregation approved of his "course and policy in Pottawatamie, and east of the Rocky Mountains." A vote was taken, and the actions of Hyde were sustained. During this conference, Hyde also addressed problems of the poor and the need to pay tithing.[89] The next year he reminisced about his service in Pottawattamie County.[90]

Local Church News. Knowing when and where meetings and conferences were being held was important to Church organization in Pottawattamie County. But to Hyde, payment of tithes and fast offerings to benefit the poor was even more important.[91] For those who hesitated to pay tithing, Hyde provided opportunities for them to give service.[92] As to fasting, an abstinence of food and drink, he set aside a specific day each spring for the practice.[93]

Although the payment of tithes and offerings was important, there were other issues that demanded Hyde's response. One issue was an attempt by Latter-day Saints in Kanesville to distinguish between "Brighamites" and "Hydeites." To those who believed Hyde and his counselors were divided in their "feelings, views, and in our counsel, &c.," Hyde assured them that "we have been *one* and united in *every single movement and principle*."[94] For those who openly opposed him and the teachings of the Church, Hyde responded by printing their names and alleged sins in the *Guardian*.[95]

As for self-proclaimed Church leaders, like Sidney Rigdon, Alpheus Cutler, James Strang, and others, Hyde referred to them as the "disaffected." Those who followed such men were called upon to repent. Hyde then advised the faithful to embrace returning prodigals and to gain greater wisdom by adhering to the word of God.[96] "The Alpha and Omega of our song is, 'KEEP OUT

88. "Second Day," *Frontier Guardian,* April 18, 1849, p. 2, col. 3.

89. "Conference Minutes," *Frontier Guardian,* May 1, 1850, p. 1, cols. 1–4.

90. See "Conference Report," *Frontier Guardian,* May 2, 1851, p. 1, col. 6.

91. See, "Tithing," *Frontier Guardian,* December 12, 1849, p. 2, col. 1.

92. See, "Tithing," *Frontier Guardian,* February 21, 1849, p. 2, col. 6.

93. See, "Fasting and Prayer," *Frontier Guardian,* April 4, 1849, p. 2, col. 1.

94. "Brighamites and Hydeites," *Frontier Guardian,* June 27, 1849, p. 2, col. 1; italics in original.

95. See, "Meeting of the High Council," *Frontier Guardian,* February 7, 1849, p. 4, col. 4; "James H. Mulholland...," *Frontier Guardian,* February 7, 1849, p. 2, col. 3.

96. "Rigdon's Confessions," *Frontier Guardian,* November 14, 1849, p. 2, col. 3; "Prospects of the Church," *Frontier Guardian,* April 4, 1851, p. 2, cols. 3–4.

OF DEBT,'" and "the practice of gaming on the Sabbath will cease."[97] He also condemned excuses for failing to worship, such as "Overslept myself. Could not dress in time. Too cold. Too hot. Too windy. Too wet. Too damp. Too cloudy. Don't feel disposed. No other time to myself."[98] Yet, Hyde believed, "The Church in Pottawatamie county was never more united than at the present time."[99]

Poetry. Poetry in the *Guardian* had historical significance to Mormons. For example, "The Wayfaring Man," "The Assassination of Gen's Joseph Smith and Hyrum Smith," "Cry of the Martyrs," "The Seer," "Praise to the Man," and "'Tis an Orphan at Its Birth" reminded readers of Joseph Smith's martyrdom. "A Journeying Song for the Camp of Israel," "California Song," "Let Me Go to the Valley," "Farwell to Kanesville," "Farewell to Iowa," and "Haste to Zion" reminded readers of the trek that lay ahead.

Local News of Kanesville. Hyde selectively printed news of greatest interest to the majority in Pottawattamie County. He instructed those "residing on the low bottoms of the Missouri river . . . to remove to higher ground."[100] He printed news of "a good Choir of vocalists" being formed.[101] But it was government issues, marriages, deaths, and advertisements that consistently appeared in his newspaper.

Government Issues. Hyde held strong opinions on local government issues, especially elections. He believed Latter-day Saints had a right to vote in all elections. Furthermore, when state officials threatened to disfranchise Pottawattamie County in 1849, Hyde printed the full text of a legislator's speech before the Iowa senate opposing the "deliberate disfranchisement of a whole county [Pottawattamie] containing, 4000 or 5000 inhabitants [who are Mormons], to condemn it to anarchy, exile and banishment, for no other assignable reason than because they voted as they pleased." When the proposed legislation failed to pass, Hyde printed, "Our readers may forget as soon as they can, the injustice which the Democrats sought to do us. Indeed, the sooner the better; but never forget that four Whig members of the Senate stood by your interests to the very last hour."[102]

Angered by the action of state Democrats, Hyde promoted the Whig Party and its candidates and encouraged his readers to do likewise. On May 29, 1850, he asked, "Are You Whig or Democrat?" To Hyde, Whigs were as the

97. "Keep Out of Debt," *Frontier Guardian,* August 8, 1849, p. 2, col. 4; "Shooting on the Sabbath-day," *Frontier Guardian,* November 14, 1849, p. 2, col. 4.

98. "Excuse for not Going to Church," *Frontier Guardian,* May 15, 1850, p. 1, col. 6.

99. "Prospects of the Church," p. 2, col. 3.

100. "Notice," *Frontier Guardian,* February 7, 1849, p. 2, col. 2.

101. "Music," *Frontier Guardian,* August 8, 1849, p. 2, col. 5.

102. "Mr. Springer's Speech, in the Iowa Senate," *Frontier Guardian,* April 4, 1849, p. 1, col. 5; "We publish today . . . ," *Frontier Guardian,* April 4, 1849, p. 2, col. 3.

"gentle rain upon the earth ... while the Democrats are like a torrent falling from a broken cloud."[103] "To the Polls! To the Polls!!" was his patriotic cry.[104]

When Hyde learned that a "poll book" containing the votes of the Kanesville precinct had been stolen, he was livid. "Down with the Poll Book thieves!" he printed.[105] However, stealing the poll book was only one crime in Kanesville. Hyde also demanded that those "aiding and abetting boys to fight in our streets" be brought to justice.[106]

For a time, he believed such vices were the sins of strangers.[107] But the more he looked into the matter, the more he blamed local Native Americans. Even though Hyde initially favored and had printed extensive reports on the culture and habitats of the Otoe and Omaha Nations,[108] he became convinced that tribes living near Kanesville were a threat. He advised locals not to trespass on Indian lands.[109] He also advised them not to feed the Indians and recommended that settlers protect themselves when necessary.[110] Such advice angered Native Americans so much that they "set fire to the Prairie, a little west of this town [Kanesville]." In response, Hyde penned, "Their [*sic*] must be a stop put to their coming upon this side of the river" and "the people should cease trading with them."[111] Unable to stop the sale of whiskey, a frustrated Hyde counseled the Saints to protect their property and the Indian agents "to curtail the further violent acts."[112]

Marriages and Deaths. It was customary to announce upcoming marriages in the *Guardian*. The name of the bride and groom and the date and place of the wedding formed a typical entry. A poetic phrase promising future happiness for the bride and groom appeared next to the marriage entry when a gift was presented to the *Guardian* staff by the intended.

Death notices were written in a brief, matter-of-fact manner. For example, "We are informed that Oliver Cowdry [*sic*], Esq., died, at Richmond, Ray

103. "Are You Whig or Democrat?" *Frontier Guardian,* May 29, 1850, p. 2, col. 1.

104. "To the Polls! To the Polls!!" *Frontier Guardian,* July 24, 1850, p. 2, col. 2.

105. "Stealing the Poll Books," *Frontier Guardian,* March 20, 1850, p. 2, col. 4; "Contested Election," *Frontier Guardian,* July 24, 1850, p. 3, col. 3.

106. "The Bars," *Frontier Guardian,* January 8, 1851, p. 1, col. 4; "Interest vs Morality," *Frontier Guardian,* January 8, 1851, p. 2, col. 2.

107. See "Emigrants and Citizens be Cautious!" *Frontier Guardian,* May 2, 1851, p. 2, col. 1.

108. "Indians," *Frontier Guardian,* March 21, 1849, p. 2, cols. 1–2.

109. See "Our citizens are particularly cautioned...," *Frontier Guardian,* February 21, 1849, p. 2, col. 2.

110. "Indians," *Frontier Guardian,* March 21, 1849, p. 2, col. 1; "Indians," *Frontier Guardian,* June 12, 1850, p. 2, col. 4.

111. "Fire, Indians, &c.," *Frontier Guardian,* October 30, 1850, p. 2, col. 2.

112. "More Indian Outrage," *Frontier Guardian,* October 17, 1851, p. 2, col. 3.

County, Missouri, on the 3d day of March last, of Consumption."[113] For those whose death brought special sorrow to the *Guardian* staff, a poetic verse followed the obituary.[114] Many obituaries also mentioned the person's cause of death, if known. The index of nineteenth-century terms on the DVD-ROM defines some of these causes in modern medical terms.

Advertisements. To promote trade in town and elsewhere along the Missouri River, Hyde offered reasonable rates that encouraged merchants to advertise in the *Guardian.*[115] He encouraged readers to fraternize establishments that placed ads in his newspaper.

To discerning readers, however, it was establishments in Kanesville and vicinity that received his highest commendations.[116] Whether the reader was looking for a watchmaker, jeweler, tailor, dentist, doctor, sign painter, gunsmith, tin maker, music teacher, or attorney, Kanesville had the service. Those needing a buggy, cook stove, ready-made clothing, cheese, or a ferry ride, should look no further than greater Kanesville.

Dependence on Newspaper Exchanges and Telegraph Dispatches. As with other papers of the day, the *Guardian* was a composite of exchanges and telegraph dispatches. National and foreign news, fictional stories, wise sayings, and humor appearing in the *Guardian* lacked originality but proved Hyde had access to such papers as the *Boston Times*, *Burlington (IA) Hawk Eye*, *Chicago Tribune*, *Cincinnati Gazette*, *Detroit Free Press*, *Grand River (MI) Eagle*, *New York Evening Post*, *New York Sun*, *New York Tribune*, *Springfield (IL) Republican*, and the *Washington (DC) Union*, as well as the *St. Louis (MO) Republican*, *St. Louis (MO) Union*, *New Orleans Times*, and *Washington (DC) Globe.*[117]

---

113. "We are informed...," *Frontier Guardian,* April 3, 1850, p. 2, col. 4.

114. See, for example, "Died," *Frontier Guardian,* September 19, 1849, p. 2, col. 6; "Died," *Frontier Guardian,* October 17, 1849, p. 2, col. 6; "Obituary," *Frontier Guardian,* May 16, 1851, p. 2, col. 2.

115. See "Terms of the Guardian," *Frontier Guardian,* February 7, 1849, p. 1, col. 1.

116. See, for example, "Business is lively...," *Frontier Guardian,* May 16, 1849, p. 2, col. 1; "To Emigrants," *Frontier Guardian,* January 23, 1850, p. 2, col. 3. Not everyone agreed with Hyde's assessment of Kanesville. The *Keokuk Dispatch* reprinted an account written by a reporter for the *St. Louis (MO) Republican* who visited the Mormon community and wrote, "I visited the Mormon settlement at Council Bluffs. I found the Saints in what they call a prosperous and happy condition; but which I (not seeing things with an eye of faith) call a most miserable and degraded state, considering that they claim to be the chosen of the Lord, an example to all nations, and harbingers of the Millenium." "Mormon Settlement in Iowa," *Keokuk Dispatch,* January 25, 1849, 2.

117. Of all the papers at his disposal, Hyde favored the *St. Louis Republican*. See, for example, "Missouri Republican," *Frontier Guardian,* March 7, 1849, p. 2, col. 3; "Correspondence of the Missouri Republican," *Frontier Guardian,* February 7, 1849, p. 2, col. 4.

Through these papers, Hyde informed readers of national events, such as the death of prominent politicians. Likewise, stories of the New York World's Fair, steamboat tragedies, railroad plans to the Pacific, and an "aerial machine now constructing in New York, to carry passengers to San Francisco" did not occasion unwarranted, lengthy editorials.[118]

But for news that directly or indirectly had bearing upon the Saints, he took an aggressive, and sometimes confrontational, stance. For example, after reporting the electoral vote that propelled Zachary Taylor to the presidential office, Hyde delighted in noting that Martin Van Buren, who would not use his presidential office to help Latter-day Saints, did not garner one vote.[119] And when several exchanges claimed Mormons in the Salt Lake Valley had more than one wife, Hyde printed, "Some of our exchanges say that the Mormon men at Salt Lake Valley have from five to twenty-five wives, If this is so, they are certainly ahead of us, and if they keep on, they will be as bad as King David and Solomon, and some others of whom we read of in olden time."[120]

When arguments were raised against admitting Deseret as a state, Hyde printed verbatim opinions from around the world. He told his readers that in Little Rock, Arkansas, Deseret was viewed as "Modern miracles—The New Mormon State." In Belleville, Illinois, the territory was an "internal organization being a Theocracy." The *New York Tribune* called it a "mystical appelation derived from their religious dialect" while the *London Times* claimed the United States would face a "great evil from contact with people so loose and radical in their notions of God."[121] Hyde then countered their arguments by writing of Deseret as a westward Zion.[122]

As to news of how Mormonism was viewed abroad, Hyde was dependent on European newspapers carried on trans-Atlantic steamers, which regularly docked at St. John's, Canada. The papers were read by telegraphers at St. John's, who sent their summaries via "telegraph dispatches" to the States. Dispatches received at the *St. Louis Republican* office were published. Hyde found that most foreign clippings had some bearing upon Church members since Mormon missionaries were laboring in England, France, Denmark, and Italy.

118. "Balloon for California," *Frontier Guardian,* April 4, 1849, p. 3, col. 5.

119. Joseph Smith met with Martin Van Buren. After Joseph explained the problems his people had suffered in the state of Missouri, Van Buren said, "Your cause is just, but I can do nothing for you." Smith, *History of the Church,* 4:80.

120. "Some of our exchanges say . . . ," *Frontier Guardian,* December 26, 1849, p. 2, col. 2.

121. "Modern Miracles—The New Mormon State," *Frontier Guardian,* February 6, 1850, p. 1, col. 4; "The Mormons," *Frontier Guardian,* February 6, 1850, p. 1, col. 5; "The Mormons in the valley . . . ," *Frontier Guardian,* February 6, 1850, p. 1, col. 5; "The London Times . . . ," *Frontier Guardian,* February 6, 1850, p. 1, col. 6.

122. "Believe not Every Spirit, but Try the Spirits if They Be of God," *Frontier Guardian,* September 4, 1850, p. 2, col. 2.

And news from Russia, Hungary, Austria, and even Tuscany was important because Mormons believed it would not be long until missionaries, perhaps themselves or their loved ones, would be called to labor in these far-distant climes.

Wise Sayings. Short pithy sayings were popular in nineteenth-century newspapers. The following are examples of the wise sayings Hyde printed: "The friendship of some people is like our shadow, keeping close to us while we walk in the sunshine, but deserting us the moment we enter the shade,"[123] "The climax of human indifference has arrived when a lady don't care how she looks,"[124] and "Every species of moral reform ought to begin with ourselves."[125]

Fiction. The reading public often demanded short fictional stories. Usually, there was little substance to them, but in the first issues of the *Guardian* the stories conveyed morals.[126] Yet as time passed and few stories in the exchanges had a moral turn, Hyde concluded to print frivolity and leave readers to judge its worth. When Hyde eventually turned to stories of romance, his subscriptions increased.[127]

Humor. Jokes were another common element in newspapers of the era. Some examples from the *Guardian* include "A person who had been listening to a very dull address, remarked that every thing went of[f] well, especially the audience!"[128]; "Why cannot California be admitted as a State? Because the inhabitants are all *miners*"[129]; and "'I have met my match,' as the Devil said when he encountered the lawyer."[130]

Conclusion

The *Frontier Guardian* followed in the footsteps of other Mormon newspapers by acting as an official organ for the Church. Hyde effectively used this medium to keep the Saints east of the Salt Lake Valley informed of Church

---

123. "The friendship of some people…," *Frontier Guardian,* May 30, 1849, p. 1, col. 6.

124. "The climax of human indifference…," *Frontier Guardian,* September 5, 1849, p. 4, col. 3.

125. "Moral Reform," *Frontier Guardian,* October 3, 1849, p. 1, col. 6.

126. See "We must ask pardon…," *Frontier Guardian,* February 7, 1849, p. 2, col. 3.

127. See, for example, "List of Monies received…," *Frontier Guardian,* February 6, 1850, p. 2, col. 6. See also the annotated list of final monies and examine the dates of subscription on the *Frontier Guardian* DVD-ROM.

128. "Going Off Well," *Frontier Guardian,* March 7, 1849, p. 4, col. 6.

129. "Why cannot California…," *Frontier Guardian,* May 2, 1849, p. 4, col. 5.

130. "I have met my match…," *Frontier Guardian,* October 3, 1849, p. 4, col. 4.

business and to encourage them to gather to Zion. More specifically, the *Guardian* offers an interesting view of the Church during this era, which is different from that in Salt Lake City's nineteenth-century *Deseret News*. The *Deseret News* tells of permanency—settling new areas and planting and harvesting crops. The *Guardian* tells of impermanency—waiting and preparing a people to cross the plains to reach a westward Zion.

The new accessibility of the *Frontier Guardian* is significant for historians, Church members, and genealogists. Publications that mention the Saints' presence in Iowa are relatively few, and their written accounts of the Mormon settlement tend to be scanty. Also, stories in the *Guardian* clarify the location of over ninety communities on the Iowa side of the Missouri River, thus revealing the large Latter-day Saint presence in Pottawattamie County[131] and reinforcing the significance that Mormons had in western Iowa.

Names published in the *Frontier Guardian* make up a valuable genealogical database. Its 109 agents traveled throughout most of the United States soliciting subscribers. Through their efforts, the names of 2,975 subscribers residing in England, Upper Canada, and the United States, were printed in the *Guardian*. Another 753 names of individuals who failed to pick up letters at their respective post offices were printed also. And over twelve hundred names of Kanesville residents and shopkeepers appeared in the *Guardian*. Furthermore, the newspaper lists Latter-day Saints leaving Pottawattamie County for the Salt Lake Valley or for California as well as those who remained behind in Iowa.

In summary the *Frontier Guardian* not only reveals the presence of at least four thousand Latter-day Saints in the greater Kanesville area during this era and contains the names of thousands of people, it also illuminates the religious, social, economic, and political aspects of a multi-dimensional Mormon society.

---

131. For example, through reading the *Guardian,* historians now know that Pleasant Grove was eight miles above Kanesville on the south side of Big Musquito and about five miles from Indian Mill in Pottawattamie County, while Indian Town was fifty miles east of Kanesville on the east fork of the Nichnebotna River near the Pottawattamie Village of Mi-au-mise. See the annotated list of places mentioned in the newspaper on the *Frontier Guardian* DVD-ROM.

Steel engraving by Frederick Piercy of Kanesville, Iowa, c. 1850s. Courtesy Church History Library.

1

General Epistles of the First Presidency of The Church of Jesus Christ of Latter-day Saints

First General Epistle of the First Presidency

First General Epistle of the First Presidency of the Church of Jesus Christ of Latter-day Saints, from the Great Salt Lake Valley, to the Saints scattered throughout the Earth,

GREETING:

BELOVED BRETHREN: Since the General Epistle of the Twelve Apostles, from Winter Quarters, December 23d, 1847, many events have transpired interesting in their nature as pertaining to the advancement of the Church, preparatory to the coming of the Son of Man; and we cheerfully improve this, the earliest opportunity to communicate to you a brief history of these events, together with such council, as the Holy Spirit shall indite.

The winter and spring of 1848 were diligently improved, by many of the Apostles and Elders, in visiting the churches and brethren in different parts of the States, counselling and setting in order the things of the kingdom, and in endeavoring to procure means for the removal of the Church at Winter Quarters, to the Great Salt Lake City; but, although some of the Saints were liberal according to their ability, yet there was not sufficient collected to defray the expenses which the Presidency had previously incurred in searching out a new location and other similar operations for the benefit of the Church, without rendering them any assistance for their contemplated journey, which was finally facilitated by the loan of teams, &c., by the brethren on Pottawatamie lands, and friends in and about camp.

The General Conference, on the 6th, of April, 1848, held, at the Log Tabernacle, in Iowa, unanimously acknowledged brother Brigham Young to be the President, and Heber C. Kimball and Willard Richards his Councillors; the three constituting a Quorum of the First Presidency of the Church of Jesus Christ of Latter-day Saints.

Brothers Young and Kimball left Winter Quarters in May, and Brother Richards in July, with large emigrating companies for this place, where they arrived in September and October, and found the Saints enjoying almost universal health. Elder Amasa Lyman also accompanied this camp, and about the same time Elder Orson Pratt, left Winter Quarters for England. Elder Woodruff took his departure for Canada, and Elders Hyde, Geo. A. Smith, and Ezra T. Benson located with the Saints on Pottawatamie Lands. Brother Richards left Winter Quarters entirely vacated: many of our cattle having been destroyed by the Indians, and many horses stolen on both sides of the river. A portion of brother Kimball's camp was fired upon at the Elk Horn river by a band of the Otoes and Omahas, and three of the brethren were wounded, two of whom are maimed for life.

On the 30th of November we received a mail from Kanesville, Iowa, by the hand of Capt. Allen Compton and three other brethren giving us the cheering intelligence that many of the Saints who were unable to proceed further on their journey had settled in various parts of Pottawatamie county, and been exceedingly blest in raising grain esculent roots, vegetables, flocks and herds, and in preparation generally for future emigration, and that union and brotherly love prevailed.

By the same mail we also learned that the unparalleled prosperity of the work had increased the Church in England, and the British Dominions adjacent, more than 7000 souls during the previous year; while the power of God, with the power of the devil opposing, had been made manifest, as in days of old, to the great joy of the Saints.

Lyman Wights' manifesto was received at the same time, which clearly demonstrated to the Saints that he was not one with us, consequently the church dis-fellowshipped him, and all who shall continue to follow him.

On our arrival in this Valley, we found the brethren had erected four forts, composed mostly of houses, including an area of about 47 acres, and numbering about 5000 souls including our camp. The brethren had succeeded in sowing and planting an extensive variety of seeds, at all seasons, from January to July, on a farm about 12 miles in length and from one to six in width including the city plot. Most of their early crops were destroyed in the month of May by crickets, and frost, which continued occasionally till June; while the latter harvest was injured more or less by drouth, by frost which commenced its injuries about the 10th October, and by the outbreaking of cattle; the brethren were not sufficiently numerous to fight the crickets, irrigate the crops and fence the farm of their extensive planting, consequently they suffered heavy losses; though the experiment of the past year is sufficient to prove, that valuable crops may be raised in this Valley, by an attentive and judicious management.

The winter of 1847–8 was very mild, grass abundant, flocks and herds thriving thereon, and the earth tillable, most of the time during each month; but the winter of 1848–9 has been very different, more like a severe New England winter. Excessive cold commenced on the 1st day of December, and continued till the latter part of February. Snow storms were frequent, and though there were several thaws, the earth was not without snow during that period, varying from one to three feet in depth, both in time and places. The coldest day the past winter was the 5th of February, the mercury falling 33 decrees below freezing point, and the warmest day was Sunday the 25th of February, mercury rising to 21 degrees above freezing point, Fahrenheit. Violent and contrary winds have been frequent. The snow on the surrounding mountains has been much deeper, which has made the wood very difficult of access; while the cattle have become so poor, through fasting and scanty fare, that it has been difficult to draw the necessary fuel and many have had to suffer, more or less, from the want thereof. The winter commenced at an unusual and unexpected moment and, found many of the brethren without houses or fuel, and although there has been considerable suffering, there has been no death by the frost. Three attempts have been made by the brethren with pack animals or snow shoes to visit Fort Bridger, since the snow fell, but have failed: yet it is expected that Cumpton will be able to take the mail east soon after April Conference.

In the former part of February, the Bishops took an inventory of the bread-stuff in the Valley, when was reported a little more than three-fourths of a pound per day, for each soul, until the 9th of July; and considerable was known to exist which was not reported. As a natural consequence some were nearly destitute while others had an abundance; the common price of corn since harvest has been two dollars; some have sold for three; at present there is none in market at any price. Wheat has ranged from four to five dollars, and potatoes from six to twenty dollars per bushel, and though not to bought at present, it is expected that there will be a good supply, for seed, by another year.

Our public works are prosperous, consist-of [*sic*] a council house, 45 feet square, two stories, building by tithing; also a bridge across the Western Jordan at an expense of $700, and six or seven bridges across minor streams, to be paid by a one per cent property tax; also a bath house at the warm spring.

A field of about 8,000 acres has been surveyed South of and bordering on the city, and plotted in five and ten acre lots, and a church farm of about 800 acres. The five and ten acre lots were distributed to the brethren by casting the lots, and every man is to help build a pole, ditch, hue a stone fence, as shall be most convenient, around the whole field in proportion to the land he draws, also a canal on the east side for the purpose of irrigation. There are three gristmills, and five or six saw mills in operation, and several more in contemplation. Mill stone equal to French burr is found here.

The location of a tannery and foundry are contemplated, as soon as the snows leave the mountains.

The Forts are rapidly breaking up, by the removal of the houses on to the city lots; and the city is already assuming the appearance of years, for any ordinary country; such is the industry and perseverance of the Saints.

A winter's hunt, by rival parties of one hundred men each, has destroyed about 700 wolves and foxes, 2 wolverines, 20 minx and pole cats, 500 hawks, owls and magpies, and 1,000 ravens, in this Valley and vicinity.

On the return of a portion of the "Mormon Batlalion," through the northern part of Western California, they discovered an extensive gold mine, which enabled them by a few days delay, to bring sufficient of the dust to make money plenty in this place for all ordinary purposes of public convenience, in the exchange the brethren deposited the gold dust with the Presidency who issued bills, or a paper currency; and the "Kirtland Safety Fund" re-signed is on par with gold.

Elder Addison Pratt arrived in company with a part of the Battalion, on the 28th of September, 1848, and found his family in health, from whom he had been absent about five years, on a mission to the Society Islands, where has been baptized about 1200 souls. Elder Grouard, who still remains at the Islands, having baptized about 620 at Aua. The confidence of these native Saints is very great in the work of the Lord, and they seek for counsel in all their ways, insomuch that Elder Grouards' labors became insupportable, and caused him to risk a voyage of 300 miles in an open boat, to bring brother Pratt to his assistance; and, although he was shipwrecked on this voyage, yet he was prospered; was taken up by a passing vessel, accomplished his mission, and returned to Aua with brother Pratt; thus by the labors of Elder Rogers, who returned and died some two years since, and elders Pratt and Grouard the gospel has been planted on some 12 or 15 of the Western Islands.

On the 1st of January, John Smith Uncle to the Prophet Joseph Smith, was ordained Patriarch for the Church, holding the keys and powers thereof same as Father Joseph Smith and Hyrum.

On the 12th of February, Charles C. Rich, Lorenzo Snow, Erastus Snow, and Franklin D. Richards, were ordained members of the Quorum of the Twelve Apostles, to fill the vacancies occasioned by the removal of three to the First Presidency, and Lyman Wight disfellowshipped. The names of the members of the quorum of the Twelve Apostles, now are, in their order as follows: Orson Hyde, Parley P. Pratt, Orson Pratt, Wilford Woodruff, John Taylor, George A. Smith, Amasa Lyman, Ezra T. Benson, Charles C. Rich, Lorenzo Snow, Erastus Snow, and Franklin D. Richards.

Of the Presidency of the Seventies, Zera Pulsifer, Levi W. Hancock, Jedidah M Grant, and Henry Harriman are in this Valley. Joseph Young and Benjamin L. Clapp are in Pottawatamie county, and Albert P. Rockwood is on a mission to the Eastern States. Joseph Young is the presiding officer of the Seventies.

Immediately after filling the Quorum of the Twelve Apostles, the First Presidency, assisted by the Twelve present in the Valley; proceeded to organize a Stake of Zion at the Great Salt Lake City; Daniel Spencer, President; and David Fulmer and Willard Snow, Councillors.

The High Council consists of Isaac Morley, Phineas Richards, Shadrach Roundy, Henry G. Sherwood Titus Billings, Eleazer Miller, John Vance, Levi Jackman, Ira Eldridge, Elisa H. Groves, William W. Major, and Edwin D. Woolly.

John Young is President of the High Priests' Quorum, with Councilors Reynolds Cahoon and George B. Wallace.

John Nebeker is President of the Elders Quorum, with councilors James H. Smith and Aaron Savey.

The Valley is settled for 20 miles south, and 40 miles north of the city. The city is divided into 19 wards; the country south into three wards, and north three wards, and over each is ordained a Bishop with his Councillors with Newell K. Whitney, President of the Bishops Quorum, Presiding; who has been instructed to set in order all the lesser officers.

About thirty of the brethren have recently gone to the Utah Valley, about 60 miles south, to establish a small colony for agricultural purposes and fishing, hoping thereby to lessen the call for beef, which at the present time is rather scarce at an average of 7 and 8 cents per pound, but will improve with the vegetation.

The wards of the city, generally, consist of nine blocks, each three square, and each ward will be fenced by itself this season, on the plan of a big field, for the purpose of saving time for cultivation.

In consequence of Indian depreption on our horses, cattle and other property, and the wicked conduct of a few base fellows who came among the Saints; the inhabitants of this Valley as is common in new countries, generally, have organized a temporary government, to exist during its necessity, or until we can obtain a charter for a Territorial Government, a petition for which, is already in progress.

There have been a large number of schools the past winter, in which the Hebrew, Greek, Latin, French, German, Tahitian, and English languages have been taught successfully.

Last fall the brethren had liberty to cut all the timber within thirty miles of the city, provided they would haul it into the city in the course of the winter. They have been diligent and done the best they could, but have made but a small beginning towards securing what there is within fifteen miles.

The month of March, and April to the 4th, was very mild and pleasant, and many small crickets have made their appearance, but large flocks of plover have already come among them and are making heavy inroads in their ranks.

For the future, it is not wisdom for the saints to leave the States or California for this place, unless they have team and means sufficient to come through without any assistance from the valley; and that they should bring bread stuffs sufficient to last them a few months after their arrival; for the harvest will not be gathered, or the grain ready for grinding. The inhabitants of the valley will be altogether dependent on the crop of this season for their support; and will have no time to leave their tillage with their teams, to bring in emigrating camps as they have hitherto done; beside[s], quite a number of men, professors and unprofessors, whose God shines best in gold, have left, and are about leaving, for the gold mines, to spend the season; the natural consequence of which will be a decrease of labor here in raising grain, while many of their families, remaining, the number of consumers will not decrease in proportion to the laborers. There are an abundance of nutritious roots in this valley, so that we have no fears of starvation, yet all the time that is expended in digging for roots, will diminish the agricultural labor, and be a loss to the next harvest.

The scarcity of grain since the settling of this valley, has caused the slaughter of a multitude of cattle, which leaves room for a fresh supply as fast as opportunity shall present; and the emigrating brethren will do well to remember that they are liable to loose many on their journey: also their cattle are good property after their arrival, and there is no fear of their bringing too many cows, young cattle, sheep, oxen, or the choicest breed of stock of any kind, to this place; for any of these articles here are better than gold, for they will purchase what is to be purchased here when gold will not do it; as will also geese, ducks, turkies, pea-fowls, guinea hens, domestics, dry goods, groceries, window glass, nails, (mostly 6, 8, 10, shingle and a few four penny,) cotton yarn, a variety of dye stuffs, particularly dye sets, paints, gums myrrh, copal and shellac, spirits of turpentine, paper, books, saws, files, screws, and sheet tin of the best quality, hardware, cutlery, iron suitable for mills and all kinds of farming utensils, sligo sheet iron, steel of various kinds, copper and brass sheeting, crockery, glasses, looking glasses, shoe leather, harnesses, harness trimming, mill saws, mechanics tools, wire of various sizes, door locks, and trimmings, cupboard and padlocks, all of which are better than cash in this city; crockery and glass of any description had better be packed in cotton, for sale conveyance, and the cotton will be very useful here; a variety of shoe leather is particularly wanted this season, and a large amount.

There are an extensive variety of grain and seeds already in the valley, but that should not prevent the saints from bringing choice seeds from any part of the earth, for every thing good that can grow here is wanted, and a large amount of the osage orange, cherokee rose tree, and English hawthorn seeds, are needed this year for hedges, and the potato or hill onion for eating, also lobelia, mulberry and black locust seed; any amount of unadulterated Silesia or French sugarbeet seed would be useful here this season.

The brethren in Pottawatamie, who cannot fit themselves out this season, as we have suggested, will do well to continue where they are, striving for the same object the next year; and the saints in the United States, Canada, Europe, Asia and Africa, will continue to gather on the Pottawatamie lands, and prepare for their future journey agreeable to our previous instruction. Notwithstanding, if there are young or single men, or men of families, (who can leave them comfortably provided for to come on next season,) who can be spared from Pottawatamie, to come on here this season, and raise grain, build houses, &c., it would be well for them to come; for *one* such man *here* can do more in providing for the future arrival and wants of the saints, than *three* can, in tarrying in Iowa; but if they have a *golden* God in their hearts they had better stay where they are. Let all these things be decided in wisdom, by the council, which is among you.

The Twelve at Pottawatamie will see that copies of this epistle are forwarded to the saints in all the Eastern Nations.

Elder Amasa Lyman is delegated to carry this epistle to the saints in Western California and cause it to be circulated among the brethren in the Western Hemisphere, as far as possible; not forgetting the Society Islands, whither Elder Addison Pratt with his family and other Elders are expecting to repair the present season.

We would remind the saints in Western California, who are not coming hither this season, that they have it in their power to do much good, by forwarding to this place their tithing and donations, to the extent of their ability, and the more liberal they are in his thing, this season, the more they will have to bring with them when they come: for their offerings are now needed by the poor saints, and the Lord has put it in your power to help them and your stewardship will, be required at your hands; and as you give so it will be given unto you.

Several Elders have already received their appointment on foreign missions, to the Western Islands, England and various nations, but wisdom dictates that their labors be retained here, at least until after the approaching harvest.

Brothers Parley P. Pratt and John Taylor, as well as Amasa Lyman and those of the Twelve recently ordained, are in this place, and are laboring night and day to do good to the church, and locate their families comfortably, so that they can again have the privilege of going forth to the nations and preaching the gospel. If the saints abroad want to see the Elders from this place, let them send us their means according to their ability, that the hands of the faithful may be let loose; that the cords with which they are bound, may be severed; and that the Elders of Israel may feel themselves free as air, and with joyful hearts leave their families and kindred and all that is dear to them here, and soar away as on eagles wings to the nations, proclaim the gospel of salvation, the day of deliverance to the oppressed; gather the outcasts of Judah, and the remnants of Ephraim from the four winds, to the place of their inheritance; that Zion may be built up, Jerusalem re-established, and the glory of the Latter Day fill the earth.

We have often told the saints, that those who came to this place, should be fully determined to keep the commandments of God, and work righteousness, otherwise they could not expect the blessing of Heaven to rest upon them; for there is nothing here which need to hinder any man from doing right, and knowing as we do the temptations and designs of the enemy of all good in endeavoring to lead men astray from the path of duty, we are constrained to say to the saints that those whose hearts are not fully set in them to work righteousness and follow the council of those whom God has appointed to lead His people in these the last days; but those who love a little shining dust, or filthy lucre, and care more to gratify their own covetous propensities, by running hither and thither, after they hare arrived at this place, like the wind upon the mountains, they had better keep away; such saints are not wanted here; God has no use for them, neither have his servants, for the Kingdom of Heaven can easier be built up without them than with them.

The saints need not suppose, that, because they cannot all gather to this stake of Zion at the present time, there is nothing for them to do. Let the Elders preach the gospel every where, as they have the opportunity, and let all saints every where watch and pray without ceasing, lest they be found sleeping, as at midnight, and the bridegroom, should make his appearance and close the door against them, for there never has been a time, since the coming forth of the Book of Mormon, when there has been a wider field opened for the exercise of faith and good works, with a prospect of success therein than at the present.

The public buildings, and other public works necessary for establishing a Stake of Zion at this place, will require a great amount of means, besides labor, and many materials, such as window glass, nails, door trimmings and fixtures, fastenings and trimmings of various descriptions will be wanted before they can be manufactured here; all of which will require means to purchase and transport; we have therefore appointed Elder Orson Hyde our agent in the United States, generally, to receive and gather tithing and donations; we have also appointed Elder Wilford Woodruff our agent to receive and gather tithing & donations in Canada, Nova Scotia, New Brunswick & adjacent islands, as he shall have opportunity; we have also appointed Elder Orson Pratt, of Liverpool, our agent to receive and gather tithing and donations in England and the British Islands and from all the Saints adjacent, and we invite all the saints in the east, to be faithful and diligent in making their remittances to these our agents, that we may speedily have means to procure such materials as are necessary to prosecute the work the Lord has given us to do; and our agents will keep an accurate and detailed account of all such tithing and donations, and appropriate the same only to our order.

On the 4th of April there was a heavy snow storm in the Valley, but the earth was clear again by mid-day of the 5th; some rain on the 6th, caused an adjournment of the Annual Conference of the church, till the 7th, and the day was spent in preaching and teaching, and conference closed on Sabbath, P. M., having been attended by a large assembly of the Saints who unanimously acknowledged the several officers mentioned in this Epistle.

To Elder Parley P. Pratt has been assigned a mission to the Western Islands, whither he is expecting to go before another winter; it is also expected during the same period that Elder Charles C. Rich will enter on the mission assigned him by locating himself and family some where in Western California.

That the saints may be faithful in every good word and work, and be diligent in all things, and yet not by haste and waste, which bringeth destruction; and, inasmuch as they cannot be prepared to come to this place, this season, let them be persevering in making preparation, and wait their time in patience, and it shall be well with them; for the Holy Spirit will dwell with them, which will cause gladness of heart and cheerfulness of countenance, so that every burden will be light and every yoke easy, which is the prayer of your brethren in the New and Everlasting Covenant and your servants, continually, for Christ's sake: Amen.

BRIGHAM YOUNG,
HEBER C. KIMBALL,
WILLARD RICHARDS.

In vol. 1, no. 9 (May 30, 1849): p. 2, cols. 2–6

Fourth General Epistle of The First Presidency

Of the Church of Jesus Christ of Latter-day Saints, from the Great Salt Lake Valley, in the State of Deseret, to the Saints scattered throughout the earth,

GREETING:

BELOVED BRETHREN:—Another opportunity is presented, whereby we may communicate to you what great things the Lord has been doing for his people; for truly has he made the wilderness to bud and blossom like the rose, and fruit thereof to come forth in its season, while the solitary places of the mountains of Ephraim are made vocal with the praises of Israel's God.

Since our last Epistle of the 12th of April, our Heavenly Father has cheered our hearts, and strengthened our hands; and the earth has yielded an abundant harvest. On the twelfth of May, peach trees, of two years' growth, were in bloom; and several trees of the same age, in various parts of the City, alternately bloomed till the twenty-ninth, then currants, peas, beans, &c., put forth their blossoms, and nature smiled with the prospect of early fruits; but on the 17th of June the snow fell freely on the surrounding mountains, followed by a severe frost on the 18th and a slight one on the 19th, which injured the vines and tender plants; more particularly on the lowest lands, yet we feel confident that this Valley will yet produce the choicest fruits, accustomed to the latitudes, as it now does the richest vegetables.

The peaches in Bro. Young's garden grew finely, until they were accidentally destroyed by the sports of the children; and the California grape is flourishing beautifully in the same garden, and other places in the City.

On the 13th of May we located a farm, one mile by two, near Jordan bridge, for the benefit of the poor, designing to build houses for the accommodation of all such as were not able to build for themselves; but on investigation we learned there were but two persons in the Valley who were unable to provide for themselves, and the contemplated farm was converted into a pasture, for the time being.

The Indians have been more quiet the present season than hitherto; though the Utes continue to steal our horses and cattle more or less, and threaten some. A band of Utes killed a small band of the Snake Indians, some time in the summer, and the white man by the name of Baker was killed by them on the twenty-ninth of May, between the Utah and San Pete vallies, though more recently they have been on their hunts, and manifested less personal hostility; yet, for the safety of the people, the drill and discipline of the Nauvoo Legion is not neglected, for we have none to depend upon for protection but God and his people; and God helps those who try to help themselves.

Emigrants from the States, and from almost all Nations, passing through the States, bound for the gold mines, began to arrive here on the 27th of May, and have continued to arrive till the present time, though most of them have passed a month since. Their numbers have been much larger than the previous year. Several have arrived in our city, who had been left, by their companions to die by the way side, and many companies and individuals have had contentions among themselves, not very creditable to civilized society, and which, contrary to the wishes of the Magistracy of our State, they have been called upon to settle. It is the urgent wish of all the citizens of Deseret, that travelers would settle their own difficulties; or rather, that they would have no difficulties so that our officers might pursue their daily avocations in peace. Were there no travellers [travelers] in our midst, we might soon forget the name of law-suit. As a people we have too much to do to attend to such matters.

Many scores, if not hundreds of these Emigrants on arriving at the Valley, and hearing the Gospel, in many instances for the first time, have been baptized for the remission of their sins, and gone no further; while others have witnessed our location, peace, union and prosperity, and though not professing to believe the doctrine of Christ, are making their way home as fast as possible, to bring their families hither, where they can enjoy health, in a land of civil and religious liberty, where they find themselves free to do right.

June 8th, a mail was received from Kanesville P.O., per hand of Thomas S. Williams, containing the first authentic intelligence from the States this season, and on the 14th commenced the printing of the Deseret News, the first Periodical in the State of Deseret.

The Nauvoo Legion, in uniform, honored the 4th of July with a public parade, which closed with a patriotic address by the Governor of the State.

The Topographical Engineers have closed their surveys for the season, and returned to Washington, as we are informed, by way of Arkansas. Rumors having been circulated in the States, that the Engineers had been received with coldness, and the object of the Expedition had been forcibly opposed by the inhabitants of the Valley, we [Valley. We] here give extracts from a letter of Captain Stansbury, (President of the Corps) to the Editor of the Deseret News, dated July 1st, '50, concerning the matter. 'How the *rumor* became prevalent, I am ignorant, * * * I take pleasure in declaring that nothing can be further from the truth. We were received by the President and public authorities with the greatest courtesy, both officially and personally, and will remember with gratitude the many tokens of kindness and regard we have received from them and the citizens of the place.

"Every facility has been studiously afforded us for the prosecution of our duties; instruments of science frankly and gratuitously loaned, and the able and faithful assistance obtained from their commencement here, of a gentleman, well known as a fearless advocate of your doctrines, and a prominent and influential member of your community." The whole letter is in the 4th No. of the "Deseret News," and a copy of the same may be found in every newspaper in the United States, that has circulated the *rumors* which drew forth the letter, provided the Editor thereof is an honest man.

The third Anniversary of the Pioneers into the Valley was celebrated on the 24th of July, by the Public Assembly, in a manner worthy of the occasion, with orations, addresses, songs of praise and thanksgiving and music, in which the Saints and Pilgrims to the mines seemed alike to participate. A synopsis of the proceedings were published in the 7, 8, and 9th Nos. of the News.

On the last of July, Brothers Young and Kimball left home on a visit to Utah and San Pete, and returned on the 12th of August; having found a place for a good settlement, located a city at San Pete, and noticed several intermediate sites, worthy the attention of smaller colonies, which we anticipate will be settled this fall, making a pleasant and safe communication from this to our most southern habitations. The San Pete settlement will also be strengthened, and others will spread on the North, to, and beyond Ogden, so that when the Emigration of this season shall close, there will be a continued line of villages at short distances, for more than 200 miles in extent; and a company is already chartered by the General Assembly of Deseret, for the purpose of running a regular line of coaches between Ogden and San Pete, to commence as early next spring as the travelling [traveling] will permit, and to be extended as fast as the settlements extend; also, from the capital to Tooele co., by way of the Great Salt Lake Bath.

The Government of the Union has been very tardy in rendering any facilities of communication between themselves and the State of Deseret, and having been left to our own resources for information, on the second of August, Br. John Y. Green was dispatched to Kanesville with a mail, and on the 15th Elder O. Hyde arrived with a mail from Kane Post Office; also, bringing with him the Frontier Guardian, the only file of newspapers we are in possession of, from any part of the earth for the past year.

The weather has been more cloudy, the nights warmer, and the showers more frequent in the heat of summer, and vegetation more rapid this season, than hitherto, consequently, artificial irrigation has been less needed; which has been a great blessing; for, during the irrigation season, there were not men enough in the Valley to water the immense fields of grain, had it been as dry as some previous seasons.

The crops have been abundant in all the settlements of Deseret, this season; and we have made every exertion to have them secured for the benefit of all: and although, from the best information obtained, we have reason to expect that our population will be strengthened, nearly, if not quite, fifteen thousand, this season, yet we are confident, if all will be prudent, there will be seed grain, and bread sufficient to sustain the whole, till another harvest.

The estimated population of fifteen thousand inhabitants in Deseret, the past year, having raised grain sufficient to sustain the thirty thousand for the coming year, inspires us confidently to believe, that the thirty thousand the coming year, can raise sufficient for sixty thousand the succeeding year, and to this object and end our energies will be exerted, to double our population annually, by the assistance of the Perpetual Emigrating Poor Fund, and otherwise provide for the sustenance of that population.

Viewing the gathering of Israel, which produces an increased population in the valleys of the mountains, an important part of the Gospel of Jesus Christ, and one of the most important at the present time; we shall send few, or no Elders abroad to preach the Gospel this fall; but instruct them to raise grain and build houses, and prepare for the saints, that they may come in flocks, like doves to their windows; and we say arise! to your wagons and your tents, O, scattered Israel! ye Saints of the Most High! rich and poor, and gather to the State of Deseret, bringing your ploughs and drills, your reapers and gleaners, your threshers and cleaners, of the most approved patterns, so that one man can do the labor of twenty, in the wheat field, and we will soon send the Elders abroad by hundreds and thousands to a harvest of souls among all nations, and the inhabitants of the earth shall speedily hear of the salvation prepared by Israel's God for His people.

Many of the inhabitants of the City, are leaving their good homes this fall, and taking up land in the country, preparatory for extensive farming operations; and many who are now arriving in our midst, are gathering in companies of tens, twenties, and fifties, to act in concert for mutual protection and assistance, in opening new fields, establishing new settlements, and in preparing to feed the friends we are calling home.

Our messengers who went east, this fall, to visit the camps of the Saints, emigrating hither, and report to us their situation, have discovered a new route from Green River, south of the old road, to the Pacific Springs, on which the feed and water are improved; also a new route on the north side of the Sweet Water River; which together with the road on the entire north side of the Platte River, from its mouth westward as located all the distance, and travelled [traveled] the most of the way by our Pioneers in 1847, is decidedly the best route for the Saints from the States to Deseret.

Crossing the Missouri River above the mouth of the Platte, and passing the Loupe Fork, which is the only river of much consequence to cross on the north of the Platte; also of the Sweet Water, except near its source in the mountains, and there are no natural obstructions on the route till you arrive at Green River; where a ferry may be expected at high water, and good fording is always found late in the season.

Our State House is enclosed; the walls are nearly ready for plastering; and we have no doubt but the several apartments will be ready for their several uses: the sitting of the General Assembly, High School, Printing Office, and Tithing, Post, and Recording Offices, the coming winter. The Warm Spring Bath House is so near completion, the visitants are accommodated at the Baths, and daily and hourly carriages are running from thence to various parts of the city.

There are several extensive store-houses completed, and near completion in our city, and goods sufficient in quantity and variety, with the exception of groceries, for the necessities of the people, till another season.

Sugar is not only a beverage, a luxury, but it is in its nature and substance, one of the component parts of our animal structure; and a free use thereof is calculated to promote health; and could the Saints have a more abundant supply, they would need less meat. Should every person in Deseret consume one-third of an ounce of sugar per-day, through the coming year, it would require about one hundred and twenty tons, more than has or will be brought by our merchants this season; and according to the best estimate we can make, three hundred tons would be consumed in this State the next year, if it could be obtained.

We anticipate some relief in the sugar market next season, from the culture of the sugar beet, and its manufacture, but this can make but little impression the first year, as we are not informed of more than one or two bushels of the genuine sugar beet seed in the valley, though we know of no country, where a greater quantity of saccharine matter is produced in vegetables than this.

About the middle of August, Brothers Young and Kimball, accompanied by Brother Hyde and others, visited Weber county, and located and gave the plan for the city of Ogden,—near Ogden river, and between that and the Weber river.

The General Assembly has held adjourned sessions, occasionally through the summer. The sittings have been very brief, though much important business has been transacted, important to our young and flourishing State. When the constitution of Deseret was adopted, and its boundaries were established therein, the actual settlers of Deseret outnumbered Western California as five to three. Notwithstanding which, a strong exertion has been made by Congress to receive California into the Union; to the exclusion of Deseret, though our petition for admission was equally before them.

******

Kane Post Office, in Pottawattamie, is the nearest office to this place, and through which all our business has been transacted with the States and foreign countries. A U. S. Mail arrived here on the 9th inst., from Independence, Mo., by which we received no news, except through the carrier, by whom we learned that a contract existed for bringing through the Mail once a month; and that President Taylor was dead.

Communications to and from our friends abroad, have been very uncertain in their transmission; and so far as it can be, it is desirable that valuable documents should be remitted by private conveyance.

The Perpetual Emigrating Funds have been judiciously appropriated the past year, under the immediate application of our agent, Bishop Edward Hunter; who is near this place, on his return from Pottawattamie, with a large company of the poor Saints.

Our annual fall Conference was commenced on the 6th of September, one month earlier than usual, so that the brethren who were obliged to go to the States, need not be exposed on their travels so late in the season; but circumstances, beyond our control, have caused unexpected delay, which, in the end, will result in good.

The Conference was fully attended, and much important business was transacted, as will be seen by reference to the minutes which are published, the most important items dwelt upon, were the Perpetual Emigrating Fund; Education: and a universal sustaining of the general officers of the Church, and of the different quorums thereof, except that Bro. Parry was added to the High Council of this Stake of Zion, in place of Bro. Grover, who is absent.

Preparations are making for the establishment of a parent school, or school for qualifying teachers; for primary and infant schools throughout the State; for enclosing the University lands, a platt [plot] of about 600 acres, directly east of the City; and for every thing else which may tend to facilitate the improvement of the old and young, in a knowledge of the arts, sciences and general intelligence.

Several thousand dollars were subscribed to the Perpetual Fund during Conference; and several individuals subscribed one thousand each. Since that time, the Perpetual Emigrating Company, of not less than thirteen members, consisting of a President, and Assistants, has been incorporated by an Ordinance of the General Assembly of the State of Deseret, with power to choose their own officers, to wit: a President, Secretary, Treasurer, Recorder, and Agents; and transact all business necessary for the furtherance of emigration; in accordance with the general principles of transacting business among States and Nations.

Brigham Young was unanimously elected President of the Company, who have since completed their organization by electing Willard Richards Secretary; Newel K. Whitney, Treasurer; and Thomas Bullock, Recorder; every member of the Company to give good and sufficient bonds for the faithful performance of their several duties; and all the Company is responsible for the acts of its officers and agents.

It is confidently reported that there is a great failure of the gold dust, the present season, in California; and many of the donations made to the Perpetual Fund, have and will be made in live stock, grain, &c., and should a proper proportion of cash be wanting, the Company will issue their paper, for the purpose of fitting out emigrants abroad, which paper will always be good; as a safficiency [sufficiency] of the stock will be retained, in deposit, by the Company to redeem that paper, at any moment; and any person coming to this place, can, with more convenience, bring the paper, than flour, stock, or even gold; which will make it an object for the brethren who have the means, and travellers [travelers] bound for Deseret, to secure the Company's paper, wherever they can find it; for with that paper, they can get such articles as travellers [travelers] most need, when money will not purchase them in this market.

The Twelve Apostles are mostly in their several fields of labor abroad. Elder Orson Hyde has been with us a few weeks on a visit, and is about to return to Kanesville, and continue his labors in the States. Elders P. P. Pratt, Geo. A. Smith, and E. T. Benson are at this place; and, with Wilford Woodruff, who is journeying thither, will spend the winter in the Valley. O. Pratt and F. D. Richards are in England. John Taylor, who left for France; Lorenzo Snow, for Italy; Erastus Snow, for Sweeden, last fall, have not been heard from since they arrived at their destination. Amasa Lyman is daily expected, with a large company of the brethren from California. Charles C. Rich is expected to continue his labors in California, and commence a settlement, with such of the brethren as wish to tarry there, in the southern part of the Territory. Orson Pratt is expected here, as early next spring, as circumstances will permit; otherwise, the Apostles are expected to continue in their several appointments, according to previous instruction; extending their labors into other countries, as opportunity presents, and as they shall be directed by the Holy Spirit.

We received a long and cheering communication from Elder O. Pratt by Elder Hyde, and we feel to say to the Saints in England, lift up your hearts and rejoice, for the Lord hath done a great work in your midst, and speedily a greater responsibility must rest upon your shoulders. The reason why a prophet is not without honor, save in his own country, and among his own kin, is the want of faith and confidence among his countrymen. Immense treasures of time and means have been expended by the American brethren, to extend the work in Great Britain; and the time has now come when we must begin to have a care for other nations, and leave you to prosecute the work begun in your midst, without continuing to send you Elders, as heretofore: God is no respector [respecter] of persons, and he is just as ready and willing to qualify your own Elders to preach and preside over Conferences, as to qualify men from abroad; and he will do it if you will give them your faith and prayers, and honor them in their calling, as you have done the foreign Elders.

We do not wish the American Elders to leave England, unless they shall particularly desire it, and that desire shall be approved by the Presidency at Liverpool; and we suggest to that Presidency the propriety of electing presiding Elders of Conferences, from the native brethren, as soon as circumstances shall render it convenient; and begin to initiate them into the practical duties of their calling; leaving the few American brethren more at liberty to visit the Conferences, and attend to general instructions.

Presiding Bishop Newel K. Whitney, died very suddenly on the 23d inst. Bishop Whitney was one of the oldest members of the Church, and we have to deplore the loss of an exemplary member, and a most upright and thorough business man; and while we thus mourn his absence, we are again reminded that the Church of Christ is built upon no man; and God is able to do his own work. Bishop Partridge was the first presiding Bishop in the Church in these last days, and died several years since; he was succeeded by Bishop Whitney, who is now gone to the world of spirits; and the voice to all is, be ye also ready. The health of the people in the Valley is generally good: there have been a few deaths, mostly of Emigrants.

Every possible exertion will be made on our part, and that of the Emigrating Company, to extend the usefulness of the Perpetual Fund in gathering the Saints: and it is important that those who anticipate help therefrom, should understand that the means sent forth are, and will be designed to furnish teams, almost or quite exclusively; and even the cases in which wagons will be furnished, will be rare. The poor, who can live in the States with little clothing, and little or no groceries, &c., can live equally as cheap on the road; and when once here, can procure the comforts of life by their industry. Souls are the articles for the Perpetual Fund to gather home, and that, too, as many as possible; and other things will be attended to in their time and place.

We are under obligation by covenant, firstly to apply the Perpetual Funds gathered in this country, to bring home the poor Saints who were driven from Nauvoo; and as soon as this shall be accomplished, we shall be ready to extend our exertions to other places and countries. Let the European Saints continue to add to their Perpetual Funds, which we doubt not they have commenced according to our previous counsel; and as soon as sufficient shall be collected to remove a suitable company, we will give instructions concerning its application, and emigration will commence.

One year ago and the Perpetual Fund was not instituted. Returns have not been completed, this fall; but so far as we can judge, they will not now fall much short of $20,000, in the Valley. Let the Saints abroad imitate the example of the Saints here, according to their ability, and let this work continue to go forward with the same progressive ratio it hath hitherto done, and the time will be short, when all the poor and oppressed of Zion will feel its cheering influence, and the cry need not be heard, "I would go up to the House of the Lord, but I have not the means."

The Perpetual Emigrating Company consists of Brigham Young, President: Heber C. Kimball, Willard Richards, Orson Hyde, Geo. A. Smith, Ezra T. Benson, Jedediah M. Grant, Daniel H. Wells, Willard Snow, Edward Hunter, Daniel Spencer, Thomas Bullock, John Brown, William Crosby, Amasa Lyman, Charles C. Rich, Lorenzo Young, and Parley P. Pratt, Assistants; Daniel Spencer, Treasurer; in place of N. K. Whitney, deceased. Orson Hyde and John Brown have been appointed Travelling [Traveling] agents; and will be in the States the coming winter. Orson Pratt and Franklin D. Richards have been appointed Travelling [Traveling] Agents; are located at Liverpool; and their particular field of operations, at present, will be the British Islands.

Thus, brethren, we have given you a brief history of the situation and prospects of the Church in the Wilderness, and the wishes of our Heavenly Father, as made manifest by His spirit dwelling in us, for your edification, comfort and salvation. The signs of the times are highly portentous of a mighty and short work in these last days; and we pray God, the Eternal Father, that he will inspire your hearts with humility, faith and patience, and dilligence [diligence] in every means within your reach, to help roll that work forward, that you may speedily be found in Zion, rejoicing with us, and the Gospel be proclaimed to the ends of the earth in the name o Jesus: Amen.

BRIGHAM YOUNG,

HEBER C. KIMBALL,

WILLARD RICHARDS.

G. S. L. City, Deseret,

September 27, 1850.

In vol. 2, no. 23 (December 11, 1850): p. 1, cols. 1–5

Addenda to the Fifth General Epistle of the First Presidency

Fifth General Epistle of the Presidency of the Church of Jesus Christ of Latter-day Saints, from Great Salt Lake Valley, State of Deseret, to the Saints, scattered throughout the Earth,

GREETING:

BELOVED BRETHREN:—Some items having escaped notice in our communication of the 7th inst., we again resume the pen, in reference particularly to the necessary supplies of sugar, molasses and honey, for the citizens of Deseret. Some experiments have been made with beets, in the manufacture of molasses and vinegar, mostly in private families, the specific result of which in minute detail, we are not informed; but we have learned for a certainty, that with little labor, any family who have a supply of beets can make themselves comfortable for molasses, though the art of removing the gas and foreign matter, is not sufficiently understood to secure so perfect an article as is desirable. Vinegar has been produced from the same source, of a good quality. Let the brethren bring all the white sugar-beet seed they possibly can for years to come.

Messrs. Beach & Eddy, of St. Louis, and Blair of Texas, have opened a general manufacturing establishment this Spring, mostly too late for sugar, but progressing in making molasses and vinegar. It is expected that this establishment will continue its operations, and be prepared for more extended labors on the approach of another harvest, but it will not be possible for one factory to supply all the sweet that will be needed; and if a practical chemist and manufacturer of sugar from the beet, one who understands the business in all its bearing, or a company of individuals who are severally versed in the various branches, could come to this place and open their sugar factories, our farmers and families would gladly surrender their domestic operations, and procure their supplies in a more perfect form, from the factories; and it would now require several extensive establishments to supply the people. It is our wish that the Presidency in England, France, and other places, should search out such practical operators in the manufacture of sugar, as fully understand their business, and forward them to this place, with all such apparatus as may be needed, and cannot be procured here.

Several swarms of bees, that have been brought from the States, are doing well in the Valley, and it is very desirable for the brethren to bring all the bees they can; for it is believed they will flourish here; and so far as honey can be produced, it will supercede the necessity of making sugar; and if there were ever so much sugar, honey is needed as a medicine, as well as a luxury.

BRIGHAM YOUNG,

HEBER C. KIMBALL,

WILLARD RICHARDS.

G. S. L. City, April 16th 1851.

N. B. Editors who have copied the Epistle, please copy the above addenda.

In vol. 3, no. 11 (June 27, 1851): p. 2, col. 4

Sixth General Epistle of the First Presidency

Of the Presidency of the Church of Jesus Christ of Latter-day Saints, from Great Salt Lake Valley, to the Saints Scattered Throughout the Earth,

GREETING:

BELOVED BRETHREN:—When the Savior was upon the Earth, and his disciples questioned him concerning the sign of his coming, referring to the Latter-days, Jesus answered them on this wise: There shall arise false Christs and false Prophets, and shall show great signs and wonders; saying Lo here! and Lo there! so that if it were possible they shall deceive the very elect: Go not after them, neither believe them; for as the light of the morning cometh out of the East and shineth even unto the West; so shall also the coming of the Son of man be.

Many of the signs and wonders, and false Christs and false Prophets referred to, have already been exhibited insomuch that many have declared the day when the Son of man would make his appearance; and many have believed on their testimony and been disappointed; while those who have been filled with the Holy Ghost, by the laying on of hands, having repented of their sins, and received remission thereof by baptism in water, have been watching the gradual progress of the work of the lord, in this last dispensation, which has been like the light of the morning, as it first gildes [gilds] the Eastern horizon, and continues to grow brighter and brighter, and spread farther and farther from the East even unto the West, and so will continue until the whole Horizon is illuminated with the clear effulgence of the noonday Sun; and the Son of Righteousness shall make his appearance in the midst of his people, according to his own declarations.

The first light of the morning in this age, and the time referred to by the Savior, was the Angel who had the everlasting Gospel, which was to be preached to all people, preaching and ministering to Joseph Smith Jr., and commanding Joseph to preach and administer to others even as he had received of the Angel; and the light continued to shine and spread as others believed on the testimony of Joseph; for they repented of their sins; were baptized by him, and he having received the Holy Priesthood from the angels, co[n]ferred the same Priesthood on the believers; and they in turn went forth proclaiming the same Gospel, administering the same ordinances, calling on all the faithful to gather themselves together, to the upbuilding of Zion, until the light has already been seen in the four quarters of the Earth, and is fast being reflected over every nation and people; and this the Gospel, the plan of salvation, is the true light that must shine from the East to the West; that is to every nation, kindred, tongue, and people, on the earth, before the end will come; and the faithful, the Saints, must be gathered together in holy places, and build Temples, and do all necessary works to open up the way of life and Salvation, to the dead as well as the living, before they can complete the work which is given them to do in this dispensation and probation.

When the Saints in Zion are sowing and reaping, and building, according to counsel, they are causing the light to shine, as emphatically, as though they were abroad in foreign nations, preaching and baptizing for remission of sins All things needful to be done, are but parts of the great whole, which must all be accomplished before men will be prepared to be restored back again into the presence of the Father; and while we again have the pleasing privilege of communicating with our friends scattered among the nations, we know not how we can with more interest, and render our Epistle more useful, than by devoting a portion to a continuation of the history of things as they do and have existed since our last letter; which is only a reflection of that light which eventually must illuminate the world; for the works of the righteous, like gold and silver and precious stones, will remain when time is swallowed up in eternity.

The Railway from this City to the mountain, was surveyed early in the season, and partly graded; and a considerable share of the timber and rails are on the ground. When the harvest approached, the work was suspended for want of laborers, but will be resumed as early as possible. The walls of the basement story of the Seventies Hall, are in progress, and the walls of the Tithing Barn are completed; also the walls of the Joiners and Paint Shop, and plaining and slitting Machine, one hundred and forty by forty-five feet on the Temple Block, preparatory to building a Temple; though all the Public Works have been hindered for the lack of lumber, materials, and laborers, and the lack has been occasioned by a majority of the brethren's neglect to pay their tithing, both at home and abroad. It mattereth not where the Saints reside, in relation to this principle; it is their duty to devote one tenth of their property, when they come into the Church, and afterwards one tenth of their income, for the support of the Public Works; for the building of Temples and other necessary purposes; and if they do not tithe themselves, they have no claim to the blessings, and endowments that will flow to the faithful through that medium.

A tithe of the tithing due from the Saints, promptly paid, would have enabled us to enclose the Temple Block, as we had anticipated, preparatory to commencing the Temple another season; but for lack of means, the plat remains open, and the commencement of the Building must continue to be suspended. It is time that the Saints understood, and it is the duty of all Elders and officers, and especially the Bishops, to instruct the Saints, that the paying of their tithing is a prominent portion of the labor which is allotted to them by which they are secure a future residence in the Heaven they are seeking after. To be prepared for a Celestial Heaven they want the blessings of a Terrest[r]ial Temple, builded [built] to the name of Israel's God, and without these blessings they cannot be prepared for the greatest glory: and should any one succeed in passing through the Temple and receive all the blessings and endowments offered to any; that person never having tithed for the building of the Temple, or other public good, would have to hear the words of Jesus, enter in at the door, and he that entereth not in at the door but clim[b]eth up some other way, the same is a thief and a robber; and the House of the Lord is the door to those who help build it; but those who have the opportunity and do it not, the words of the Savior remain true, if they enter therein; and from henceforth the living may not expect the blessing of the Temple unless they help built it. Your tithing we value not, only as it affects your salvation and the salvation of the dead.

The Council House is completed. The Tithing Store House is in progress of finishing, and will be ready to be occupied the coming winter, for the several purpose designed, instead of a Joiner's shop as hitherto. The foundation of a Tabernacle, on Temple Block, one hundred and twenty-six by sixty-four feet, is nearly completed, and we expect the building will be completed this Fall. The Deseret Pottery is in successful operation, some good light yellow ware was drawn from the Kiln June 27th, and white ware is soon expected. It is anticipated that the Valley materials for making crockery and China ware, will be equal to any other place; and that the Pottery will soon be able to supply this market. Good Potters are wanted. A Carding Machine is in operation and doing extensive business in this Valley; also one in Utah, and others in progress.

There are four grain and five saw mills in operation, or nearly completed in Great Salt Lake County; also two grain and two saw mills in Weber County; one grain and two saw mills in Davis County; two grain and three saw mills in Utah County; One grain and two saw mills in San Pete County; one grain and one saw mill in Iron County; and one saw mill in Tooele County; and an increasing desire and exertion to promote domestic manufacture prevails throughout the Territory.

We have visited the various counties and settlements generally, this season; and found the Saints industrious and prosperous, extending their farming operations as far as possible, and preparing food for the brethren who are coming hither. The harvest will be abundant for all who will have occasion to eat thereof, though many fields have suffered by the drouth [drought]; the mountain streams having been unusually low this season, and help scarce at the time, most needed for irrigation. Harvesters are much wanted, and more thrashing machines, and labor saving machinery of all kinds, could be used to great advantage in our midst.

A High Council was organized at Manti, San Pete County, April 30th, Isaac Morley is Patriarch of that Stake of Zion. Chalk, stone coal, salt, and iron ore, abound in the region of Iron County; also a substance resembling white clay which answers a good purpose, as a substitute for soap. We decided on locations for settlements on Salt Creek, in Jewab [Juab] Valley, and Corn Creek, in Parowan Valley, between this and Iron county; and companies will leave immediately after Conference, to form those settlements.

The birth day of the Nation, July 4th, was celebrated by the citizens of the Valley, in a most patriotic manner, on the banks of the Great Salt Lake, abont [about] twenty-four miles from the City, attended with every expression of joy and gladness, that could flow from the hearts of a free and virtuous people.

The 24th of July was celebrated as the Anniversary of the entrance of the Pioneers into the Valley of the mountains, and in this, much interest was added over former celebrations, by the appearance of the Pioneers in the procession, each carrying the tools, or emblems of tools, utensils, and implements used by them on their route, and after their arrival, even to sheaves of grain the products of their labor. The remembrance of this day is sweet to the Saints, as was the Passover to ancient Israel; and the demonstrations of gratitude and thanksgiving on the Anniversary were pure, virtuous, holy, and without alloy.

Several depredations have been committed by the Indians during the Summer mostly in Tooele Valley, where it is computed that more than five thousand dollars worth of cattle and horses have been stolen, and mostly killed or destroyed. So great was the destruction of property, that annihilation of the settlement seemed inevitable, unless the savages were met and resisted; which resulted in the death of one white man and a few Indians, which produced a cessation of thefts for a season. Some minor thefts have been committed in other settlements; though, in general, the Indians about the settlements, have neither the disposition or courage to fight the settlers.

A band of Indians, living on the muddy, between Iron County and San Diego appear more hostile of late, and no doubt killed Br. Isaac Brown, when on his return from California last Fall. The Indians on St. Mary's River, have committed many depredations on travelers the past year; and as is supposed, killed eight emigrants about one hundred and fifty miles north of this, a few weeks since; and the California Mail, which was expected heare [here] ten days since (Sept. 4) has not been heard from.

Elder Orson Hyde arrived in the Valley, on the 17th of August, direct from Kanesville, accompanied by Elder Carrington and a few others, all of whom were robbed and plundered by the Pawnee Indians. During the great amount of emigration from sea to sea, through the mountains, the Indians have received some insults and abuses which they are sure to resent, and the

Saints and others who may have occasion to pass through these tribes referred to, will do well to be prepared to act on the defensive.

Doctor John M. Bernhisel, and the Hon. A. W. Babbitt, returned to this place on the 19th of July, accompanied by several officers of the United States Government for the Territory of Utah, which was chartered last September, and the General Government having now received this Territory unto their postering [fostering] care. The citizens will be relieved of many burdens, hard to be borne by them in a new country, to which they were compelled to immigrate, while destitute of many of the comforts of life. Dr. Bernhisel, was appointed by the President of the United States, Special Agent, to expend an appropriation of five thousand dollars, granted by Congress for the purchase of a Library for Utah; which appropriation he expended by selecting books in the eastern cities, during the past winter, and the Library is now on the way to this place. Many gentlemen in the States, through the solicitation of the Doctor, have donated books, magazines, pamphlets, maps, and papers, which will add greatly to the value and interest of the Utah Library, and elicits our warmest thanks. Dr. Bernhisel was unanimously elected delegate to Congress by the Territory, on the 4th of August, and on the 1st of September, left in the Mail Coach for Washington City; the same day that a commencement was made to lay the foundation of a State House, on Union Square, in this City, towards the erection of which Congress has appropriated twenty thousand dollars.

The Valley is well supplied with a general assortment of merchandize at the present time; but the exportation of cash having been far greater than the importation, the past year, it is to be feared that many articles will remain unsold, which might be used to advantage were the circulating medium suited to foreign markets in the possession of those who would like to purchase. Shingles are now extensively manufactured, and would be very extensively used, could nails be procured, but it is not supposed that one half, and probably not one fourth enough of shingle nails will be brought this season, to supply the market; and the present prospect is that many buildings will have to be delayed before another market season, for lack of assorted nails. If a company of brethren could be formed in England, Wales, Sweden, or any other country, to come and make Iron from the ore, (magnetic ore of the best quality) and machinery for rolling, slitting, and cutting nails, and drawing off wire; it would be one of the greatest auxiliaries, for advancement in building up the Vallies [Valleys] of the Mountains; and the Presiding Elders in those countries are instructed to examine this subject and forward such a company with the least possible delay.

School Houses have been erected in the Wards generally, and Schools have been in operation the present season. The Parent School has been suspended a few weeks, for lack of a commodious room; but a house is in progress of erection, for its accommodation, and the School will be resumed the coming winter. A portion of the wall around the University Land is completed, and a portion has been delayed for want of laborers, a difficulty we often meet with, and which might be avoided, if a few score of thousands of the Saints who are abroad, would rise up in the name of Israel's God and come home, and help us to do what is required at our hands, and it is as much the duty of the Saints to gather, as it is for sinners to repent and be baptised [baptized] for the remission to repent sins, and every Saint who does not come home, when he has an opportunity, will be afflicted by the Devil. And why? If you will stay on the enemy,s [enemy's] ground, after you have had a chance to escape, that enemy will claim and exercise power over you; while your faith will fail, because you have been disobedient to the counsel to gather yourselves with the faithful, unto holy places, where the Holy One of Israel presides in the midst of his people, and where the power of Satan is destroyed, broken, or brought in subjection; therefore, if you shall tarry, after a way has been made for your escape, and lose your life, or the lives of your household, or your property, whose fault will it be? And whose loss? You must bear it.

Seth M. Blair, Esq., and President Joseph Young are each preparing mills and presses in our City, for the purpose of extracting the juice of the beet, of which many have been raised this season; and although we wish them success, and anticipate that they will do much to abate the scarcity of saccharine matter, for culinary purposes; yet we know of no one in our midst who is sufficiently versed in refining the beet juice to make a perfect article of sugar; but we expect this lack of information will be soon overcome by their experience; and also by the early arrival, next season, of a company of manufacturers from France, as we are informed by letter from Elder Taylor. We are also informed from the same source, that a large company of Woolen Manufacturers, will come at the same time, from the same country, bringing all the necessary machinery, and the best of sheep, all of which are much needed here; and we hope that nothing will interfere to hinder the arrival of those companies against our next Beet and Wool crop. A small Woolen Factory is already in progress of erection in our Valley, and there are many sheep here, but thousands more are wanted.

Experiments at tanning hides, and making leather, have, as yet, been very limited in the Valley. Much leather is needed in this country, and many thousands of the best hides have rotted or been wasted, for want of sufficient help to errect [erect] tanneries, and convart [convert] those hides into leather. There are plenty of materials containing tanning to prosecute the business to advantage, and prevent the necessity of heavy importations, at an enormous expense; and if some of the brethering [brethren] who are tanners, would come home and attend to their calling here, they would receive the blessing of many souls. Some attempts are now making at this business, but more help is wanted. Brethren, the harvest here is great, but the laborers few.

We have made arrangements, during the past year, with a gentleman in Wisconsin to come hither for the purpose of manufacturing paper. Report says that he is on the way, and we hope to see him here this Fall.

Books, papers, and every medium of intelligence through the press, are unusually high at this place, owing, in a great degree, to the heavy transport, which will be remedial to a great extent, when the rags in the Valley can be converted into paper. A large Printing Press has recently arrived, and all necessary materials for a respectable newspaper, and a small Book Bindery, all of which, will probably, be brought in requisition the coming winter.

The Warm Bath-House has been open to visitors through the season. Excellent salt is made by boiling 3 to 1 of the Lake water. Good lime is burned in Red Bute Kanyon. Plaster of Paris is dug within two miles of the City, and is much used at the Pottery, and for finishing houses. The Saleratus from the Lake four miles east of Independence Rock, is much used in the Valley, and the Saints will do well to bring what they can when they come; and the borax from the Lake, west of Independence Rock would be much used by our mechanics, if they could get it.

The Church Pasture on the north of the City is fenced; and the farm for the benefit of the poor on the West of Jordan, is nearly surrounded by a ditch. Many houses and other buildings have been erected in the city and country, this season, and many more would be if materials and laborers could be procured.

Ogden, Provo, Manti and Parowan cities have organized under their respective charters, and are governed by municipal law. The nights have been warmer than usual the past three months; winds more frequent and stronger than common in the Valley; and there was a frost on the low lands on the night of the 28th of August.

The United Sates mail leaves, Great Salt Lake City and Independence, Missouri, on the first of each month, exchanging at Fort Laramie. Also the mail leaves Sacramento and this place on the first of each month; and a mail is exchanged between this and Dallas in Oregon once to two months. We have a weekly mail from hence to San Pete, and a semi-weekly from hence to Brownsville. A Post office is established at Parowan, Iron County, but no mail route is yet established between Payson and Parowan; though at the next session of Congress we anticipate the establishment of a post route from hence to San Diego, passing through Parowan, which ronte [route] will be passable at all seasons of the year.

A Post Office is established at Honolula [Honolulu], Oahu, Sandwich Islands, and letters post paid to San Francisco, will be forwarded every opportunity. A letter from Elder Hiram Clark, President of the Sandwich Mission, dated Honolula [Honolulu], January 27, contains our latest intelligence from those Islands. Elders Clark, and Whittle, were stationed at, Oahu; Elders H. W. Bigler, and Thos. Morris, at Molokai; Elders John Dixon and Wm. Farrer, at Ranai; Elders Hawkins & Blackwell at Hawaii; and Elders Cannon & Keeler at Maui; having entered on their respective labors about the 20th of December. There are many whites on those Islands, but they have little regard for gospel privileges. The Natives generally can read and write, and are under the influence of Missionaries, whose policy it is to keep the natives in subjection to their theories by personal influence, and by means of the Press, which issues a weekly paper. Three or four editions of the Bible have been issued in native Sandwich, which in the end will prove a blessing to that people. No special and direct communications have been received concerning Elder Addison Pratt, and the Mission at Society Isles; since his return thence or from the other Missions, in and about the Pacific, though report says the work is very prosperous in Australia, and other places in that region.

By the Star of July 1st, we learn, there were 42 Conferences composed of 642 branches of the Church in the British Isles, and 3874 Elders and Priests, and more than 32,000 members, and the gospel is continuing to spread, and believers to multiply faster than ever. Near 1000 have emigrated the past season, and 50 were baptized on board the ship Olympus, on its passage from Liverpool to New Orleans; Elder Wm. Howel, Presiding. Elder Wm. Burton, of this city, died at Edinburgh, last March. This is the third death among the American Elders while on the British Isles. Elder Flanigan died at Birmingham at a previous date, and Elder Barnes same years since; and the fourth of all that have died on Foreign Missions in this dispensation. Elder Hanks died at sea, on his passage to the Society Isles, in the year 1843. The London Conference numbers over 3000, and is receiving more than 100 per month by baptism.

In Italy the work is gradually progressing under the Presidency of Elder Lorenzo Snow, and the deep rooted tradition of ages, is beginning to give place to sober reflection and light of truth. Elder Snow is translating (if not already completed.) the Book of Mormon into the Italian language. The Waldenses are beginning to look after the truth, and Switzerland is becoming glad in the hope of Eternal Life. Elder John Taylor is in France, preaching and translating the Book of Mormon into French, though probably the translation is complete, before this, and the prospect is flattering in that country. Elder Erastus Snow, continues his labors in Denmark, and has translated the Book of Mormon into the Danish language, so that, that most important of all Books, to this generation, may now be read by the greater portion of the inhabitants of the earth, in some language with which they are familiar. Much opposition has been manifested towards the Gospel in Denmark, and adjacent countries; yet the truth has triumphed and will prevail, and Satan will continue to oppose, and fight, until he is bound; and that opposition is good to prove the faith and integrity of the Saints; and that is one reason why it is necessary there should be a Devil, even to prove men, and make manifest who the righteous are, Miracles are wrought, the sick are healed, the lame leap, the poor have the gospel preached to them, and God is with his saints. The gospel has recently gone from Germany to Iceland.

At no time since the proclamation of the gospel in this age, has the Church been in a more prosperous state, than at the present. At no time have the saints been more ready to follow counsel, and do those things which are required of them, and God is blessing them on account of their obedience; and yet there is room for improvement, for advancement in every thing that is good; and that man who does the best he knows how today, should so continue to live in the exercise of faith and intelligence, which will produce good works, that he shall know more, and be ready to carry that knowledge into practice, so as to [be] better and more useful to-morrow; and so on, from day to day, till he is prepared to enter into the presence of the Father. It [If] men would be great in goodness, they must be intelligent, for no man can do good unless he knows how; therefore[e] seek after knowledge, all knowledge, and especially that which is from above, which is wisdom to to direct in all things, and if you find anything that God does not know, you need not learn that thing; but strive to know what God knows, and use that knowledge as God uses it, and then you will be like him; will see as you are seen, and know as you are known; and have charity, love one another, and do each other good continually, and for ever, even as for yourselves.

But if a man have all knowledge, and does not use it for good, it will prove a curse instead of a blessing, as it did to Lucifer, the Son of the Morning. If a sinner is advised to repent, and be baptized for [a] remission of of his sins, and does it not, it will prove to his condemnation instead of a blessing, and he cannot receive the laying on of the hands of the Elders for the reception of the Holy Ghost. If a Saint who has received the Holy Ghost, is counselled to gather with the Saints, to come home, and he neglects to come, he has no further claim to the blessings promised unto the faithful, who obey all the commandments; his light becomes darkness, and remaining in this state, where God is he cannot come; for the ordinances in the house of the Lord, in Zion, and her Stakes, are as necessary for a full salvation, as baptism is for a a partial salvation; and the voice of the good Shepherd is to all Saints, even to the ends of the earth; "gather yourselves together, come home; and more especially to the Saints in Pottawatamie, the United States, Canada, and the British Isles; *come home! come home!!*"

O ye Saints in the United States, will you listen to the voice of the good Shepherd? Will you gather? Will you be obedient to the heavenly commandments? Many of you have been looking for, and expecting too much; you have been expecting the time would come, when you could journey across the mountians [mountains] in your fine carriages, your good wagons, and have all the comforts of life that heart could wish; but your, expectations are vain, and if you wait for those things you will never come, you will leave your carcas[s]es to rot in the midst of the Gentiles, and your faith and hope will depart from you.

How long shall it be said in truth "the children of this world are wiser in their generation, than the children of light." Some of the children of the world, have crossed the mountains, and plains, from Missouri to California, with a pack on their back, to worship their God—gold [.] Some have performed the same journey with a wheel-barrow, some have accomplished the same with a pack on a cow. Some of the Saints, now in our midst, come hither with wagons or carts made of wood, without a particle of iron, hooping their wheels with hickory, or raw hide, or ropes, and had as good and safe a journey as any in the camps, with their well wrought iron wagons; and can you not do the same? Yes, if you have the same desire, the same faith. Families might start from Missouri river, with cows, hand-carts, wheel-barrows, with little flour, and no unnecessaries, and come to this place quicker, and with less fatigue, than by following the heavy trains, with their cumbrous herds, which they are often obliged to drive miles to feed. Do you not like this method of travelling [traveling]? Do you think salvation costs too much? If so, it is not worth having. Sisters, 50 and 60 years old have drove ox teams to this valley, and are alive and well yet; true they could have come much easier by walking alone, than by driving a team, but by driving the oxen, they helped others here; and cannot you come the easier way?

There is grain and provisions enough in the Valley for you to come to, and you need not bring more than enough to sustain you 100 days, to ensure you a supply for the future: and let those who are coming with teams and have the means, bring nails, glass, paints, oils, wire No. 9. osage, orange, and other choice seeds, and such articles as are most needed in a new country, to exchange with the brethren here for bread: and start earlier than usual, even as soon as teams can possibly be supported on the prairie, so as to avoid the spring rains and floods, and be here to assist in harvest.

Dispense with all useless rubbish on the journey, and provide young stock of the best quality, so far as you are able to bring any; and silver instead of gold, for change is scarce, and silver will be more useful. The funds for the emigration of the poor use continually increasing, by the exertion of the Saints in the valley; and it is the duty of Saints in the States, and other places to add to those funds according to their ability. President Orson Hyde will return to Kanesville this Fall, and make preparation to remove his family to this place the ensuing season. Elders Ezra T. Benson, and Jedediah M. Grant, will repair to Kanesville, immediately after Conference, and superintend the emigration the coming season. They are sent expressly to push the Saints to the Valley.

Elder Woodruff will remain at this place at present; also Elder Geo. A. Smith, unless circumstances shall occasion his return to Iron County. Nothing definite has been heard of Elders Parley P. Pratt, Amasa Lyman, and Charles C. Rich, since they passed Little Salt Lake last spring; though the papers report their arrival in California with 140 wagons, and it it is supposed that Elder Pratt is pursuing his mission on the Islands and coasts of the Pacific; and that Elders Lyman and Rich, are marking a settlement in California, between this and San Diego, and gathering the Saints thereto, and that they will appoint missions to the Elders, as the Spirit shall direct. They are also instructed to extend settlements toward Iron County, at every desirable point, with as little delay as possible. Elder Orson Pratt is on the way from the States; and about 500 wagons, mostly of the Saints who are emigrating to this place; but they started too late, were hindered by heavy rains and floods, and it will be very late before the last camp will arrive.

By recent communication of President F. D. Richards, of England, we learn that the prospect of immediate emigration of the European brethren to San Diego, as we had anticipated, is in no wise flattering, there being no regular shipping from England to that port; therefore, Elder Richards will continue to ship the Saints by way of New Orleans to Kanesville, as hitherto, only be particular to start them earlier in the season, so that they can be at Pottawatamie in season to build their hand-carts, and walk or ride over the mountains as they may have means, before snow falls. Many of the English brethren and sisters think it a trifle to walk 15 or 20 miles to hear preaching on the Sabbath, and return home at evening, and then stand at their labor the remainder of the week; and can they not walk 20 miles per day, for 50 days, for the sake of getting to their Father's house; to the home of the Saints, in the Valley of the mountains? Some may have teams, some cows, they can kill buffalo, and other game by the route, and when weary, rest a day, if the Sabbaths are not long enough; and can not they fare as well as ancient Israel, when journeying towards Canaan? They were traveling 40 years, but the Saints can walk from Kanesville here, in twice 40 days, and harm no one. Now is the time for the Saints to come, except such, as are counselled to tarry, and preach, and the like, and they who can come will never find a better time. If some of the Saints would bring shepherd dogs, they would be of great use in the Valley; shepherds are needed here.

Elder Richards will also appropriate so much of the emigrating fund in his possession, as may be necessary to forward two ship loads of the Saints to Kanesville, where they should be, in April, ready to prepare for their journey over mountains. Let your selection be made in wisdom, having regard to those who are faithful, and have borne the burdens in the heat of the day; and also in some measure to their professions or trades, according to our need of the various mechanic arts, as we have suggested, and your information of circnmstances [circumstances] here shall prompt; committing them to the care of agents, wise men, who will receipt for all moneys, and will take receipts before landing, of every individual, of the amount he has been helped by the funds, with a promise to refund the same as soon as he can procure the means; and let each company remain together until they arrive at this place, when it shall be told them what to do.

Start no more Saints on account of the Poor Fund, than you forward means, by the Agents in charge, to see their respective companies safe through to the Valley. And let no funds go into the hands of those who are helped, but let all moneys expended be paid out by the Agents, for passage, provision, and such things as are indispensible [indispensable]; taking receipts of all, in the harbor of New Orleans, and also at Kanesville; and let all shose [those] receipts, funds on hand vested in oxen, cows, or other property in the hands of the Agents, or in use of the company, be reported at our office immediately on arrival. It is expected that every person assisted by the Fund, for the emigration of the poor, will help themselves to the utmost of their ability; and not one bring stores of merchandize, to the expense of another's tarrying behind. No! let him who has chests of goods, or money, pay his own passage, and let those be helped, who cannot help themselves, or, but in part; and many can furnish every necessary thing but their passage money, and many, a portion of that. If those assisted by the Poor Fund expect to ride in carriages and wagons over the mountains, the number you can forward will be very small; but if they have faith to walk through, a few teams loaded with flour, will make a multitude comfortable, and many can be removed at little cost. The funds now on hand amount to more than $13,000 raised almost entirely in the Valley; and if the Saints in England and other places, shall be as diligent the coming year, in donating to the Fund, as have the Saints here, a great ingathering may be expected to follow.

The Semi-annual Conference of the Church, commenced at the Bowery in this city, Sunday, Sept. 7th, at 10 A. M., and continued from day to day, till Wednesday the 10th inst., when it adjourned to the 6th of October, next, to meet at the same place. President Brigham Young presided during the Conference, which was composed of a vast assembly of the Saints, from all the settlements; and the various proceedings were marked with strong feelings, in preachings, teachings, testimonies, and in sustaining all the general authorities of the Church, as they were last April, except Lewis Abbott, deceased, and Elisha H. Groves, removed to Iron County, and William Snow, and Winslow Farr, were appointed to fill the vacancies in the High Council, Nathaniel H. Felt and John Banks were appointed Presiding Travelling Bishops, to travel in the Church and among the branches, counselling the Bishops, and seeing they are faithful in their calling, in gathering, tithing, and causing it to be forwarded to the general office, in keeping correct accounts: and they settle with the several Bishops, from time to time, and reports the same to the Presiding Bishop.

E. T. Benson and Jedediah M. Grant were appointed Agents to gather the poor, and President Orson Hyde's, Agency was continued. Elders Samuel W. Richards, Wilard Snow, Abram O. Smoot, Dorr P. Curtis, and Vinson Shirtliff, were appointed missions to the British Isles, and Daniel Carn, to Germany. President John Young, received a mission to Ohio, to preach the gospel, and gather the Saints, and Elder John L. Dunyon to preach the gospel in the States. The Conference voted to observe the words of wisdom, and particularly to dispense with the use of tea, coffee, snuff, and tobacco, and in this thing, as well as many others, what is good for Saints in other in the mountains, is good for Saints in other places, and if all who profess to be Saints would appropriate the funds, lavished on luxuries, and articles unwise to use, to the benefit of the Public Works, we would soon see another "Temple of the Lord."

The Conference also voted to commence anew the tithings and consecrations; and that within 30 days, each Saint should make a consecration of one tenth of his property, and one tenth of his interest or income ever after, and that all who will not thus tithe themselves be cut off from the Church.

A fire is kindled in the earth, and who shall quench it? A light is shining, and who shall extinguish it? The nations of the earth are fearing and trembling; the fire burns, and the light dazzles, but they know not what to make of it. God has set his hand to restore Israel, and save the remnants of Ephraim, but they know it not. The oldest and most powerful governments are shaken to their centre, and kings know not the cause. The way is fast preparing for the introduction of the Gospel into China, Japan, and other nations, which for ages have sat in darkness, and stood aloof from celestial science, and foreign intercourse; and it is the business of the Twelve Apostles, to fill every open door, and push to the right and left, with the horns of Joseph, until every heart shall feel; and blow the trump of salvation, till every ear shall ring with the glorious intelligence, that there is a God in the heavens, who guides the destinies of all men, and who would that all men should come to the knowledge of a crucified Savior, and be saved.

Brethren pray for us! Sisters pray for us! Be humble, prayerful, watchful, diligent, and persevering, in every good word and work, and in the end you shall overcome all evil, and sit down with us in our Father's kingdom. Elders of Israel lift up your voices like trumpets, open your mouths wide, and proclaim salvation to all the meek of the earth, and you shall bring many souls to Zion.

It is our wish to see all the members of the Quorum of the Twelve Apostles, at the General Conference in this city, on the 6th of April, 1853. And we hope the brethren will be able [to] arrange the affairs of their various missions, in such a manner, that no injury will be sustained by the Saints, while they shall spend a little season with us in council. And we pray God, the Eternal Father, to bless the Saints, throughout the earth, in the name of Jesus Christ. Amen.

BRIGHAM YOUNG,

HEBER C. KIMBALL,

WILLARD RICHARDS.

In vol. 3, no. 21 (November 14, 1851): p. 1, col. 2–p. 2, col. 2

2

Counsel from Brigham Young and the First Presidency to the Saints Scattered Abroad in Pottawattamie County, Iowa

Letter from the First Presidency [Great Salt Lake City, April 9, 1849]

By the following letter from the Presidency of the Church, it will be seen that tithing, donations, &c., are desired in the Valley to build up the place, and to make such improvements as may be necessary. Any person that may be friendly disposed towards the Saints, who may have a heart and a purse to aid them in that lonely Valley to improve it, and to make it a desirable place, can forward to us their tithing, donations, &c., &c., for those purposes. This is the place to pay your tithing and to bring your gifts and offerings for the benefit of the church in the Valley. Elder Woodruff has a similar appointment in the Eastern States, and Elder Orson Pratt a similar one in England. We know of none others that have such an appointment on the East side of the Rocky mountains.

To all persons interested:

This letter certifies that Elder Orson Hyde is a duly appointed and authorized agent of the Church of Jesus Christ of Latter Day Saints, to receive, solicit and gather tithing and donations in the United States, and he is hereby instructed to keep a detailed account of all such receipts, specifying the amount, name and residence of each individual making remittances, and forward the same to us by some faithful brother, or appropriate the same to our order. And should Elder Hyde leave the States, he is instructed, to countersign and transfer this letter to some faithful brother whom he shall select as agent in his stead, and this letter thus countersigned shall be good authority for said agent to transact the above business as though Elder Hyde had done it himself.

Given under our hands and seal at Great Salt Lake City, Great Basin, North America, this 9th day of April, 1849, for and in behalf of said Church.

~~ BRIGHAM YOUNG.

{ SEAL.}HEBER C. KIMBALL,

~~WILLARD RICHARDS.

Presidency of said Church.

In vol. 1, no. 11 (June 27, 1849): p. 2, col. 2

Letter from the First Presidency [Salt Lake City, October 16, 1849]

GREAT SALT LAKE CITY,

Oct. 16, 1849.

PRESIDENT ORSON HYDE:

Beloved Brother: The Lord has been devising, or rather making manifest ways and means to facilitate the gathering of his Saints in these last days, and we lose no time in cheering your heart with the intelligence, and offering such suggestions as may be wisdom for you to follow, in helping to roll on the glorious work of gathering Israel.

The saints are prospering in this valley, which is a very natural result of their good endeavors to keep the commandments and work righteousness. The desire of the brethren to see Zion built up, is constantly increasing: and their labors are tending more and more to this one great object. Of our proceedings, the circumstances of the saints, and things in general in this region, you will soon learn by our late epistle; and we write you more particularly at this time, concerning the gathering, and the mission of our general agent, for the PERPETUAL EMIGRATING FUND, for the coming year, Bishop Edward Hunter, who will soon be with you, bearing the funds already raised in this place; and we will here state our instructions to Bishop Hunter, so that you may the more fully comprehend our designs.

In the first place; this Fund has been raised by voluntary donations, and is to be continued by the same process, and by so managing, as to preserve the same, and cause them to multiply.

Bishop Hunter is instructed to go direct to Kanesville, and confer with the general authorities of the church at that place, and by all means within his reach, procure every information, so as to make the most judicious application of the funds in the purchase of young oxen and cows, that can be worked effectually to the valley, and that will be capable of improving and selling after their arrival, so as to continue the fund the following year.

We will give early information, to those whom we have directed to be helped, and such others as he shall deem wisdom, being aided in his judgment by the authorities among you, so that they may be preparing their wagons, &c., for the journey.

Wagons are so plenty here, that it is very desirable not to purchase with the perpetual fund; but let those to be assisted make wagons of wood, when they cannot get iron, such as will be strong and safe to bring them here, so that all the funds may be appropriated to the purchase of such things as will improve in value, by being transferred to this place.

The poor can live without the luxuries of life, on the road, and in the valley, as well as in Pottawatamie and other places; and those who have means to purchase luxuries have monies to procure an outfit of their own, and need no help, therefore let such as are helped, receive as little assistance in food and clothing, wagons, &c., as can possibly make them comfortable to this place, and when they arrive, they can go to work and get their outfit, of all things necessary for comfort and convenience, better than where they are, and even luxuries.

As early in the spring as it will possibly do. on account of feed for cattle, Br. Hunter will gather all his company, organize them in the usual order, and preside over the camp, traveling with the same to this place; having previously procured the best teamsters possible, such as are accustomed to driving, and will be gentle, kind and attentive to their teams.

When the saints thus helped arrive here, they will give their obligation to the Church to refund to the amount of what they have received, as soon as circumstances will permit; and labor will be furnished to such as wish on the public works, and good pay; and as fast as they can procure the necessaries of life, and a surplus, that surplus will be applied to liquidating their debt, and thereby increasing the Perpetual Fund.

By this it will readily be discovered, that the Funds are to be appropriated in the form of a loan, rather than a gift; and this will make the honest in heart rejoice, for they love to labor, and be independant [independent] by their labor, and not live on the charity of their friends; while the lazy idlers, if any such there be, will find fault, and want every luxury furnished them for their journey, and in the end pay nothing. The Perpetual Fund will help no such idlers; we have no use for them in the valley; they had better stay where they are; and if they think they can devise a better way of appropriating the emigrating funds, than we propose let them go to work, get the funds, make the appropriation, set us a better pattern, and we will follow it; and by that time we are confident they will have means of their own, and will need no help.

Brother Hunter will return all the funds to this place next season, when the most judicious course will be pursued to convert all the cattle and means into cash, that the same may be sent abroad as speedily as possible on another mission, together with all that we can raise besides to add to it; and we anticipate the Saints at Potawatamie and in the States, will increase the funds by all possible means the coming winter, so that our agents may return with a large company.

The few thousands we send out by our agent, at this time is like a grain of mustard seed in the earth: we send it forth into the world, and among the Saints, a good soil; and we expect it will grow and flourish, and spread abroad in a few weeks so that it will cover England, cast its shadow on Europe, and in process of time compass the whole earth: that is to ray, these funds are designed to increase until Israel is gathered from all nations, and the poor can sit under their own vine and inhabit their own house, and worship God in Zion.

If from any cause, there should be a surplus of funds in the hands of our agent, when he leaves the States with a company, he will deposite [deposit] the same with some good house, subject to our order, or bring it with him as wisdom dictates.

We remain your Brethren
in the Gospel,
BRIGHAM YOUNG,
HEBER C. KIMBALL.
WILLARD RICHARDS.

In vol. 1, no. 24 (December 26, 1849): p. 2, col. 5

Letter from Brigham Young [Great Salt Lake City, November 19, 1849]

The following extract we copy from a letter written at Great Salt Lake City, Deseret, dated Nov. 19th. 1849, by President B. Young, to Elder Orson Hyde.

You had the company's well fitted out with breadstuffs, &c., many of them wish now they had instead of their two barrels of flour, half a barrel of sugar, for we have wheat, barley, rye, oats, and buckwheat, with potatoes, turnips, carrots, beets, pumpkins, squash, &c. &c., in abundance. Do I say potatoes plentiful? Yes! for I see many use them constantly, and let me state, that a brother, the other day brought thirty-three bushels of potatoes to the tithing office, being the tenth of the increase of one bushel of seed. He raised upwards of three hundred and thirty bushels, another brother (Halliday) raised from one bushel of seed wheat one hundred and eighty bushels, so you see we have plenty of eatables; sustenance for man and beast in abundance, and we wish you to send on all the help you can. Labor is high and laborers are hard to find. We pay common laborers one dollar and a quarter per day, mechanics from two to three, and pay them in the above mentioned produce, likewise in coffee, tea, sugar, domestics, clothes, boots and shoes, meat, &c. &c., or the pure gold if they wish, and we anticipate next season it will be the same with us, only a little more so, that we invite all to come who can find their way to this place, and are willing to stay when they get here and labor to build up Zion. May the blessings of Heaven rest upon you while helping to build up the Kingdom of God is the prayer of your affectionate brother in the Gospel of Jesus Christ.

BRIGHAM YOUNG.

In vol. 2, no. 12 (July 10, 1850): p. 3, col. 1

Letter from the First Presidency [Great Salt Lake City, April 13, 1850]

We clip the following extract from a letter written at Great Salt Lake City, April 13, 1850, by the Presidency of the Church, to Elder Orson Hyde. The extract is brief, but it comprehends a great deal, and our brethren and friends would do well to read it and treasure it up:

"We have not much to say, or not much time to add to what we have written. It is a very busy time with us. The weather is fine and the brethren are very busy putting in the wheat, and from present appearances, we shall need double the hands at harvest we now have. We anticipate a visit from you (Elder Hyde,) * * * this summer, and hope you will bring a great many reapers along, for we shall need them. The public works are languishing for help, and we want the Saints at home.

"Push the Saints to Zion, and persuade all good brethren to come, who have a wheelbarrow, and faith enough to roll it over the mountains, &c.,

SIGNED,

BRIGHAM YOUNG,

HEBER C. KIMBALL

WILLARD RICHARDS.

In vol. 2, no. 13 (July 24, 1850): p. 2, col. 4

Letter from the First Presidency [Great Salt Lake City, September 21, 1851]

Great Salt Lake City,

Sept. 21, 1851.

To All the Saints in Pottawatamie,

Beloved Brethren: We send unto you our beloved brethren Ezra T. Benson and Jedediah M Grant, for the special purpose of counselling and assisting you to come to this place, and we desire you to give heed to their counsel in all things and come to this place with them next season; *and fail not.*

Come all ye officers in the Church and all ye officers in the State or county. There is no more time for Saints to hesitate what course they will pursue. We have been calling to the Saints in Pottawatamie ever since we left them to come away; but there has continually been an opposing spirit, whispering; as it were—Stay another year, and get a better fit-out, until many who had means to come conveniently have nothing left to come with, even as a former Prophet said, "if a man will not gather when he has the chance, he will be afflicted with the Devil," his property will go to waste, his family fall by sickness, and destruction and misery will be on his path; even so has it been with some of you, and soon will it be with more of you, if you do not hearken to this call and come away.

What are you waiting for? Have you any good excuse for not coming? No! you have all of you, unitedly, a far better chance than we had when we started as Pioneers to find this place; you have better teams and more of them. You have as good food and more of it; you have as much natural strength as we have had to come; our women and children have walked here, and been blessed in walking here, and barefoot, too, only as they could occasionally get a skin from the Indians to make a moccasin, and can you not do the same? You can. And we say again, come home! And if you can get one good wagon and team to five families, and five teams to 100 souls; or no teams at all, more than cows and calves to your handcarts, you can come here with greater comfort and safety than the Pioneers come here who had nothing to come to; while you will have every thing; and here is the place for all the Saints to get their fit-out for Zion, even from all nations, therefore we say again, *Arise and Come home.*

Elder Hyde will return to your place, with Brs. Benson and Grant, and act in his calling as usual; but you must not depend too much on him, for he has his private affairs to settle and prepare to bring on his family, and come with you; and we have sent Brs. Benson and Grant to bless you, and counsel you and relieve Br. Hyde. Therefore we wish you to evacuate Pottawatamie, and the States, and next fall be with us all ye Saints of the Most High, and it shall be well with you if you will keep all the commandments.

Oh ye Saints, give not your heritage to reproach, neither sell your improvements in Pottawatamie to strangers for nothing. No! rather sell your improvements for their value or give them into the hands of those you shall be counselled to, for the benefit of the poor Saints who are coming after as consecration, for the benefit of the poor.

It is a day of sacrifice, and those who are ready to sacrifice and do their duty, and come home, they may save being burnt. How long will the Saints in St. Louis, remain where they are? Arise and come with the Saints of Pottawatamie, and you shall be blessed.

We remain your brethren in the
New Covenant,
BRIGHAM YOUNG,
HEBER C. KIMBALL,
WILLARD RICHARDS,

In vol. 3, no. 21 (November 14, 1851): p. 2, col. 6

3

Minutes of Church Conferences Held at Kanesville, Iowa (April 6, 1849–October 6, 1851)

Conference Minutes [April 6–7, 1849]

First Day.

Pursuant to the Semi-Annual adjournment of October, 1848, the Conference of the Church of Jesus Christ of Latter-day Saints, on the 6th of April, A. D., 1849, convened at the Stand, prepared for that purpose in the Hollow, about 60 rods northwest of the Tabernacle, at 2 o'clock, P. M. The morning having been so rainy, that they could not assemble.

Present of the Twelve, Orson Hyde, George A. Smith and Ezra T. Benson.

President O. Hyde addressed the assembly relative to the prosperous condition of the Church, and our duties to our Heavenly Father, the manifestations of his kind providences: the present aspect of the weather; the severity of the past winter, and the local affairs of the Kingdom of God.

The Conference then organized—President George A. Smith, moving, that Pres't. O. Hyde act as President of said Conference. (Carried.)

Pres't. O. Hyde mentioned, that E. M. Greene and James Sloan be clerks of said Conference. (Carried.)

Pres't. Geo. A. Smith moved that Robert Campbell be Reporter, to report speeches, according to the best of his ability. (Carried.)

Pres't. Geo. A. Smith moved that James Craigan and Philemon Merrill act as Marshall's during this Conference, in seeing that the congregation is properly seated, horses and wagons kept off from the ground; all things kept quiet, and that they call to their aid as many good men as shall be necessary. (Carried.)

Pres't. O. Hyde, said there were some items of business to be brought up before the Conference; but in consequence of the late hour and the wind should not bring them up this afternoon. He would leave it for Brs. Smith and Benson to touch upon the items, that the people may have them to reflect upon; said he wanted some good sermons preached to warm up the hearts of the brethren. As the cold winter is now past, and the sun begins to climb the northern latitude, to warm the earth with his benign rays; so may our hearts be warmed with the Spirit of God. Spoke relative to prayer: said, it was the ancient order of things for the Saints to kneel before the Lord, to pour forth their fervent desires unto him; but we have been through so much, and passed through so many trials, and placed in so many different and difficult circumstances, that it has become very common for us to pray standing up. But let us kneel. He then knelt with the assembly and poured forth a fervent prayer; imploring the divine spirit to conduct and guide the affairs of the Conference; to bless the Saints in the Salt Lake Valley and those scattered abroad.

The Brethren sung, "Come all ye sons of Zion."

Pres't. E. T. Benson moved, that A. Burnham be requested to act as Chorister during the Conference. (Carried.)

Prest. O. Hyde proposed that seats be reserved in front of the stand for the singers, and that all who are singers, no matter whether they understand the rules of singing or not, come forward to those seats and mingle their voices in harmonious songs of praise to God our Heavenly Father. He further said, there had been complaints brought to them (referring to Presidents G. A. Smith, E. T. Benson and himself,) about the dam that had been erected across the Mosquitoe Creek, by Mr. Meeks. Said, the Church has nothing to do with it, but the law was open on this as well as other matters, and there was plenty of jurisdiction in the county. He would recommend that the people living down there, who are incommoded, meet, and with Mr. Meeks agree on some three or five good men, disinterested; who shall examine the affair, and then say what is right; and let both parties agree to abide their decision, and then do it. I do not like for men to lose their labor, neither do I like for settlements to be exposed to sickness and disease by stagnant waters.

Pres't. Geo. A. Smith, said, notwithstanding it was windy, he thought best to lay before the Brethren some items of business for their consideration. Spoke on church policy; thought it best for all to work for each others general good; recommended that the Brethren keep up their organized meetings of the High

Priests' Quorum; and also of the Seventies; and that one or more officers from each branch attend said meetings, so that a continual semi-monthly report of intelligence may be had with each branch. Spoke concerning administering to the poor; locations of the Saints coming in the present expected emigration. The large farmers and those who are able, leaving with their teams, and leaving the poor without teams He wished to organize a body of Elders to travel and preach through the county, so that each branch may have preaching every Sabbath.

Prest. E. T. Benson spoke on the drift of emigration. He went in for the salt instead of the gold.

Prest. O. Hyde said, we were always right and always safe, when we go in the channel of the counsel of this church.

Prest. G. A. Smith spoke relative to the gold mines, &c. Also requested the brethren to invite in those who are from a distance, and not prepared to take care of themselves.

The Brethren sung "Come let us anew," &c., and adjourned until 10 o'clock, A. M. tomorrow.

Second Day

SATURDAY, April 7th, 1849.

Pursuant to yesterday's adjournment, the Conference convened at the stand, at the appointed hour. Present, Presidents O. Hyde, Geo. A. Smith, and E. T. Benson. The High Council seated in order, in front of the stand.

The Choir comfortably seated, and the Marshalls performing promptly their duty. The Band also was present. The weather was beautiful.

The Choir sung, "Come, come, ye Saints,' &c.—with music.

Prayer by Prest. O. Hyde, and the Choir again sung, "Let Zion in her beauty rise," &c.

Pres't. O. Hyde addressed the Conference, calling the minds of the people to a remembrance of their duties to the Divine Ruler, with thanksgiving for life and health. I rejoice to see so many countenances sparkling with health; and if I may judge from their expressive smiles, a good spirit inhibits each bosom. Spoke relative to riches; the work of removing the Saints to the Valley; the arrival of emmigrants. If the rich all go away, we who stay, will be on the Bishop's hands, (Geo. A. Smith said the Bishop is going,) then we shall be left free. The wages offered for hands to go in the Government Trains, will be inducements that will take away the nerve and strength of our settlements. Is this good policy? Some will go to California or Oregon, on an 18 months' trip, probably at $40 per month which will be $720,; and when they return having paid their expenses and the debts that their families have contracted during their absence, it will swallow up their wages, and they will be no better off than those who remained at home with their families, and will not have half so many chickens, pigs, calves, &c. Is it wisdom, when we are not demanded, when our country is not invaded, for us to leave? Is it wisdom on another hand, for the strength of our people to leave! I tell you, if you go in this way, I will go too. I am willing to play my part, but I want some of the strength and nerve of the people to be yoked with me.

After much counsel on this matter, we have come to the conclusion, that it is best for us that every man, that don't go to the Valley stay at home, and raise grain to feed the hungry. We want every man that is a farmer, who intends going to the Valley to put in a good crop, and if you cannot sell it, leave it with the proper authorities for the benefit of the poor. We are placed here to do good to each other. We can do no good to God, but we can do good to his Image here on the earth. I had rather trust the chance of the salvation of that man that remembers the poor, than the man that has his £20,000 sterling a year for preaching. Do not let the California gold or government wages entice you away. Related Br. H. C. Kimball's dream of the bear with golden claws and golden teeth, which may be explained in the high wages of Government, and the gold of California. We will not say, you shall not go to California or in the Government service, but we, as your humble servants, recommend that you do not go. My exhortation is more particularly intended for those who purpose going to California and Oregon. If a man can get in a good crop, and leave his family comfortable, have his pigs, &c., growing, and go for a few months, we have no objections.

Pres't. Geo. A. Smith, moved, that A. P. Rockwood, Lyman Stoddard and William Snow be a Committee to receive reports of Branches from their Presiding officers. (Carried.) Reports to be made by to-morrow noon.

Pres't. O. Hyde nominated, Hiram Clark, to baptize such as wish to be baptized for the remission of sins during the Conference.

Pres't. Geo. A. Smith, moved, that Joseph Young, George Coulson, H. W. Miller and Joseph S. Clarke, be a Committee to ordain during this Conference.

Pres't. O. Hyde said, in relation to ordinations. Don't ordain them for their own accommodation, but ordain such as sustain just and equitable characters, and ordain them for the strengthening and building up of the kingdom of God.

Pres't. Geo. A. Smith, moved, that some Elders be appointed to travel and preach through the county. (Carried.)

Pres't. O. Hyde said, we wanted men that would devote their time to it, and moved that Joseph Young, Lyman Stoddard, J. M. Benson, Hiram Clark. H. W. Miller, and James Snow be said Traveling Elders. (Carried.)

Pres't. Geo. A. Smith, moved, that those six men, be a Committee to devise the plan of their appointments, and carry out their measures; calling to their aid such of the High Priests, Seventies and Elders, as shall be necessary. (Carried.)

The Quorum of the High Priests will meet at this place the first Sabbath, and the Seventies the third Sabbath of each month.

Pres't. Geo. A. Smith, spoke relative to the business of the Conference, and the plans to carry out our measures to sustain and carry on the work of the Kingdom of God; urged the necessity of the Brethren that go to the mountains to assist in getting in spring crops, and if they cannot sell them leave them for the poor. This is the best place for Mormons to make a fit-out. From the experience of the past we find it is best that each man make all preparations as though he was going to stay.

Moved, that it was the mind and council of this Conference, that every man that intends going to the Valley, do something in the way of labor, to leave for the benefit of the poor who shall stay behind him. (Carried.)

President E T. Benson said, he rose to bear testimony to what had been said, and to the correctness of the business that had been done. We talk about moving to the Valley, about our labor, our stock, calves, &c., because it is our religion. We are called to pass through trials and tribulation to make us perfect. Jesus passed through all these to make him perfect, yet he was without sin. I can bear affliction when I can have the sympathies and confidence of this people. We have many things to present to this Conference. Every man that has named the name of Christ wants salvation. Every man and woman must learn their duty, and not be slothful servants; spoke on anticipation and the millennium. If you want an exaltation press forward, be diligent and follow counsel. Ye Elders of Israel, what is your calling here? To hoe potatoes. But anticipate when you get to the Valley. What then? Why, you will be sent to the nations of the earth. Do you think of it? I think of it; I pray about it, and I want you to pray about it too. Before I get through I shall touch the hearts of the rich. We have some Church property to carry to the Valley, and we are going to roll it off from our shoulders and you must bear it. A year ago last fall and winter, it is known that numbers of Elders were sent to the East to collect means to help off the Presidency last Spring to the Valley. Br. Erastus Snow was traveling in New York, and I was in Pennsylvania, and when Br. Snow had been laboring in a certain Branch, and the Brethren were ready to respond to the call, a certain Elder and a good man too, gets up, and said to the Brethren, you need not respond to that call; I have been to Nauvoo, and among the Saints, and I know that when any of the authorities want anything the Brethren immediately hand it out to them. Now I mean that Elder shall eat his words, he is here in the congregation—I have seen him to-day; now let him come forward, and give some cattle, and help to roll off this property. If he don't want his name exposed, he may come privately—Nicodemus like. I believe all things will work right. And now Brethren I want you to get the good spirit. When a man has been legally baptized into this Church, he becomes a legal heir to the Holy Ghost, and need not complain of being lonesome, for he can commune with the Comforter when he is about his work. Faith is the gift of God, and there is but one principle on which he will give it. Some will say, if we carry the church property will you pay us for it? I will tell you; the man that helps us in sending the church property shall have our blessing. We want to strengthen the hands of the Brethren in the mountains; they are raising crops, and let us do our part.

Pres't. O. Hyde moved to adjourn one hour and one-fourth, and meet at the same place.

Dismission by Pres't. Geo. A. Smith.

In vol. 1, no. 6 (April 18, 1849): p. 2, cols. 3–6

Conference Minutes

Sunday, April 7th, 1850.

10 o'clock, A. M.—Conference convened at the stand, a large congregation assembled of the brethren, and many of the California Emigrants.

PRESENT.—Prest. O. Hyde, the High Council, Benj. L. Clapp, and Seth M. Blair upon the stand[.] The band and Choir present

MARSHALS—J. C. Wright, Isaac Allred and Elisha Everett.

Music and singing while the congregation were assembling.

This morning opened with an almost cloudless sky, and soon spreading his genial rays on the large rural amphi-theatre of the Conference ground, situated on the S. E. end of Chadwick street, and which was capable of containing 20,000 souls. At an early hour the carriages, buggies and wagons began to arrive on the ground and the audience comprised a large number of emigrants, gold diggers and strangers as well as the Saints.

The meeting was called to order by reading and singing "The Savior lives no more to die."

Counsellor Coulson addressed the throne in thankfulness for the favorable weather and for the blessings of health, &c.

The choir then sung "Let every mortal ear attend."

Prest. Hyde said it is with peculiar feelings I rise to address you this morning. It is difficult to speak in the open air, but by the assistance of your faith and prayers, I will endeavor to say some things that may be for your consideration hereafter. I look around through the congregation. I see many strangers that are passing through with expectation of bettering their condition. Many are wealthy and have a competence, but still men that are ambitious will go through any danger to be more powerful and more wealthy. There are many, I may say thousands, that will be swept away in a few years, and leave their places to be filled by others. There has been much said in these times with regard to the communion of spirits. The subject may be somewhat novel; but as the spirit of truth will bring things to my understanding, it may be profitable. Much has been said with regard to spirits. The doctrine is being incorporated among the learned that angel's visits are few and far between, but in former times it was not so. Angels in the latter times we claim have visited our earth. I will here state that my curiosity has been awakened with many others by accounts in the Eastern Newspapers of visitations of spirits from the unseen world, had been heard—mysterious knockings, and unsatisfactory accounts given about them. I have paid little or no attention till I had seen an account by a private letter. There seems to be mysterious knockings and that cannot be accounted for; some think it is ventriloquism and some one thing and some another. The philosophers and priests are staggered by it, but they have come to the conclusion that it is supernatural agency. I bring forth this for the purpose of presenting things of this nature in their proper light, that we might know what is transpiring among us. Has the Almighty manifested things mysteriously, or has he come out in open daylight to our understanding. Witness the case of Lot and the Angels, in the form of men, and their visits to him—and the hurrying him and his family out the city—and the city being wrapt in flames of fire. The time when our Savior was born, God sent messengers to the Shepherds that were watching their flocks. What was the intelligent language employed on that memorable occasion. "Glory to God in the highest, peace on earth and good will to man.["] There was nothing mysterious, all was light and no darkness at all. By and by an angel was sent to Mary: saying, I am Gabriel, &c.; every thing was open, frank and free that emanated from the Almighty. Does anything that emanates from the powers of darkness bring things clear to the understanding—no all is darkness. I will here mention one thing that was written by a hand on the wall in the King's palace "Mene, mene tekel upharsin." The wise men of the nation were struck with terror and astonishment at the unknown writing upon the wall; but Daniel, the prophet of the Lord declared to the king, "thou art weighed in the balance and found wanting, &c." We will come to the Savior who proclaimed salvation to the people, and what did he say! "Oh Jerusalem, Jerusalem, thou that stonest the Prophets and killest those that were sent unto thee," &c.; by and by the Savior was put to death, and strange sights were seen, and these sights and scenes were prophecied [prophesied] of by the people as good omens, and they thought promised protection, when the very symbols were signs of the city's speedy overthrow. Witness also the heifer bringing forth a lamb. "They had eyes but did not see—minds that could not understand, and they were subject to any spirit that might visit the earth. They could see the sights but could not understand them. A man was seen running about the streets of Jerusalem, and continually cried for some days "Woe unto Jerusalem, &c. They would not correspond with the glad tidings brought by the angels, and proclaimed by the Savior—here was something good. We may learn from the past and draw correct conclusions by them of the future. How is it in our days. An angel has come bringing us a message of mercy through Joseph

Smith and he who has brought this to us has been murdered in cold blood, in Carthage prison, and perhaps your humble servant may have to share a like fate; but my life is not in my own hands; but the testimony has been reiterated from one end of the Continent to the other and the great mass have cried away with him, they have cried Joe Smith—false prophet—away with him. Where has he gone. He has gone to Heaven and his counsels may have some weight in directing the counsels of Heaven in the affairs of the Church. We have gone preaching the gospel without money and without price, sometimes we have slept in barns and under apple trees; our clothes been worn out, and our feet sore and bleeding. Sometimes we have met with a smile and a happy greeting, and sometimes a favor. We have been called every thing; we have been kicked round the earth till we have become almost case hardened. We owe no ill-will to any, but good will to all mankind. How was it in Jerusalem before its final overthrow, strange sights were seen and they were divided one against another &c.. There seems something like it in our own country. I am sorry to speak it. Would that it were otherwise. Not only is division in our Halls of Legislation; but the signs are ominous that the States will split against each other. The North against the South. What is the condition. Let the rock be but once split, and the demon of confusion and bloodshed will run universally. When we consider these signs they do not portend good, inasmuch as it is all mystery[.] We are forced to the conclusion of this kind. What are we to do. Why, the Savior has said when these things come to pass, lift up your heads and rejoice, for your redemption draweth nigh. Not to rejoice over their destruction, but rejoice that our names are written in the Lamb's Book of Life, for the time will come when the Savior will say, come ye blessed of my father, inherit the kingdom prepared before the foundation of the world. When God sends a message it is plain, and no mystery or mysterious knockings; it is all peace and good will to men; But the other looks like the witch of Endor raising up Samuel, it does not mean any good.

Prest, Hyde was at the conclusion of the foregoing remarks requested to relate the circumstances of his visiting Jerusalem, as John E. Page had been heard to say that he had never been there. He then related his travels from place to place, and that he was kindly treated there by the Missionaries had eat and drank with them, and they have borne testimony that I have been there and now this man says I have nont [not] been there—I reproach him not—for my feelings pity him. If any man thinks I have not told the truth they may question me.

Music and singing.

Prest. Hyde introduced as business of the Conference, the first Presidency:

Prest. Brigham Young, you know his policy. Some may be discommoded for the present, who have sent off their teams and wagons and they have not been retu[r]ned. But what have they done? Have they not sent back means to help off the poor and they have pledged themselves to do so until every soul has been removed. Wait with patience and you[r] turn will come. (Susta[i]ned by a general expression of the people.)

Prest. Kimball, was unanimously sustained as First Counsellor to Prest. Young.

Prest. Williard Richards was sustained as Second Counselor to Prest. Young, and Historian to the Church.

Prest Orson Hyde, said: I want to know if you approve of my course and policy in Pottawatamie, and east of the Rocky Mountains, and I want you to speak your sentiments freely. (Voted unanimously.) I intend to take a course that will deserve your good will. I will pray for you, and want you to pray for me.

P. P. Pratt, was sustained as one of the Twelve Apostles.

Prest. Orson Pratt—I had expected him here to-day. It would do us good to see him. His labors have been as efficient in England as any man that has ever been sent there. He has introduced a system of philosophy that has been a battering ram to the learning and philosophy of the present age. According to a letter from England there has been an increase of 11,000. Though he is a small man, he is made of good stuff, and the best of all is, God is with him. May God bless him. Amen (Voted unanimously.)

John Taylor has been sent to open the Gospel in France; but the gospel has been opened for him. He will always pass. (Voted unanimously.)

Wilford Woodruff. He has charge of the Eastern Branches. I expected to see him to-day. (Voted unanimously.)

Geo. A. Smith—may the Lord bless his memory. Amen. (Voted unanimously.)

Amasa Lyman, he presides over a company of good boys that have been digging in the gold mines; may he be successful, blest and protected in the land where he is. (Voted unanimously.)

Ezra T. Benson was sustained by a unanimous vote in his Apostleship.

C. C. Rich—sent to take Amasa's place, may he be prospered in his labors where he is. (Voted unanimously.)

Lorenzo Snow, has gone to the Pope's Dominions. It is a hard place for a man to preach—he has gone with his life in his hand, may he have our prayers. (Voted unanimously.)

Erastus Snow has gone to Denmark—may he be successful. (Voted unanimously.)

Franklin D. Richards has gone to England, he is a good man—may he be blest in his labors. (Voted unanimously.)

The Presidents of the Seventies, viz: Joseph Young, Levi Hancock, Henry Herriman, Zera Pulsifer, Albert P. Rockwood, Benjamin L. Clapp and Jedediah M. Grant were each acknowledged and approved in their office.

The High Councilors were then presented in a body, viz: James Alred, Ira Oviatt, Aaron Johnson, Geo. Coulson, Wm. Snow, James McLellan,

Geo. W. Harris, Lyman Stoddard, Jacob G. Bigler, Henry W. Miller, Noah S. Bulkley and Jerome M. Benson. These were acknowledged and approved in their office, with the exception of two contrary votes. Br. Jesse Haven voting in the negative—explained saying he had been informed that Br. Coulson had stated publicly that Joseph Young was on the ground of apostacy, and this had given him feelings so that he could not conscientiously vote for him, for he believed that Br. Joseph Young had a good spirit and of the right kind, and he thought that Br. Coulson should say whether he had made these statements or not.

Br. Clapp said he did not vote, not that he had any personal feelings, but from a sense of duty as it was for the whole people, that these votes were cast, and from general dissatisfaction that he found where he had labored this winter towards Jerome M. Benson, in regard to his competency and teachings, and insulting course.

Counsellor Coulson made some explana[t]ions concerning his remarks before the Branch where he presided relative to the spirit of apostacy, and that that same spirit had in a certain measure manifested itself here among us, and referred to the course that hand been taken by Br. Joseph Young and some others, and he protested against it.

On motion, Br. Benson's case was referred to the next sitting of the High Council on next Saturday. Br. Benson requested [t]he presiding Elders and teachers of the different branches where he has preached to the present.

Remarks from several.

Br. Clapp said there had been some remarks relative to himself or the saw-mill association, to which he felt to respond.

Prest. Hyde, said he was not personal, he did object to the saw mill combination in too. He then called upon Br. S. M. Blair, to give the feelings of the Government upon the subject of the saw mill.

Br. Blair said he presumed he knew the situation of this as well as any man, he had done as much for it, and that at his own expense, he had taken the model, and presented it at Washington to the commissioner of Patents, and that his other business led him to leave the city before the patent was to be issued, and was informed by the Clerk that the patent would be issued in eight days, and he telegraphed to that effect, but Capt. Day had since wrote to him that the model was rejected on the ground that the principle would not work.

On motion, Bishop Aaron Johnson and his counselors, Jacob G. Bigler and Lorenzo Johnson were acknowledged and approved in their office.

On motion, the President of the High Priesthood, Wm. Snow was acknowledged and approved in his office.

On motion, the President of the Elders, Joseph S. Clark, was acknowledged and approved in his office.

On motion, the Patriarch here, Wm. Draper, Sen., was acknowledged and approved in his office.

On motion, the official acts of those in the Valley, so far as we know them, are approved.

Br. Hyde spoke relative to Father Cutlers going to the Valley this season according to the request of the presidency or that he come up here and show that he has a desire to go. He said he verily believed if Father Cutler really wants to go to the Valley and had not the means, that he could be helped so that he could go.

On motion, the Conference voted that if Father Cutler does not go to the Valley, or come up here and show that he has a disposition to go, that he is disfellowshiped by this conference.

Bishop Aaron Johnson spoke relative to tithing and the poor.

Br. Hyde said, as the Lord had made it an article in his Law, he hoped that every person would make it one in their creed to pay their tithing.

Br. Edward Hunter from the Valley spoke relative to the Perpetual Fund and the gathering to the Valley.

Col. C. M. Johnson spoke relative to the organization of the County, and the people paying their taxes, that it should be done without coercion, for the good of the people, and that he had given them all reasonable time, &c.

On motion, the Conference adjourned for one week to meet at this place if the weather is favorable, but if unpleasant, until the first pleasant sabbath thereafter at 10 oclock, A. M.

After singing and music the congregation was dismissed, having been detained six hours without recess, and were very attentive.

Supposed to have been between two and three thousand persons upon the ground.

Only 22 branches were represented.

ORSON HYDE, CH'MN.

E. M. GREENE, CLERK.

In vol. 2, no. 7 (May 1, 1850): p. 1, cols. 1–4

Adjourned Conference [May 19, 1850]

WEDNESDAY, MAY 29, 1850.

ADJOURNED CONFERENCE.

SUNDAY, MAY 19, A. D., 1850.

The adjourned Conference convened at the Stand, South-East of the Printing Office; it was a fine morning and the sun shone delightfully, a large congregation had gathered at an early hour. Present of the twelve Prest. O. Hyde, O. Pratt., W. Woodruff. The members of the High Council, the Marshal,

J. C. Wright, and many influenced brethren. The meeting was called to order by the Prest. O. Hyde. Singing by the choir and music by the Band. Prest. O. Hyde remarked it was a very important time with us and all people from here westward, spake of the words of the martyred Prophet, "Plagues shall go forth and shall not be stayed, also relative to the poor Saints that have landed in this place. The grog shops, &c., also relative to the drouth [drought], said the first thing to obtain rain was for each person who can, take a poor family and become a benefactor and temporal Savior to them at this time, and said *will you do it.* General cry, *yes! yes!* Prest. Hyde then said shall the sins and pollutions of those raised up drunkards, turn on the heads of the keepers of grog-shops, whether Jew or Gentile, the people said, *yes!* He then said if the brethren were willing to take in poor and succor them, to manifest it by raising their hands, also those who would take their stand firmly against those grog shops, drunkenness and all vices, (all hands were up.) No opposition.

Prayer by Prest. O. Pratt.

Music and singing. "Thou art gone to the grave." Prest. O. Hyde said, the out and in emigration caused so many changes, it required new officers to be appointed to keep all things right; Bishop Aaron Johnson was going to the Valley, and it was necessary for this Conference to choose a man to fill his place, and proposed that Bishop Aaron Johnson make a nomination.

The Bishop nominated Wm. W. Lane, was seconded by J G Bigler, and carried by a full vote. Prest. O. Hyde, proposed an agent of the High Council to travel among the branches.

On motion, it was voted that one man fill that agency.

On motion it was voted that Lyman Stoddard fill that office.

On motion, it was voted to appoint a Committee to settle the poor Saints who have just arrived.

On motion, Jacob Bigler, J. M. Benson, Isaac Bullock were chosen said Committee, and David Candland clerk.

Councillor Geo. Coulson spoke of the Indian affairs, the shooting of those Pawnees last spring, &c., said Prest. O. Hyde, had had an interview with the chiefs of tribe, and on their agreeing that all difficulties were settled, and that they should not molest our emigrants or the Californians as they pass through their lands he paid or caused to be paid the sum of $50, and called the people to sustain it by subscription.

Isaac Bullock, Daniel Mackintosh, James Sloan, T D Brown[,]. Jacob Bigler and John Needham, were appointed to pass through the congregation, and $48 was received.

Charles Allen and Rebecca Winslow came to the stand and were joined in marriage by Prest. O. Hyde. Music and singing.

Br. W. Woodruff dismissed with prayer for one hour. The same night a copious shower of rain fell.

Sunday, 2—P. M.

Elder Orson Pratt spoke at some length, giving cheering accounts from England, of the progress of the work of the Lord. He was followed by Elder Woodruff from the East, who made a few happy remarks.

Conference adjourned until October 6th.

In vol. 2, no. 9 (May 29, 1850): p. 3, col. 1

Adjourned Conference [April 20, 1851]

SUNDAY, April 20, 1851.

Convened at the Grove at half past ten o'clock, weather rather chilly with showers of hail and rain occasionally. The choir sung a hymn. Prayer by Elder Hyde; after which President Hyde, stated, that in consequence of the unsettled state of the weather, we would have to proceed immediately to the business part of the Conference; and further said: it must needs be that offences come, but woe to them by whom they come; but if they should come, we must endure hardship as good soldiers.

The Apostle Paul said: "I know this, that after my departure grievious [grievous] wolves shall enter in among you not sparing the flock, also of your own selves shall men arise, speaking perverse things to draw away disciples after them.["] Of necessity there must certain men rise up; and I look at them as if they were inspired of God, and raised up in the same way that Pharoah [Pharaoh] was raised up, that God might show forth his power through them. Though Satan is fallen, he is control[l]ed by our Heavenly Father, and is used for some good purpose as those who have affinity to him.

On motion, President Brigham Young was sustained in his office as President of the Church, by a unanimous vote.

Moved that Heber C. Kimball and Willard Richards, be sustained as his Counsellors.

Elder Hyde stated with regard to the others officers there, that they were under the control of the first Presidency—hence no need for an action in their case. He also stated that there was another character before them, and that his course and conduct were always before there vision.

On motion, Orson Hyde was sustained as President of the Twelve Apostles by a unanimous vote—and upon the presumption that the quorum were one in all things, there was no reason why they should not all be presented at once,—their several localities were named,—the motion put, and carried unanimously in the affirmative. The Elder then stated that his highest ambition was, to do right.

Moved by President Hyde and seconded, that his Counsellors be sustained: carried unanimously.

On motion, Bishop W. W. Lane, and his Counsellors was sustained, carried.

On motion, W. Draper, Sen., be sustained as Patriarch of the Church in Pottawatamie carried.

The President adverted to the case of Father Cutler, and after some salutary remarks, moved that he be cut off from the Church, carried by a unanimous vote.

On motion, D. P. Raney, W. Redfield, Nathan A. West, Walter W. Cox, and Amos Cox, were cut off, for aiding and abetting Father Cutler, and promulgating his insidious views.

President Hyde stated; it will be recollected that last year the case of Father Cutler was brought up before the Conference; we said if he would move up among us, and manifest a wish to go to the Valley, I would pledge myself that he should receive the means to go with. He has never been here, but endeavored to exercise an influence to draw away people after him. He now says; that he received his commission from Br. Joseph, because he thinks that Br. Brigham will not sustain him in his foolish operations.

The Choir then sung, "Now let us rejoice in the day of Salvation."

The President then arose and said: I Want to say something about emigration. I expect to go myself; but will not go until the emigrants get across the river. I have an anxiety to speak unto you freely; but I do not feel that this is the day to speak upon the subject in consequence of the weather,—but a few words touching emigration. It is with us, as with our Fathers: we are strangers and pilgrims on earth. There never were any people that received promises from heaven, but had to be the same. For instance. Abraham: Did he live in his father's house and home all his days? It was said to him, as recorded in the acts of the Apostles; "Get thee out of thy country, and from thy kindred, and come into a land that I will show thee." I will give it to thee for an everlasting possession: yet Abraham died, and did not receive (if Stephen's testimony be true) one foot of it; for he, and his seed had died not having received the promises, but saw them afar off and were persuaded of them and embraced them, and confessed that they were strangers and pilgrims on earth;—they sought a city which had foundations whose builders and maker is God. John says, "he saw the city descend from God out of Heaven, as a Bride adorned for her Husband, and then he said: behold the tabernacle of God is with men, and he will dwell with them, &c. The reward is reserved for those who come up through great tribulation, and have washed their robes, and made them white in the blood of the Lamb.

After a lengthy discourse on tithing he referred to the Revelations in the Book of Doctrine and Covenants on the subject, and promised peace, health, and prosperity to those who crossed the plains, and also to those who remained, inasmuch as they did their duty, and what the law of the Lord required, and abstain from murmuring and ingratitude.

Br. James C. Snow, having been appointed as traveling agent for this High Council to settle all difficulties arising in the branches of the Church, of a moral or spiritual nature, was confirmed in this office and calling by a unanimous vote. By the consent of parties, he may also act as traveling Bishop to settle differences arising out of demands of dollars and cents, or any property of value.

The Bishop and his counselors are the most suitable men to settle matters of difference arising out of dollars and cents, because it is more in accordance with the nature of their office and calling, to transact temporal business. By the consent of parties, the Bishop may also settle differences of a moral or spiritual kind. This arrangement is not designed to be applicable any farther than this Bishoprick [Bishopric].

President Hyde continued, and said: I hope that you, who are able, will turn out some cattle or money or both to the aid of the Perpetual Emigrating Fund. Turn out your cattle and money and vest it where it will rebound to your everlasting honor, and the poor will bless you, and God will bless you. We want to increase the Fund and extend its operations abroad, and in other countries, and other lands.

You that want cattle from the poor fund, whose names have not been published, call and get them, and feed them well on corn and hay, and prepare yokes and break them to work, or you may not get them. Others may importune us so strongly that we shall let them all go.

The Elders who are going out on missions, are requested [to] meet at the New Hall on Hyde street, at 3 o'clock, P. M. On motion, the Conference adjourned to meet on the 6th of October next, at this place. Dr. George Coulson, of Council Point, closed by prayer.

A great concourse of people was present; and although the day was very unfavorable, the people anxious to hear, remained on the ground till the final close. Harmony, union, and the spirit of God ruled the meeting. And happy are we to say, that not a dissenting vote was given to any measure proposed. All was right, and all was well. The Lord be praised, and let the people say Amen.

DANIEL MACKINTOSH,
Reporter.

In vol. 3, no. 7 (May 2, 1851): p., 1 col. 6–p. 2, col. 1

4

Accusers of the Brethren

William Smith

We have just read a letter from Br. Appleby, of New Jersey, which he requests us to publish. We should be pleased to comply with his request, if the subject of his communication was not such a melancholy picture of human weakness, depravity, and woe. William Smith was excluded from the church in Nauvoo, for saying that his brethren had wronged him and sought his life. This was a slander upon the church which they would not endure. He said this to excite a sympathy in his favor that merit would never award to him. As bad as he represents the church to be, he was written two or three letters to us, confessing a part of his sins, and desiring to get back into this *"wicked and abominable church:"* but the church would not receive his confession, and consequently would not receive him. He would confess many things that he was not guilty of; but the church required him to confess fully the things that he was guilty of. He never wished the priesthood for any other purpose than to use it as a key to sensuality, avarice and ease. Being righteously cast out from the church, he seeks the ruin of those who did it, by trying to transfer his own sins to their account.

The people in New Jersey know him so well that he can do no harm there, neither in Philadelphia. We do not wish to disgrace the columns of our paper by admitting any of his low blackguard and vulgarity. He cannot harm you Bro. Appleby, neither the cause of our Master. A pure and noble mind will never dwell upon such scenes of depravity, as he seems to take delight in.

Your letter speaks of three dollars being sent on subscription. This was a mistake. The letter contained only a one dollar note on the "Trenton Banking Company." The ten dollar sent in a former letter, mentioned in your last, was duly received. But we send you the papers.

In vol. 1, no. 1 (February 7, 1849): p. 2 col. 2

Alpheus Cutler

It is frequently reported to us that Father Cutler and the Silver Creek Branch of the Church are going widely astray, and that they are saying and doing many things—that some of them are holding secret meetings in Missouri, &c; and we are called upon to take further action in their case: But we here State, that Father Cutler's Mission was suspended at the April Conference. The action of that body was forwarded to the Valley by Elder Egan with all the whys and wherefores. Elders George A. Smith and Ezra. T. Benson will be there to represent, in person, the way Father Cutler has treated the action of the Conference in reference to his mission, also in reference to his holding in fellowship a man that was disfellowshipped by the Conference; and will also faithfully and truly represent to the Presidency of the Church the spirit by which that branch and its leaders are actuated. We decline any further action until we get official returns from the Presidency which we shall look for, in part, by Elder Babbitt, whose return we look for about the middle or twentieth of this month.

Every wise man knows enough to keep away from such as are rejected because of their vanity, self-will, self-righteousness and self-sufficiency: But those who are kindred spirits of theirs, will cling to them, sympathise with them, and will make with them their home, while a heated zeal holds them together; but when this gives way to calm and sober thought, the ties are broken, and one goes to the world, another becomes an infidel, a third goes to Texas or to the gold mines. Be patient and all things will be done in their time and in their season Pray earnestly that ye enter not into temptation, and commit all things to the care of Him who will deal justly with all men.

In vol. 1, no. 14 (August 8, 1849): p. 2, col. 3

Sidney Rigdon and James Strang

CENTERVILLE, Sept. 15, 1849.

DEAR BRO. BARNEY: I now take the liberty to address a few lines to you, hoping at the same time that you will pardon me for intruding so much upon your time. The subject that I am about to write upon I deem of great importance; especially to us who have named the name of Christ and should be one, for he hath said that unless you are one ye are not mine. My ears have often been saluted with these words—"Brighamite and Hydeite," now I would ask what is a Brighamite or a Hydeite? I know what it took to make a Rigdonite or a Strangite; Rigdon once belonged to the true Church of Christ, and was in high standing; but be sought for great power and authority to build himself up; and departed from the principles of truth and righteousness, and all those that followed after him were justly called Rigdonites—the same with the Strangites. We see then that the materials that it took to make a Rigdonite or a Strangite was apostacy and dissension.

Is not President Brigham Young striving with all his might, mind and strength to carry out the measures of our beloved Prophet and Seer, Joseph Smith, who was murdered in Carthage jail, for the testimony of the truth which he had bourne? And is he not doing all in his power, together With the Council to build up the Kingdom of God on the earth—that his will may be done here as it is done in heaven; and is not Br. Hyde following in the wake and doing all that is in his power to roll on the work of the last days! Yes, verily yes! Then let all those who truly follow after these men whom God our Heavenly Father hath placed at the head of his Church, let them be called saints of the Most High; let the name of Brighamite and Hydeite cease forever, and every one, both male end female, strive to do all that is required of them. Let us hold up the arms of Moses and Israel will prevail; the Kingdom of our God will be built up, and his knowledge and glory cover the earth as the waters cover the sea, and all will know him from the least to the greatest.

Yours, respectfully,

DAVID CLUFF, SEN.

To Edson Barney.

P. S. I hope to prosecute the remainder of my journey in the coming spring to the Valley of the Mountains—if the Lord will; where I hope to enjoy the sweet society of my brethren. D. C.

Mr. Barney handed us the above private letter which we give a place in our columns, and all we can say to confirm the above is that Elder Hyde, (who is now absent,) and Brigham Young, are one, and their sentiments are one, and their policy is the same in all things, and if there is any who claim to be a Brighamite or a Hydeite we do say that the spirit of the Lord is not with that man, woman, or child; and we will quote an old saying of St. Paul when there were contentions among the corrinthians, which is recorded in the (1st

Cor. 3d Chap., 1st to the 10th verses:) "And I, brethren, could not speak unto you as unto spiritual, but as unto carnal, *even* as unto babes in Christ. I have fed you with milk, and not with meat; for hitherto ye were not able *to bear it,* neither yet now are ye able. For ye are yet carnal: for whereas *there is* among you envying, and strife, and divisions, are ye not carnal, and walk as men? For while one saith, I am of Paul: and another, I *am* of Appollos; are ye not carnal? Who then is Paul, and who is Appollos, but ministers by whom ye believed, even as the Lord gave to every man? I have planted, Appollos watered; but God gave the increase. So then neither is he that planteth any thing, neither he that watereth; but god that giveth the increase. Now he that planteth and he that watereth are one: and every man shall receive his own reward according to his own labor. For we are laborers together With God; ye are God's husbandry, *ye are* God's building."

This is applicable to those who claim that they are Brighamites or Hydeites, and we can say with the Appostle [Apostle] that it mattereth not about these, whether one planteth and the other watereth, the spirit of the Lord is in the whole matter, and he will give the increase, and bestow upon those who keep an eye single for the upbuilding of his kingdom, and his commandments a reward with the righteous.

And furthermore we will quote the saying of President Hyde, upon this same subject: "Who is Hyde or who is Brigham but your humble servants and brethren in Christ Jesus, our Lord? Those who are saved, are the disciples and followers of Jesus Christ. He is the Great Head of the Church, and after his name are the sanctified called. Brigham is the man to receive the word of the Lord for the Saints—the legitimate channel through which it comes; and Hyde is the man to carry out that word according to his best ability. How many disciples has Christ in Pottawatamie County that will receive this word through this channel? *Every one will do it.*"

The above is conclusive proof that there is no such thing as a discordant note in their whole course. And we can further say that the same policy and counsel that has been given the Saints here, counsel to the same effect has come from the Presidency at the Valley, and this should be evidence sufficient that the Presidency of the Church in Pottawatamie County is moved upon by the spirit of God in all their actions. And all would do well to cease their contentious about the matter, for surely the spirit of Lord cannot dwell where there is contentions.

In vol. 1, no. 18 (October 3, 1849): p. 2, col. 2

Accusers of the Brethren

By letters that we receive from various sources, we learn that the followers of Strang, Brewster, Wm. Smith and several other strange *accusers* of the Saints, are becoming cloyed and sick of the kind of food that has been given them for the last five years: And as the Saints have not been destroyed by the Indians nor by crickets as they predicted—nor have their bones bleached upon the prairies as they declared they would; the poor things are getting weak in the faith, and seeing the prosperity of the good folks in the Valley, they are becoming restless and uneasy at their own condition. They have also seen that the desperate and wicked efforts of their leaders to convince the United States that we are their sworn enemies, has had no effect—has not made "one hair white or black"—has not advanced them nor thrown us in the rear. The result is, that many of them intend coming here and going from here to the Valley in the Spring. They have tried hard to destroy us, yet if they have found repentance and will manifest it to us, we will forgive them, and ask our Heavenly Father to forgive them also. They have not injured us particularly; but the wound they sought to inflict upon us has fallen upon their own flesh and spirit.

To all whom it May Concern.

This is to certify before God and man—that we never took any oath, neither have we ever been brought under any covenant against the Government of the United States, as some vagabonds declare, who only profess the Mormon creed to bring disgrace and dishonor upon those who conscientiously follow its precepts. The crown which they could not place upon their own head, they seek to trample in the mire and filth. We know of no Mormon that has ever taken such an oath, or been brought under any such covenant. Neither do we know of one that ever intends to be.

If these vagabonds had said that we were combined against unjust and unlawful oppression, and against mobocracy by which we have suffered the loss of almost all things;—if they had said that we were combined to pray, and teach our children to do the same, that a righteous judgment might come upon those who have shed the blood of the prophets, and who have sought our destruction, they would not have merited so severe a censure.

If the foregoing is not the truth, and the honest and undisguised sentiment, and feeling of our heart, then we are incapable of telling the truth upon any subject. If a nation fail to do its duty, the power that gave that nation birth, may chastise it. We say no more. Our yea is yea, and our nay is nay, touching this affair.

In vol. 1, no. 26 (January 23, 1850): p. 2, col. 2

William Smith

Cause for which William Smith was Excluded from the Church?

It is a law of the church that its members shall pay over one tenth part of their property which they may have at the time they join the body, and annually thereafter, one tenth part of their increase. This is called the law of tithing. This tithing is appropriate for the benefit of the poor, for public purposes, &c. The temple at Nauvoo was built by the tithing of the people. After the death of Joseph and Hyrum Smith, the Twelve came into power, and they formed the council that were to apply this tithing, or to create a bishop to apply it. William Smith was, at that time, nominally one of the Twelve, and he claimed that it was his right to have one-twelfth part of the tithing set off to him, to be appropriate to his own individual use, or in any way that he thought proper. This was not allowed any one of the Twelve; and he was the only one that ever asked or expected such a thing; and we were conscious that none but a prodigal in every sense of the word, (which we considered him to be,) would indulge such a wish. This being positively denied him, he went up to Galena and published there, or at some other place, a pamphlet, in which he laid many false and grievous charges against the whole Twelve; but more particularly against Elder Brigham Young. This pamphlet was read in part to a large collection of people in the Temple, and he was then and there excluded from the society and fellowship of the church by a unanimous vote of the entire body, among whom were assembled almost the entire authorities of the whole church. To present the cause of his expulsion from the church in a few words, it is this. A wish to appropriate the public funds of the church to his own private use—for publishing false and slanderous statements concerning the church: and for a general looseness and recklessness of character which ill comported with the dignity of his high calling.

In vol. 2, no. 1 (February 6, 1850): p. 2, col. 2)

James Strang

The Mormons.

We clip the following from one of our exchanges, and would apprize the public, that we have no fellowship with the party styling themselves Mormons, who are about to erect a Temple on Beaver Island, in Lake Michigan, James J. Strang is their leader, and they are generally known by the appellation of Strangites, although they denominate themselves Mormons, or Latter-day Saints.

The Mormons are about to erect a Temple on Beaver Island, in Lake Michigan. It will be about one hundred and sixty by sixty feet.

In vol. 2, no. 17 (September 18, 1850): p. 3, col. 3

Reflections for the Disaffected

When the Church was broken up in Illinois many strange spirits appeared to claim their own One went with Rigdon, another went with Strang, another to Brewster, and another to Bill Smith. These all claimed to have the right and power to lead the Church. With one or two exceptions, the Twelve hung to the President of their Quorum, and were united: and if we could have been shaken or moved by the exertions of these disaffected spirits, I am sure that we should have been morally annihilated.

By the united voice of the people, and by their good will, Br. Brigham Young was duly appointed President of the whole Church. He is now appointed Governor of Utah Territory in spite of the most vindictive opposition of these strange and wicked spirits. The Providence of God has prevailed with that man; and Governor Young is far from being that tyrant, murderer, and knave that these wicked persons have represented him. Men have perjured themselves before the Courts of Justice concerning that man, and it will soon appear in the face of the world, that in their zeal to do him a wrong, they have ensnared themselves. God has foiled our enemies, and placed the Cepter [Scepter] over his people in the hands of his chosen, through the agency of the American Government; and may Providence smile upon the Government for their liberality in respecting the wishes of the Saints.

Now, all who have turned away from the Church in times of persecution and trouble, through the darkness that prevailed, may return and find pardon if the will repent, except those who have wickedly and maliciously forged and manufactured revelations, and ascribed them to the Holy Ghost; thus blaspheming against that Celestial agent; and those also who have corrupted themselves, and turned the grace of our God into lasciviousness. You all see that Zion in the wilderness has really prevailed, not withstanding your hatred, your false assertions, your cruel opposition and your crafty and untiring labors to hedge up her way. God is with her in deed and in truth. We have been there and seen them,—have felt and realized that God loves that people in the Salt Lake Valley. We would therefore say to all those who have left us in times gone by, in consequence of the wicked devices of evil men, they may return to the

Church and find favor if they are inclined to do so, after they have fed on husks till they are convinced of the difference between them and corn.

In vol. 2, no. 23 (December 11, 1850): p. 2, col. 2

James Brewster, James Strang, Sidney Rigdon, and Alpheus Cutler

Prospects of the Church.

The Church in Pottawatamie county was never more united than at the present time. Since some disaffected and murmuring ones have left, and gone to the Valley, where they will be dealt with for their own good, the various branches have seemingly melted down into a union, that, we trust, will continue without interruption. There now appears a bright prospect of an early Spring; and the farming interests of this country are being pressed forward with zeal and animation by a large portion of the inhabitants; while another portion are making active preparations for the Valley of the Great Salt Lake.

Our exchanges say that Brewster is broken up, and his company dispersed at Santa Fe. If this is untrue, it is not untrue that he soon will be. Strang will make his own snare and be taken in it. Cutler and his followers are so upright that they, like the boy's tree, lean a little the other way. They who gather not with us, scatter abroad; and the first and most prominent signs of Apostacy [Apostasy], are relations of terrible bad news or tales from the Valley—all sick and dying there—starving to death—Indians killing them, &c., &c. Besides, they are quarrelling at the Bluffs or somewhere else. We would advise all such characters, to save their breath to cool their porridge; and not think the Saints have gone astray because condemnation and fear have filled their own hearts. The cause of truth is on the increase in Pottawatamie and Mills counties. A goodly number of our Methodist friends in Mills county have recently been baptized into our church, and in this town there are more or less baptized almost every week. The cause is prospering in England, Wales, and in Scotland; also on the continent of Europe—in Italy—in Denmark and in Norway; and quite a branch, we hear, is built up in Calcutta. His majesty, the King of Denmark, has accepted the Book of Mormon who, with other members of the Royal family, is examining it. The Book of Mormon will be at the World's Fair, in the English, French and Danish Languages by the industry and perseverance of our Missionaries is those countries. They have strong prejudices to face and to overcome; there is an ARM on which they can lean for help which is more mighty and powerful than the traditions and prejudices of the age; and while immortality beams upon the eye that is single, the sword of truth can be wielded to cut asunder the cords which have bound, so long, the inhabitants of the earth in ignorance, superstition and folly. May the Angel of Mercy sustain those laborers abroad, and nerve them with power and wisdom adequate to every emergency that may arise before them! Let the prayers of the faithful ascend on high that these swift messengers to the nations may light up the world so bril[l]iantly that the honest in heart may see clearly, and not stumble! "How beautiful upon the mountains are the feet of him that publisheth glad tidings, &c." Hope inspires activity—activity produces the means of life, and sets all the wheels of improvement in rapid motion. "Fly swifter round ye wheels of time, and bring the welcome day."

But a few years ago, little was said about slavery and Abolitionism. It was considered then treasonable to think or talk of dividing the Union; But how rapidly has restraint, upon these subjects, fled away! States now talk of seceding from the Union—of arming themselves for the fight: Men in high places, call the Union a damnable humbug, and others set the laws at defiance with a reckless security and desperate carelessness. After the ties are cut asunder which held religionists, of the same creed, together: How long before political bonds will be thrown off like the surplus clothing of two about to engage in mortal combat? The days are numbered, and the Almighty knoweth the times of visitation and trouble. If these things were done in the green tree, what will be done in the dry? And if judgment began at the House of God, what shall the end of them be that obey not the Gospel of God? We say not these things because we wish misery and confusion in the land! No, America is our home and country. We know no other—we seek no other; and while we live, may the "Stars and Stripes" that have floated on the breeze to please the eye and gladden the heart of every son and daughter of Columbia, continue to grace the American name while the constellations of the heavens shine upon our land and upon our sea! But we say them because the Prophets of old have said them; and we, their children, wish to sustain the honor of our fathers, and lead many of our brethren to see and embrace the truth.

"He shall send forth his angels and gather out of his Kingdom all things that offend, and that do iniquity." He has angels for all purposes that he wishes to accomplish. Some are vessels of honor, and some of dishonor. Hence the necessity of a Strang, a Brewster, a Rigdon and a Cutler, to gather the offensive ones out; as the Buzzard diligently removes putrid flesh, because he loves it, and by his labors, he secures to us a pure and fragrant air, the inhaling of which gives life and health.

In vol. 3, no. 5 (April 4, 1851): p. 2, cols. 3–4

5

Conflict between Orson Hyde and Almon W. Babbitt

The Bribery Case

Because we informed our friends last year by letter from Burlington that Col. Warren would tell them when and where to vote, many have come to the conclusion that the Mormon votes were sold, and were to be delivered wherever the purchaser might direct. The facts of the case are these: At the time that letter was written, we had no evidence that our country was made into precincts, attached to any other county. We did not know how, or in what shape our organization might be made; and as we regarded Col. Warren as a high-minded and honorable man, we requested him to communicate with our friends, and let them know where they could legally vote, if they could vote at all: and when the time of the elections would be, as we expected to be absent ourself, and knowing that our people had been in an Indian country so long, shut out from all the common sources of intelligence, that they had lost the track of elections, and would esteem it a favor to be correctly informed. We therefore wrote them as we did, and as A. W. Babbitt, Esq., has labored so faithfully to convict us of bribery and corruption, we here state in sincerity and truth, that this same A. W, Babbitt, Esq., is the only man on earth that ever offered us a bribe; and he did say to us in Burlington in July last, we think, (the exact day and hour we cannot determine,) that if we would go in for the election of

Gen. Cass, he would ensure us a press and type, as good as we desired, without taking any further trouble. We replied that we believed Gen. Taylor was the right man, and we intended to go for him press or no press; and we even told him that forty presses would not divert us from our purpose.

We envy not Mr. Babbitt the honor nor the glory that he has won in commencing, an unprovoked crusade against us.

In vol. 1, no. 6 (April 18, 1849): p. 2, col. 2

Letter of A. W. Babbitt [Kanesville, May 23, 1849]

JOSEPH YOUNG, Esq.,

DEAR SIR: I perceive from a number of the "Keokuk Dispatch," published in September last, that I am made to say, that Orson Hyde showed me a draft upon the Whig Committee at Washington for the sum of $1000. This statement made by the Editor of the Dispatch is false. I have made no statement to any person, or in any place contrary to those made in my letter to the Hancock Patriot in October last.

I am yours very respectfully,

A. W. BABBITT.

In vol. 1, no. 9 (May 30, 1849): p. 2, col. 1

Joseph Young, Esq.

If the statement, denying the publication of the "Dispatch," had been made at the time it appeared, we confess that it would have altered the tone of some of our letters in relation to Mr. Babbitt. If an angel from Heaven had declared that we showed him a check on Washington or on any other place or on any person under heaven, for a thousand dollars, we should have been forced to say that he told a falsehood. We borrowed the money to get our press, and we expect to pay it again honorably and fully. We have no feelings against Mr. Babbitt that we are unwilling to lay aside, neither are we disposed to extort, or exact from him the last farthing.

Mr. Babbitt's statement to Mr. Young, puts the veto upon the bribery speculation charged upon the Whigs. In this, Mr. B. has done himself justice, has honored the truth, and liberated us from unmerited censure. There were several tributary causes of difficulty between us, arising in a great measure, out of a misunderstanding of each other's position, and the consequences were, a pretty brisk and spirited fire at each other. We have concluded to drop and settle the matter, and be friends so far as the Church is concerned. Yet we confess that we have not made a Whig of him; and we think that he will do us the justice to say that he has not made a very deep democratic impression upon us.

In vol. 1, no. 9 (May 30, 1849): p. 2, col. 1

A Day of Rejoicing

On Saturday week there was a great day of rejoicing and gathering among the inhabitants of this town and vicinity, occasioned by the arrival of A. W. Babbitt, Esq., with the United States' Mail from Salt Lake, and the intelligence brought of the good harvest at that place. And also manifested their gratification in regard to the formation of a State Government at Salt Lake; and the new State of "Deseret" was welcomed with smiling faces and gladdening hearts.

The day was beautiful in the extreme, being one of the balmiest days of the season. Soon after the dawn of day the note of preparation commenced, and all seemed to del[i]ght in what was about taking place. The Committee of Arrangements were also busy in completeing the arrangements to ensure the order which is so characteristic among the Saints. About eleven o'clock, A. M., the procession commenced its formation under the direction of J. E. Johnson, Chief Marshal; David Candland and T. Williams as aids, on horseback, with blue sashes and while badges, "Truth and Liberty," with the American eagle in the centre as relief.

The banner for the occasion was designed and painted by Robert Cam[p]bell, of this town, which was magnificent. The design was the Stars and Stripes, in the centre was a r[illegible]g star represented, and in the centre of that was a bee-hive with flowers for relief, in the two side points were the bees all busily engaged, and on the upper point was an eye, made to represent the all-seeing eye of Jehovah. The whole decorated with an excellent display of blue tassels. In the white stripes of the flag, was these words, "The Constitution of the United States, may it live forever and ever," "Liberty and Truth will prevail." This was carried at the head of the procession; next in order was our splendid band of martial music, under the direction of Mr. Pitt, which done great honor to the occasion. Immediately after was the President of the day with his Vice Presidents, with red sashes trimmed with white, badges with "Truth is Liberty," and "Zion is our Home," inscribed, next in order came the Committee of Arrangements with purple sashes, and badges "Truth is Liberty," next followed the members of the High Council in citizens dress; next came the ladies with their smiling countenances, three abreast, which gave a complete charm to the occasion; and next followed the gentlemen, three abreast, preceded by a beautiful banner; and at twelve o'clock the procession commenced marching in the following order: marching and counter-marching on Tabernacle street, thence down Race street, up Hyde street to Main street, thence down Main street, and after marching some distance counter-marched to the stand erected for the occasion in the public square, when Mr. Babbitt was introduced upon the stand by Col. C. M. Johnson and Dr. Andrews, and was received in behalf of the vast assembly by Henry Bishop, Esq., in a very neat and appropriate speech, welcoming him upon his safe arrival to this place, and as a member of Congress from the new State of Deseret, after which Mr. Babbitt, made a most eloquent and heart stirring speech, of considerable length, in substance as follows:

Mr. Babbitt said, had I the vanity to believe that these marked attentions from my fellow citizens were heaped upon me in consequence of some great work or exploit of my own; nature would be too weak to respond; but believing it to be the rejoicing of the soul in behalf of the rising State of Deseret, I shall respond. I look upon the inhabitants of the County of Pottawatamie not as a detached portion; but as an integral part of the people of the Valley of the Salt Lake: a part in feeling and in destination. I believe that the rejoicings of this day eminates from the dispersal of the cloud which has broken from the Valley. It makes the hearts of all rejoice. I shall adopt the circumstances of the day for my subject, I see the motto of your banner is "Liberty and Truth." I might ask, what is Liberty and Truth? The question, what is truth, was asked by one of the ancients. Many would follow truth, if they knew it. I answer. Liberty is the enjoyment of truth, I know our land is boasted as the Land of Liberty, that feeling is what has brought us here to-day. That has sent our friends to a distant land; it has carried me through much toil and many privations and shall still bear me on. Some here are well read in the history of the past; but you are not fully apprized of what has passed among our brethren who have emigrated to the Valley; and knowing that you desire a knowledge and that your feelings are, to join with them, I shall give you the knowledge and also my views, concerning their moves. Our brethren have organized in a State Policy, and are acting under the same; and will act until further provided for, by Congress, and under this act your humble servant has been appointed a delegate to Congress. You will ask, is not this premature? I answer it is not, the Bay Country and New Mexico have done the same. A Governor has been appointed by the President and he has instituted his Government; and it is revered, no law to that intent not withstanding. It is on common law principle and to be handed to Congress for their approval. The eye of Government has been upon us; and why? Because we were reported to not be Republicans. When is the man that ever heard the Prophet Joseph Smith condemn the constitution. The constitution originated by the spirit of God. But as says Judge Story it may parish through the negligence of its keepers. The Constitution is good, it emanated in the bosom of eternity and those who signed it have sworn to protect our citizens, &c. I do not say here, what I would not say, were I in the Halls of the Republic. It is not to advocate any particular form or party, but to present these things to you, and wish to call your mind to these points. I am glad to be able to lay before you the, degeneracy of those who seek the posts of honor. We wish to restore true liberty, &c. Dr. Franklin at the Declaration of Independence delivered a political prophecy, and if people will not hear the ancient prophets, I will quote to them a modern prophet. He objected to a fixed salary being given to the president. He said let him be an honorable man, and the people will take care of that; but you fix the post of honor and profit, and it opens the door to all who are disposed to set themselves up at auction, and it will be bid for by many; but it will be bold and avaricious men, that through that channel will thrust themselves upon you; and when it is so, comes the decline of our Government, &c. What should be the law of the State of Deseret? Their laws should be those of Jehovah, and their rulers should be those who can judge in equity and not after the hearing of the ear. We want to build up the Kingdom of God—that object has carried our brethren to the Valley. I was present on the 24th of July, when they held the Anniversary of the entering of the Poineers [Pioneers] into the Valley, it was like the landing of the Pilgrims on Plymouth Rock, they arrived there destitute, and when they had raised bread enough to satisfy the demands of nature, they rejoiced, and I rejoiced with them; they rejoiced and shouted "Hosanna;" and my soul rejoiced exceedingly. I rejoiced in view of the future. The Lord has opened unto us the windows of Heaven and bestowed bountifully the fruits of the earth. Two tables were spread one mile and a half in length, and seven thousand persons sat down to the feast. The Liberty Pole was raised one hundred and sixty-five feet in the air, and the Banner floated sixty-three feet. I report then a place where the honest can live in the enjoyment of truth, &c. I might say much on the storm that has [was] bursting over the nations for the two years past. You that are acquainted with ancient history, look back, can you show any time of such general revelation, when has there been so much blood and carnage? Trace the revolutions of Rome, what has caused that holy See to move its quarters. I now call upon you to sustain the little State of Deseret, that it may be added a star on the Banner of the Union.

This is neither a political or a religious speech; such an one as the circumstances of the day call forth. This people has given the greatest proof to our Government of their truly Republican feeling in their sacrifices, having offered fathers, sons and brothers upon the alter of duty, who after having gained for their country, a territory highly important both as to wealth and commerce; many have again re-inlisted to support the American Flag in that country. I hope to hear from your honorable committee. And may God bless you is the prayer of your humble servant. A. W. BABBITT.

Prest. Orson Hyde remarked, friends and brethren I shall not long detain you, but I cannot withhold my hearty response to the moves of our brethren in the Valley—peculiar has been the incidents leading to these movements and the formation of the Government in the State of Deseret. Which in accordance with our feelings we also feel to hail our brother who has bourne news to that distant Valley and back. We have a good day and all is right and we feel to rejoice before the Lord, &c., may God add his blessing. Amen.

After the several speeches the mass [of humanity] were formed as before, and marched to the bountifully filled tables near the Tabernacle, which after a blessing was asked of our Heavonly [Heavenly] Father upon the food, all partook till satisfied. Several spirited toasts were given which we were not able to procure—the following toast struck our attention as forcibly, we cannot refrain from giving it:

"May the new Star Deseret, be as the Star of Bethelem [Bethlehem], a guide to the wise of all nations."

Immediately after the dinner was over, those who were disposed, both old and young, entered the merry dance together, and enjoyed themselves till near 11 o'clock at night, when the dance broke up. The President of the day delivered a short and pleasing speech, after which, all went home rejoicing, for the blessings they had enjoyed during this day. Nothing occurred to mar the harmony and peace of the occasion, and will be a day long to be remembered by those who participated in its enjoyments.

In vol. 1, no. 17 (September 19, 1849): p. 2, cols. 3–4

A. W. Babbitt, Esq.

It is known by our friends and by the public, that there was a time when some considerable difficulty existed between us and the above named gentleman; but that difficulty was fairly settled in our Church; and though politically opposed to each other, we think that he cannot feel himself very highly complimented by the recommendation of William Smith as a candidate for Governor of the State of Deseret.

It matters little to us who the Governor of that section may be, if indeed a government should be there organized; if he is only a good man, and will not see his subjects unlawfully murdered in cold blood as they were in Illinois.

In olden times a wicked and familiar spirit spoke in praise of the servants of God; but they rebuked that spirit, and would not suffer it to speak in their favor. We also read, that that which was written aforetime, was written for our learning, that we through patience and comfort of the scriptures might have hope. Would not William like to be Governor of that country? No! for he is already a notch higher in his own estimation. He is PRESIDENT of the Church.

Jesus said, "my sheep know my voice and they follow me, but a stranger they will not follow." William's sheep neither know his voice, nor will they follow him; but will run away after us, strangers, oppressors, tyrants, usurpers of power, traitors to the Government as he declares us to be.

We have seen in the course of our life a deranged man who really owned in his estimation, every house and all the land in the country—he owned several banks, besides a great many ships at sea; and would count over his wealth, in his own mind, with far greater pleasure and satisfaction than William can have in his exalted notions of being the head and leader of the Church, from the fact that his delusion was an innocent one, while William's delusion is criminal because it is spurred on by a vindictive and revengeful malice that corrodes and cankers his own bosom while he affects a consciousness of right.

In vol. 1, no. 22 (November 28, 1849): p. 2, col. 1

Circular of A. W. Babbitt [St. Louis]

Mr. Babbitt has printed a circular at St. Louis in which he has undertaken to construpate our course, and also all those who stood for right, and if we had considered that the letter had been calculated for the benefit of this people we should not have sold much, but he has endeavored to sow disunion in our midst, also to falsify our course; but we find by looking over the Valley news that he is censured at that place for telling the emigrants what was palpably not true, and if he will falsify in one thing he is very apt to in others. We have no good opinion of Mr. Babbitt's political veracity or his course, for his effort has been against the people of this county, from the fact that they are not willling [willing] to support men like Thompson, who, we understand, had the stolen poll books in his possession while in Washington City, and would make Mr. Miller procure an original copy of them, and who has called the people of Pottawatamie county, *indiscriminately* aliens, foreigners, and not twenty-one years of age, roving gipsies [gypsies], and without an abiding place, &c.; and Mr. Babbitt would make you believe that Mr. Thompson was your friend, after making all these statements before Congress, but if this was the first statement of the kind Mr. Babbitt had tried to palm upon us, we might believe him in earnest, but his object has been and now is to break down, President Hyde and the church organization of this county. When Mr. B. came here, he wanted to know if we intended to publish Miller's letter in *phamplet [pamphlet] form*? We replied to him that we would publish it in just such a form as suited our own convenience. He then asked us if we would publish anything for him in reply? We replied that we would if we had time. He then asked us if we would do it for money. We made the same reply as before. We are prepared to prove that we told Mr. Babbitt that he could have a chance to reply in our regular edition, over his own signature, but he never asked the privilege. We make the following extracts from his circular:

"During my late visit among you, a libelous letter over the signature of Daniel F. Miller, was published in the Frontier Guardian, Extra, and as many know, all contradiction was denied me through that organ, *until the election was over.* ["]

All know that he arrived here on Saturday, and our publication day did not occur till the following Wednesday, just two days after the election.

"The object, in my opinion, was to support falsehood at the expense of truth. The election is over and the operators of the *Guardian* did not realize their expectations; and having failed at three successive elections, they may well begin to reflect whether their nett [net] is not on the wrong side of the ship, for they have toiled three years and caught nothing.

But the general election is over, and the Editors of the *Guardian* and its *pets*, have labored in vain, and brought forth in trouble; and now comes the special election, between Miller and Thompson; you may ask which shall we vote for? In answer, I will say, you know my advice has been given on two former occasions, [the people of this county did not take your advice.—Eds.] not to vote for either party. My motto is, between two evils, choose neither. But if there is still a disposition to bring out the people to vote, my advice, is vote for Mr. Thompson. [Consistency, thou art a jewel, Mr. Babbitt advises you not to vote, the next sentence he advises you to vote for Thompson.—Eds.] I have proved him for three years, two of the time[s] smarting under the lash of your vote, and I must in all justice to him, say he has ever shown himself ready to do you justice: do so by him. Again, he has been three years in Congress, is acquainted with all the members, and with parliamentary rules, and can do more good for the time he has to serve than any new member, however friendly he may be. I say then to the friends of Deseret, (or Utah as may be,) support Mr. Thompson, and I will vouch for a liberal friend to her immediate interest."

When Mr. Babbitt found that we were determin[ed] to publish Mr Miller's letter, he attempted to prevent its publication by threats of the most aggravating nature, and said that he had money for the office which he would not pay if we published the letter, and we suppose that it was Locofoco hush money to buy the press into silence, if nothing more; but he found it could not be done, and he tried every scheme that he could to traduce the press. If the money that he had in his possession was in reality for this office, we caution persons from putting money in his hands for us.

Mr. Babbitt, says: "the object in my opinion, was to support falsehood at the expense of truth." Now let us take a view of the different points in Mr. Miller's letter, and see how much of it was false, if any. Mr. M. says: in the

1st place, that Babbitt said that he "was on his way to Pottawatamie county to break down Hyde;" well every one knows that it was his endeavor while here to induce the people to believe that President Hyde, had no right to advise the people which was best for their interest, and that he (Mr. Babbitt,) was the only man that should be heard in this matter, because, we suppose, that he had received a large sum of money to secure the election, if possible, of a Democrat Congressman from this district. 2d. "As regards the people of Pottawatamie county he said he had the money to bring your people all out and make them drunk and vote against the Whig ticket."

As regards to horses, the citizens of this place well knew that he had a splendid span while here, and he also stated in a public speech that he had spent *five hundred dollars*, to prevent the people from voting the Whig ticket. As for getting the people drunk; deducting the voters of Trading Point, or as they term themselves the *Spartan Band*, and which they say numbered sixty, leaves a balance of sixteen Democratic votes, which we are willing to admit that Mr. B. obtained; whether he obtained them by whisky or otherwise, we are not prepared to say; We understand, however, that he had a cask of brandy tapped in one place, and in another that he paid the bill for all that was drank, which run freely during the whole of election day; and about the close of the day he thinking they had not been surfeited enough with liquor he began to break open the Champagne and wine bottles, and his *friends* began to crowd upon him rather heavily for the wine, he then began to pitch it into the street, by the box, a dozen bottles in each; and after so profusely using the liquor he obtained but 16 votes, making an expense of 31 dollars per vote, to him or his party; we are inclined to believe that it must be some portion of the Locofoco corruption fund. Mr. Miller says that he unjustly slandered the people of this county. We have only to refer you to the sentiments expressed by him in his public speeches, when here, for proof. He calls all those who voted for the Whigs at the late election, the *Guardian's pets*; we hardly know what disposal will be made of those 16 *pets*, that he obtained while here at the expense of 31 dollars each; but we believe that the 446 *pets* of the Guardian will show him that they cannot be *petted*, by his slanderous tongue. And they will rally to the polls on the 24th of September, and show that they have no fellowship with demagogues, and those who have robbed from them the most sacred of all rights, their voice through the ballot-box. We refer the readers of this to an article in another portion of our paper, concerning Mr. B., from the Deseret News.

In vol. 2, no. 17 (September 18, 1850): p. 2, col. 4

This Once, and We are Done!

Daniel F. Miller says that Babbitt declared that Hyde had sold himself and had been guilty of all kinds of fraud and villainy, and that he (Babbitt) was then on his way to Pottawatamie to break him (Hyde) down;—that he had the horses to carry him there and the money to bring the Mormons all out, make them drunk and vote against the Whig ticket! Mr. Miller says the above over his own signature; and expresses the wish that it may be made public. Nothing secret here, nothing designed to operate against Mr. Babbitt in an under current. But Mr. Miller shows himself honorable, frank and open.

Now for Mr Babbitt's own evidence, touching the character and conduct of Daniel F. Miller. As early as July 4th 1848, Mr. Babbitt gave us a history of Mr. Miller and his general conduct towards our people. At that time we knew little or nothing of Mr. M. having, for years, been in foreign countries. Mr. B. will recollect that he had a party in the Temple at that time, and Mr. Miller was invited to attend, but could not. About this time Mr. B. declared to us that Daniel F. Miller was a most excellent man;—that he had ever showed himself a faithful and consistent friend to our people "*through thick and thin;*" Indeed, he spared no pains to inspire us with the most dignified and exalted ideas of his nobility of soul and devoted friendship to the Mormons in the day of their trouble. Why, said I, is Miller a Mormon, or does he ever intend to be? No, says Babbitt, he is not a Mormon, and I do not know that he ever intends to be, but it is the nature and disposition of the man to succor and relieve the distressed among all people, and to strengthen the weaker side. In short, he told us that Mr. Miller was every thing that a gentleman and an honorable man could be, and advised us by all means to vote for him. Mr. B. has repeated the same in substance on more than one occasion in Kanesville since that time. Now, did Mr. B. tell us the truth or did he not? George A. Smith, Father John Smith, and a hundred others at the Salt Lake Valley who were well acquainted with Daniel F. Miller can say whether Mr. Babbitt's testimony of him is true or false.

Did Miller tell the truth on Mr. Babbitt at Crippin's Tavern in Charleston? We believe that he did, from the fact that when he (Babbitt) arrived on Silver Creek and in Kanesville, he attempted to do just what Miller declared that Babbitt said he would do. He tried to break Hyde down, and to frighten the boys in the office in various ways to prevent them from publishing; but on finding that he was, "*barking up the wrong tree,*" he told them that he had gold in his pocket for the office, but he should not pay it over if they published Miller's letter. The boys said they could not help it,—the letter had to be published. Whisky, brandy and champaign ran just as freely as water in two house here, at his expense, or at the expense of the Democratic party for all that could be drummed up to rally around his standard. Thus did a *professed* minister of God, (we blush to own it,) seek to blind men[']s eyes, to stop their ears and to palzy [palsy] their senses, by pouring down them the poisonous flood that drowns men[']s souls in perdition and woe. By it, the most depraved and debased passions of men were aroused. Such were his associates, his abbettors [abettors] and fellow helpers: and since he left this section, some have had to be excluded from the Church for intemperance and drunk[en]ness.

If Miller, as an opposite lawyer, had to abuse Paine because he was a Mormon; most likely it was to counteract an influence that asserted friends had raised against him by calling him a Mormon: Or if this is untrue, Mr. Babbitt cannot be altogether a stranger to the fact that lawyers sometimes blew hot or cold according to the "*size of the pile*," and the interest of the client.

We now *prophecy politically, not religiously,* (for we will not desecrate religion so much as to lug it in here) that Mr. Babbitt will not again be elected representative of the people of Utah Territory, particularly after offering such a gross insult to this people as to recommend them to give their votes to the very man who is so intimately connected with that stolen Poll-book affair. Then it will be seen whether certain Senators in Congress will reject every measure of the people of Utah if it does not come with the endorsement of A. W. Babbitt Esq., according to what his vanity has led him to intimate. How can he be a representative from Utah when he resides in Illinois, and never resided in Utah? He needs still to learn the Mormon Creed; "mind your own business!" and not seek to divide the peope of an other's charge upon *any subject,* neither attempt, by threats or flattery to control the *individual* property of another in his absence; the *Press.* But Mr. Babbitt was angry because the boys would not hold still and allow him to break down Hyde and destroy his influence without opposition, according to "Dan Miller's" letter.

In vol. 2, no. 23 (December 11, 1850): p. 2, col. 1

Platte Argus

This Paper says that Governor Young is an unnaturalized foreigner. Where did he get his information? He probably has so much on most subjects that he felt himself able to make the above statement without any information at all.

The Governor's Father was a soldier in the American Revolution—and when we saw him, he drew a pension. His Mother was an American Lady, and gave him birth on the Green Mountains of Vermont. So Mr. Argus has not hit the truth in this case; but has probably hit it in the following, in the very place where he missed it in the above.

"Mr. Babbitt, a distinguished member of the Mormon Church has renounced his connection with the same and come back to the States." What say you Br. Babbitt, is it so?

After writing the above article, we showed the manuscript to Mr. Babbitt, and he authorized us to say that it was unqualifiedly false so far as relates to his renunciation of the Mormon Creed.

In vol. 3, no. 22 (November 28, 1851): p. 2, col. 3

Governorship of Utah

We have just received a letter from a responsible source, intimating that Mr. Babbitt is in Washington, seeking the appointment of Governor of Utah. We can hardly think so; still, we do not know. We would suggest the propriety of waiting a little, to see if Governor Young be removed. Gov. Young is the choice of that people. He has braved the dangers of the wilderness—encountered the savage foe; and still a foe more fearful,—hunger and want,—with hundreds around him, suffering the same. He and his people have endured—have overcome these obstacles,—and plenty of the staple articles of life now abound there by perseverance and industry; and the Valley of the mountains has become almost like the Garden of Eden. We trust that the Government may not find it necessary to remove Governor Young. Were he to be removed, we should not know whom to recommend to fill his place. We should be forced, therefore, to be silent touching the matter of re-appointment in case of his removal.

In vol. 3, no. 26 (January 23, 1852): p. 2, col. 4

6

Poetry

"On the Death of the Phrophet [*sic*]"

Joseph, Farewell! thy spirit pure,
  Is new beneath the Altar crying,
Unto that God of mercies sure,
  On whom thou call'dst when thou wert dying.

Thy cry is heard, and vengeance certain,
  Will fall on those who caused thy death;
For God will raise the secret curtain
  And blight thy murderers with his breath.

We felt thy loss! Yea, tears of sadness,
  Filled every eye in Zion's land;
We would have met thy fate with gladness,
  Could we have staid thy murderers'hand!

But fare thee well! thy woes are ended
  And perfected at suffering's shrine;

Thy name with holy martyrs blended,
  Shall in eternal glory shine.

In vol. 1, no. 1 (February 7, 1849): p. 2 col. 4

Lines Written by Miss Eliza R. Snow, upon the Martyrdom of Joseph Smith, the Prophet and Seer.

[Editor's note: this poem was actually written by William W. Phelps. Eliza R. Snow later edited a primary songbook and attributed the poem to Phelps.]

TUNE—*Star in the East.*

Praise to the man that commun'd with Jehovah,
  Jesus' anointed "that Prophet and Seer,"
Blessed to open the last dispensation;—
  Kings shall extol him, and nations revere.

CHORUS.
Hail to the Prophet, ascended to heaven,
  Traitors and tyrants now fight him in vain,
Mingling with Gods, he can plan for his brethren,
  Death cannot conquer the hero again.

Praise to his mem'ry, he died as a martyr;
  Honor'd and blest be his ever great name;
Long shall his blood, which was shed by assassins,
  Stain Illinois, while the earth lauds his fame,

CHORUS—[Hail to the Prophet, &c.

Great is his glory, and endless his priesthood,
  Ever and ever the keys he will hold;
Faithful and true he will enter his kingdom,
  Crown'd in the midst of the prophets of old.

CHORUS—[Hail to the Prophet, &c.

SACRIFICE brings forth the blessings of heaven:
  Earth must atone for the blood of that man;

Wake up the world for the conflict of justice,
   Millions shall knew "brother Joseph" again.

CHORUS—[Hail to the Prophet, &c.

In vol. 1, no. 23 (December 12, 1849): p. 2, col. 4

"Signs of the Times"

Change upon change, succeeds in rotation,
   Defying the power of millions to tell
What yet will transpire in this generation,
   Among the great mass that desire to prevail.

The past only furnishes series of trouble,
   Millions have died, within the last year,
Friends and acquaintances, freed from the bustle,
   At present are sleeping—whose names we revere.

The old and the young are lying together
   The rich and the poor both wearied, now rest;
The bereav'd and distressed are left to consider
   That life's like vapour, soon vanished at best.

Kingdoms and thrones are continually falling,
   Rulers and Judges are hurl'd from their seats,
Nobles and statesmen, deserting their calling;
   And fleeing for refuge, from mobocrat threats.

Famine and plague, are making their inroads;
   Distress and perplexity, stalking abroad;
Anarchy, wrath and confusion's the Tripod,
   That vice has erected to worship her God.

Signs in the Heavens, the wise men have notic'd
   On earth, blood and fire, and vapor of smoke,
They are but omens, and sent to admonish
   Mankind of their danger before the great shock

Great partisan zeal, and selfish ambition,
   Have severed the links of friendship and truth,

Till tumult and war in every direction,
Are sweeping their thousands to misery and death.

Well might the prophets pause and reflect, on
The picture displayed in vision to them,
And mourn over man for sin and transgression,
Understanding the wrath reserved for some.

A prophet's been raised by the council of Heav'n,
To guide the affairs of the children of men,
Unto him the keys of knowledge were given,
To open the door of salvation to them.

Although he is dead, his priesthood is living,
Ministering still, not withstanding he's gone,
Through agents on earth, ordained to this calling,
The Gospel is offered to all that will come.

Ye nations! wake up, embrace its salvation!
Secure to yourselves, and your children, the truth,
Then you like a rock, in the midst of the ocean,
Shall stand 'mid the surges that time ushers forth

The spirit of Jesus will also be with you,
And in you abiding continually too;
Provided that you in his doctrine continue;
This promise is offered to gentile and Jew.

In vol. 2, no. 1 (February 6, 1850): p. 4, col. 1

"Let Me Go to the Valley"

Let me go to the Valley, for there I have been,
Where the Sun's ever clear, and the sky's never dim,
And the streams from the mountains in grandeur do flow,
'Tis the home of the Mormon! Oh, there let me go.

Let me go to the Valley that lies in the West.
In the far distant mountains tha' I now love the best,
For the Saints will be there, and the Twelve they will go,
While the outcasts of Israel together will flow.

Let me go to the Valley in which I delight,
With my brethren and sisters again to unite,
Where the glory of Zion in her beauty shall glow,
Beneath our own fig tree! oh there let me go.

Farewell all ye mobbers, we bid you adieu,
The Saints you have driven, our brethren you slew,
And the blood of the prophets to heaven doth cry;
The widow and orphan you're caused to sigh.

Let me go to the Valley, where the Salt Lake doth flow,
At the foot of the mountains that's covered with snow,
Where no gallies with oars are seen of her streams,
Where no gallant ships are there to be seen.

In vol. 2, no. 2 (February 20, 1850): p. 4, col. 1

"Far[e]well to Iowa" by Lake W. Gallup

Farewell to Iowa, whose scenes are bright and gay,
We now must leave thee far behind;
And soon be far a way to spend the joyous day,
In yonder valley to our mind.

We look upon the view, and lingering bid adieu,
To lands that's been our home awhile,
Then turn and move along, the road before us long,
While other things our time beguile.
Reflect upon the past, and to me stand aghast,
For yonder scene of long ago,
Breaks in upon the mind with all its varied kind,
And forms a picture of our woe.

Behold our foes at hand, whose evil deeds will stand,
For as to view so drear and sad,
But while we move along, let us forgive their wrong,
To make the picture scene more glad.

We leave a land behind which be bourne in mind,
And years to come when far away,

This parting scene now took of hours and its last look,
Will be as if 'twas but yesterday.

So must we part from all, to go at nature's call,
Where're we end our journey here,
To find the destined port, beyond this world of sport,
Among our friends forever dear.

We seek a mountain land, with this our little band,
And bid farewell to Iowa,
But yet we'll have to roam, through life to find home,
Beyond this earthly one of clay.

'Tis soon we move our way rejoicing with the gay,
That have to cross the distant plain,
Leading to Deseret, where we desire to get,
And with the good and virtuous reign.

And now once more adieu, our lands are lost from view,
So when this life on earth is o'er,
May we in pleasure leave for him who shall receive,
The saints to live forever more.

In vol. 2, no. 11 (June 26, 1850): p. 4, col. 1

"Who Is It That Takes the Guardian?" by James Taylor

I'll tell you who it is and why,
At least I'll take my pen and try,
The good may laugh, the rest may cry.
For they won't take the Guardian.

They who are always discontent,
And run the way that Judas went;
Who for the cause can't spare a cent,
These never take the Guardian.

Those who pretend to be so good,
Whose deeds are dark when understood,
They're always drunk or some such mood,
These never take the Guardian.

Those who are poor but meek in heart,
And always first to take a part
In any good that God may start.
These always take the Guardian.

Those who are found with means of grace,
Who Zion-ward do keep their face;
Its holy cause they ne'er disgrace,
Because they have a Guardian.

Those who christ's coming would abide,
Though my afflictions sorely tried,
Will come and help our Br. Hyde,
And take the Frontier Guardian.

In vol. 1, no. 23 (December 12, 1849): p. 4, col. 1

"The Printer"

Among the ranks of human kind,
Some go before, and some behind,
But mark them well and you shall find
  Not hindmost is the Printer.

Of numbers oft he takes the lead,
And is a gentleman, indeed,
For whom the world has utmost need,
  This very self same Printer.

The lessons which you learn at school,
That you might not grow up a fool.
Had all, in scientific rule,
  Been published by the Printer.

How do your Presidents and Kings
Govern so many thousand things?
'Tis by the types, and screws, and springs,
  Belonging to the Printer.

The farmer, and mechanic, too,
Would, sometimes, scarce know what to do;

Could they not get a certain view
Of work done by the Printer.

The doctor cannot meet the crooks
Of all his cases, till he looks
Upon the pages of the books
Supplied him by the Printer.

The lawyer for a wit has passed,
But high as he his head may cast,
He would be but a dunce, at last,
Were it not for the Printer.

Who is it that so neatly tells
The various goods the merchant sells,
Inviting all the beaux and belles?
Who is it but the Printer?

Two classes of the human race,
Of different size, of different face,
Appears in this and every place—
Now obvious to the Printer!

One sings the base on sharps and flats,
Bedecked with pantaloons and hats,
And long-tailed coats, and smooth cravats;
Of this class is the Printer.

The other sings the treble sweet,
Adorned with frocks and bonnets neat.
And look! now beauteous and complete,
And lovely to the Printer!

'Tis Hymen's will, of course you know,
These classes should in couples go,
And, since the world will have it so,
So be it, says the Printer.

There's not a man below the skies,
Who better understands to prize
The charms that grace a lady's eyes,
Than does this very Printer.

Young Maidens, then, without debate,
'Tis hoped you'll duty estimate,
Before in fact it be too late,
  The value of the Printer.

In vol. 2, no. 14 (August 7, 1850): p. 4, col. 1

"How Softly on the Bruised Heart" by C. D. Stuart

How softly on the bruised heart,
  A word of kindness falls,
And to the dry and parched soul
  The moistening tear-drop calls;
Oh, if they knew, who walk the earth
  'Mid sorrow, grief, and pain,
The power a word of kindness hath,
  'Twere paradise again.

The weakest and the poorest, may
  This simple pittance give,
And bid delight to withered hearts,
  Return again and live;
Oh, what is life if love be lost!
  If man's unkind to man—
Or what the heaven that waits beyond,
  This brief and mortal span?

As stars upon the tranquil sea,
  In mimic glory shine,
So words of kindness in the heart,
  Reflect their source divine;
Oh, then, be kind, whoe'er thou art
  That breathest mortal breath,
And it shall brighten all thy life,
  And sweeten unto death.

In vol. 3, no. 2 (February 21, 1851): p. 4, col. 1

"Remember the Poor" by P. E. Brocchus

Remember the poor, whom misfortune detains,
From the place of their holy desires;
Whose hearts follow those who are crossing the plains,
And who surround the distant camp-fires.

Oh! many have traveled from homes far away,
From Fond ties and from scenes that are dear;
Though the voices of friendship and love bade them stay,
Through great toil they have come, and are here.

Yes, far o'er the main where Atlantic's rude waves,
Along the shore sweep their threatening crest,
They have sighed a farewell to dear friends and dear graves,
For a home in the beautiful west.

Like pilgrims, who long for a dear promised land,
Over mountain and plain they have come,
But here, by the fiat of Heaven, they stand
Still away from their bright future home.

Remember them then, should pale sickness appear,
And trials upon them descend;
Drive grief from their hearts, from their eye wipe the tear,
To their sorrows and wants give an end.

When Winter shall come, and firece [fierce] storms are around,
And make dreary the dwellings of men;
When the forests are sere, and snows bleach the ground,
Oh! comfort them, comfort them, then.

And when spring shall return, haste, haste them away,
To the valley of peace and of rest;
To the mountains that rise, and the streamlets that play,
Through their beautiful home in the West.

In vol. 3, no. 12 (July 11, 1851): p. 2, col. 5

"The Frontier Guardian" by North Pigeon Joe

There is no paper in the land
That ever yet has come to hand
That takes as just and bold a stand,
   As the noble Frontier Guardian.

Truth's the motto she doth hold
And the same to me she doth unfold;
Richer far than Western gold,
   Is the noble Frontier Guardian.

In every part of this wide world
Her noble banner is unfurled,
And every Saint throughout the world,
   Should praise the Frontier Guardian.

Orson Hyde stands at the helm
The cause of error to o'erwhelm
And clear away its nasty phlegm,
   All through the Frontier Guardian.

Night and day he's known to labor
All for the good of his friend and neighbor
That he to them might prove a Savior,
   All through the Frontier Guardian.

And if on earth there is a sheet
That with all others doth compete
Giving men the truth complete,
   It is the Frontier Guardian.

Come then ye Saints both great and small
And gather up before next Fall
And take it with you one and all,
   The noble Frontier Guardian.

And every one that expects to start
And in the emigration take a part,
Should stow away all in their carts,
   The noble Frontier Guardian.

And now these lines I send to you
As a token in the Covenant new
And as a tribute justly due,
  The noble Frontier Guardian.

And for the present I'll say farewell,
Yet perhaps some other day I'll tell
The reason other papers can't excel,
  The noble Frontier Guardian.

In vol. 4, no. 1 (February 6, 1852): p. 4, col. 1

7

Letters from the Mission Field

Letter of Elder Addison Pratt [Sandwich Islands]

DEAR BROTHER SMITH: Having learnt by my wife that you have written me several letters since I left Nauvoo, and notwithstanding I have received none of them, I will write to thank you for your kindness. I suppose that you have been apprized of our proceedings among the Society Islands by way of our letters up to the time I left, there for the Paumotu group. This cluster lies between Tahiti and South America, and on account of their being low coral islands, they are very dangerous to sail among, and of course not much known to navigators, Chain Island, or Aua, is the metropolis of that group, the inhabitants of that Island have conquered the whole group, they carried on a war of extermination for more than twenty years, and their mode of warfare was to depopulate every island they could conquer. They not only butchered the inhabitants, but cut down all the cocoanut trees, so that if any [illegible] ever get back, they would have nothing to live upon. But now the remnants of the vanquished are permitted to return and plant cocoanut trees and build houses upon their lands, and some of those Islands are now getting tolerably inhabited.

But it is even now distressing to see their "morais" or places of human sacrifice. I visited one that I paced off and found that I could trace it 18 paces when it was lost among the roots of the cocoanut trees. This place was prepared by setting up curb-stones in a trench wide enough to receive a human skull and in this trench they were deposited touching each other, and were then covered with two or three inches of dirt. Every war chief had one or more of these "morais." And when they went to war with the neighboring Isles, after their battles were fought, they would take off their hands, and take off the under jaw, for then the head can tell no tales—cook and eat the bodies; and the heads they would tie by the hair and string them on to a rope and tie it to the masthead, frequently having enough to fill the rope, these they would carry home, make a feast, have a war dance, offer the heads as a sacrifice to their gods, and then bury them in the trench. It was among those people that I went to assist Br. Grouard, after I left the pleasant Island Tubuai. The reason of my leaving Tubuai, was on account of Br. Grouards starting after me in a native canoe, and was cast away on a small Island called Metia, 60 miles to the north-east of Tahiti. He left there in a French vessel and arrived at Tahiti, and sent for me to meet him there, or he would come after me in his open canoe, when it was repaired, and if he was lost in the attempt his blood should be required at my hands, and as Tubuai is 300 miles south of Tahiti, and no land between. I made an possible dispatch to hinder his hazardous undertaking, we left Tahiti, in a French ship, bound on a pearl diving voyage among that group of Islands, which afford the richest pearl fishery that I have heard of in the Pacific. We arrived there in February of 1846. The people were overjoyed to see us, and expressed it by inviting us to every town on the Island, where Br. Grourard had organized branches, which were five. They feasted us on cocoanuts, fowls, fish and hogs neatly dressed—and roasted whole.

Those Paumotu Isles have but few vegetables aside from cocoanuts, but these grow in the the greatest abundance,—coral reefs seem to be the fittest place for them. After we had visited all around, we were much anoyed by the contentions of the governors of the various villages to see which of them we should live at. I told Br. Grourard, I saw no other way to stop that, but to divide the Island into two circuits, he to take charge of one and I of the other, and then spend a week in a place. We did so and that put an end to all controversy—he took two towns and I took three. Those islands are of a curious formation, are of an oval shape. Aua or Chain island is some fifteen miles in length, averages about one mile wide, forming an oval circle around a body of water, some six miles wide and thirteen long with various places where the tide ebbs and flows into it. This you see forms a curious inland sea, called Lagoon, and is one of the finest places to take a pleasure ride in a sail boat, and my circuit required much of that exercise, and consequently (as I was a man of dignity) it required a dignitary to wait on me, and one of those war chiefs, who owned one or more islands that he had conquered in the "tau hetene" or times of heathenism, volunteered his services to wait on me, and would not probably have attained to this "honor," had he not owned a new and commodious canoe with an excellent cotton sail, therefore he was permitted to be my boatman. He was a very large and stout man, and as often as we arrived in port on the ebb tide and the canoe could not reach the landing place because of shallow water; you would see him trudging off with me on his back with all the magnificence of his office and would set me down upon tera-firma with the heartfelt satisfaction that he had been the [illegible] things to the people, and in the midst of an anxious multitude who were as anxious to get the first opportunity to shake hands with me as he was to be the honored bearer of their long looked for guest.

Before Br. Grourard left there to come after me, he had often told them of me, and they would enquire every particular concerning me, and when they found I was an elderly man, they inquired if my teeth were good so that I could live on cocoanuts, for said they, white mens' teeth decay much sooner than natives do. He told them that I have some missing ones, but still he thought there was enough left to grind cocoanuts. And when their canoe was repaired and came to Tahiti, after Br. Grourard, I had got there before them to their great joy. They gathered around me with great curiosity, and as I was busily engaged with them, Br. Grourard was standing a little way off diverting himself with our interview, when all of a sudden he burst out in a loud laughter, and when I asked an explanation, "why, said he, they are looking in your mouth when you laugh, to see if you have teeth enough left to eat cocoanuts."

After we had baptized nearly 200 more, and had arranged matters on the island, Br. Grourard, took a notion that he could be spared to go on a mission among that group, and that I could take charge in his absence. I told him I had come to help him do the work that he was not able to do alone, and now we had enlarged the field he wished to leave me in charge of the whole! Oh! said he, you have a better faculty to preside than I have, and I like to pioneer better than you do," and after more persuasion I consented. He left me about four months and returned so as to attend the October Conference at Aua. At [illegible] should return to America, and get my family and a recruit of elders. They wished from 5 to a 100 sent to them, so that they could have a supply. Br. Grourard, visited some eight or nine islands and baptized in all 116 souls, left some native elders to preside. In November I prepared to leave; I went [a]round, by request, to each town to preach and bid them adieu, and as is customary each town made me a feast, sometimes roasting three or four good sized hogs whole, they are roasted underground, and I think the best way to roast pork I ever saw. It is done by excavating in the earth a cavity large enough to receive the quantity of food they wish to cook, some wood is then laid across the hole, and some stones of a convenient size are laid on the wood, and it [is] set on fire. As the word burns out, the coals and hot stones fall down together, and with a stick or spade, most of the hot stones are taken out, then some bounded banana stalk is spread over the coals for a two-fold purpose;

first, to keep the food out of the ashes; secondly, it affords an abundant supply of well flavored juice, which raises a steam as the food is cooking, on to this is laid a layer of food, perhaps meat and then a layer of hot stones, then a layer of vegetables, and then of hot stones, and so on in conical pile, till it is all deposited, then it is all matted over with large green leaves that those Isles' produce for the purpose, and then the whole is covered with a thick layer of dirt. Here it remains till it is well cooked and then it is carefully taken out in the nicest manner. Each parcel is carefully wrapped in leaves before it is put in. And I can assure you that food cooked in this way is the sweetest and most delicate you ever tasted.

They also made me many presents of mats [illegible] hens and coacoanuts. And when I had taken leave of my friends, I obtained passage free of cost, on board of a vessel belonging to some American merchants living at Tahiti, of which Mr. Chapman, American Vice Consul at Tahiti, was one.

I had a pleasant passage to Tahiti, where I found my friends well and in good spirits, for business was brisk and money plenty. There were several men of war lying there; one frigate of 64 guns, several sloops of war and some cutters, under the French flag. One steam frigate, the Salamander, and a cutter under the English flag; one Danish frigate, and a number of English, French and American merchant and whaling vessels. But the war between the French and natives was still raging. But in December of '46 the French conquered and peace was restored, and as there was no vessel bound direct to California, I commenced preaching to the natives on Tahiti, and soon began to baptize. I organized a branch there of 27 members, all natives, and in March, I obtained a passage for San Francisco, where I arrived in June, touching on our way at the Sandwich islands. I staid in California one year, and then started for Salt Lake City. I arrived in the Valley the 28th of September, where I found my family; they had arrived one week before me. To find them all alive and in good health, was a blessing that I felt was from the hand of the Lord. But I will not try to describe the sensations of our meeting, after a separation of five years and four months. But let those that feel curious on that point, try it, and they will then know for themselves. We have spent the winter very pleasantly among our friends here. I devoted a part of it in teaching a Tahitian school, for the benefit of those that expect to be sent on that mission. Among my scholars was your brother John, and he has made good proficiency, and I expect he and his wife will be among the number that will be sent there, and I could gladly wish that you were here to go with us, as I hear such hints dropped, that one of the Twelve, are to be appointed to preside over all missionary operations in the Pacific Ocean. If you were on hand I should have fond expectation it would fall to your lot.

You see that my paper is getting pretty well used up, and I must taper off. My [illegible] of the friends there, I wish to see and here [hear] from them.

I, as ever remain your brother
and fellow laborer in Christ
Our Elder Brother,
ADDISON PRATT.

In vol. 1, no. 10 (June 13, 1849): p. 1, cols. 1–3

Letter of Elder Orson Pratt [Liverpool, England, July 23, 1850]

DEAR BRETHREN:—Through the blessings of a kind providence I have been preserved to once more meet with the Saints in the British dominions. I have been absent from you about four months, during which time I have preformed a lengthy though pleasant, journey to Council Bluffs, on the extreme western frontiers of the United States. The facilities for traveling within a few years must have increased to such a degree, that it seems apparently to have decreased the distances upon the surface of our globe. To cross the Atlantic, and travel some two thousand miles into the interior of America, would have once been considered quite an undertaking, but now it is only a pleasure excursion. The power of steam seems to have almost united the continents into one.

In less than three weeks the servants of God can go from St. Louis to Liverpool—a distance equal to one-quarter of the circumference of the earth. They may well be termed, in the language of Isaiah, "*the swift messengers of the nations.*"

It has fallen to the lot of the Latter-day Saints to live in one of the most momentous ages of the world—an age in which wickedness rains predominantly upon all the face of the earth—an age in which God has determined to rend in pieces and overthrow all the governments and kingdoms of this world, and establish his everlasting kingdom in the hands of his Saints, who shall bear rule under the whole heavens. For about six thousand years the inhabitants of our world have displayed their wisdom in the establishment of various forms of human government; but wickedness has triumphed among them all. The wicked have had their day for rule, but it is now drawing swiftly to a final close. Their sun is setting no more to rise: a long night of darkness as awaits them. God has set his hand to turn and overturn, and to give the kingdom unto his Saints—to redeem the earth from oppression and violence—to consume the wicked as chaff, that righteousness [illegible] may be exalted.

To bring about this great change in gover[n]ment affairs, one of the most important revelations that have ever saluted the ears of mortals, has been given namely, the BOOK OF MORMON. It is sent forth as a last message to the nations of the wicked; it is sent to establish a kingdom which shall break in pieces all other kingdoms; it is sent to gather out the righteous from all nations, and establish them in one; it is sent to fulfil[l] the times of the Gentiles, and bind up the law and testimony among them, that if they will not repent; they may be delivered over unto destruction; it is sent to gather Israel from their long dispersion; it is sent to make known the gospel in greater plainness and ful[l]ness, that contentions upon doctrine may ease and the watchman of Zion see eye to eye; it is sent as the great preparatory work for the second advent of the Son of God; it is sent that the Saints many know the signs of the times, and not be in darkness, and that great day come upon them unawares.

When this message shall have been proclaimed to all nations, tho [the] Son of God shall come to sit upon the throne of his power and reign forevermore. Already twenty years have elapsed since the setting up of the kingdom of God; the proclamation has already been sounded in the ears of many nations: tens of thousands in America, in Great Britain, in the Isles of the Pacific, and in various quarters of the globe, have received glad tidings, and with penitent contrite hearts have been baptized preparatory to the coming of the Great Bridegroom. Already tens of thousands have gathered out from the United States, Great Britain, and Islands of the sea, unto the vallies [valleys] of the mountains in North America; there they are building cities, temples, and public buildings, converting the fertile vallies [valleys] into gardens, and vineyards, and well-cultivated farms, spreading themselves abroad into all the surrounding country. Where before resounded the warhoop of the savage, and the howling of wild beasts, now are heard the voice of civilization, and the melodious songs of the righteous.

Let the poor afflicted Saints in this land cheer up their drooping spirits, for they shall in due time be gathered; if they cannot obtain means in this land, they shall be helped from afar; for the Lord will surely deliver His people, and no power can stay His hand. Already a sound of deliverance begins to be heard from a distance. Hark! It is a voice from the mountains. It is not a voice of savage triumph; it is not the voice of tyrants, clad with terror; it is not the voice of a nation bowed down with oppression; it is not the voice of mourning and lamentation; but is the voice of freedom, rejoicing in the high places of the earth. Behold her standing on yonder mountain tops, clothed with celestial light. With out-stretched arms to the nations, and with a voice of lovely compassion—she calls—Listen! she calls to the Saints in affliction: she invites them to her dwelling place. Her voice is heard! see the Saints arise: see mighty ships waft them o'er the main—see countless numbers track the western plains; the everlasting hills re-echo with their songs. Lo! a vast multitude assembled, enrobed in garments pure and white; They pray—the heavens listen—the powers above are marshalled [marshaled]. All things prepared—the Saints return to Zion, the Lord goes before the camp—the nations fear and tremble; ZION IS REDEEMED, and becomes the joy of all the earth. Praise ye the Lord.

Our latest news from the Salt Lake Settlements was dated the 12th of April. All things were then prosperous in the Valley. They were ploughing, sowing, planting, and making every preparation for an abundant harvest. Tens of thousands of emigrants for the mines, together with immense numbers of horses, mules, and cattle will pass through the Valley this season, which will afford a ready market for all the provisions that can be spared. Large quantities of merchandise, both in dry goods and groceries, are being taken by the merchants to supply the demands of the country; they are paying forty guineas per ton for the transportation of goods from the Bluffs to the Valley. The Lord is truly beginning to favor Zion, and to abundantly supply all her wants, although he takes his own way to accomplish it. Oh! that the Saints may not forget the Lord in the days of their prosperity. How great are the responsibilities resting upon them! and how fearful the consequences of abusing the privileges and blessings bestowed from heaven?

Elder Woodruff, with most of the Saints from the Eastern and Middle States, is now crossing the plains. It is judged that our emigration to the mountains this season will amount to some three thousand souls, taking with them from 800 to 1000 wagons. The Saints who still tarry at the Bluffs are generally poor, but they are in rich and fertile country, and with perseverance and industry will soon be able to pursue their journey over the plains, leaving the country for others of their brethren who may come on and wish to tarry there for a season. There are some three or four thousand Saints in St. Louis, who are apparently doing well, much better than the poor in England. At this present time there seems to be in America a feeling of friendship and good will towards the Saints in almost every quarter. Our poor find employment sooner than any other closs [class] of people; they have been proved and found trustworthy; hence they are sought after in preference to others. The Lord has seen the afflictions of his people, and softened the hearts of that nation towards them for a season. How long his friendship will continue we know not; it cannot be long; for the nation has rejected the message of heaven, and they must be rejected of God; they will from time to time harden their hearts against the people of God, and will desire their destruction, but God will deliver them out of their hands.

About two years have elapsed since I was appointed to preside over the Saints in this land. I have endeavored, during the time, to inform myself concerning your condition, and to offer such counsel as I thought best adapted to your circumstances. If, in the multiplicity of business which has pressed my mind, I have at any time erred, it has not been intentionally. It has been my constant prayer and study to know the will of God concerning you. It affords me great pleasure to know that the churches have greatly flourished since I have been in your midst, and that many thousands have been added to your numbers. Peace and union have also prevailed in almost every branch; while the Holy spirit has been abundantly poured forth upon you, as is evident from the miraculous manifestations of the healing power, together with numerous other blessings enjoyed throughout the land. These tokens of the goodness of God towards his saints are calculated to make the faithful servants of God rejoice.

The wise and judicious management displayed by the presidents of conferences, and the traveling elders under them, has been the principal means in the hands of God in extending the cause of truth in the British Isles. The extensive circulation of the printed word has also given an impetus to the rolling of the great wheel of salvation. Strictness of discipline in plucking off dead branches—in purifying the church of corrupt members—and in laying the axe at the very root of every species of wickedness, has also a powerful tendency to strengthen and confirm the meek and humble, and to enlighten the eyes of the honest inquirer.

Let the presiding elders of every conference endeavor to inform their minds relative to the condition of every branch under their respective jurisdictions. See whether your flocks are in a healthy condition or not. The Lord has made you the shepherd over his sheep; if you lose the sheep, or suffer them to perish through your neglect, they will be required at your hands. Teach the presidents of branches to look diligently after all the members. Counsel them to enforce strict discipline, and to root out all backbiting and evil speaking one against another; for this is a great evil, and tends to quarrels, divisions, strifes, apostacy, and death. If the backbiter or evil speaker will not, after proper admonitions, reform and cease his evil practices, let fellowship be withdrawn from him, and let all know that the church of God is not the place to injure and devour one another. If any officer or member under your charge be found teaching or practising [practicing] unvirtuous doctrines, let him be dealt with strictly by the law of God; and if the president of a conference shall transgress, or teach or practice any iniquity, let the same be reported to us, accompanied with the proper evidences; and if one of the Twelve, or the President of the Saints in Great Britain, shall transgress the law of virtue, and teach or practice unrighteousness, let the presidents of conferences inquire into the same, and collect the testimonies thereof, and forthwith transmit the documents unto the First Presidency at headquarters, that all may be dealt with according to the law of heaven. The time is come when too much light and knowledge have been given to the Saints for them to suffer themselves to be imposed upon by men who are carried away with their lusts. And we say, in the name of the Lord, that the displeasure of heaven shall overtake the adulterer unless he speedily repent, and his name shall be blotted out from among the people of God. "Woe unto them that commit whoredoms, saith the Lord God Almighty, for they shall be thrust down to hell." Woe unto them who shall betray the confidence reposed in them, and shall make use of their authority to seduce and lead astray ignorant and silly women, for, except they repent, their authority shall perish quickly like the dry stubble before the devouring flame. Woe unto them who lie and bear false witness against their brother or sister to their injury; it were better for them that they were sunk in the depths of the mighty ocean than to offend the children of God. Woe unto them who steal; for their deeds shall be made manifest, and justice and judgment shall lay hold on them in an hour they think not. Woe unto them who love slander, and will not cease to speak evil of their brother and sister, for they shall be hated of God and man, and their hopes shall wither away and perish. Woe unto all those among the Saints who shall turn from their righteousness and do iniquity, for the great day of the Lord is at hand, and their portion shall be among hypocrites and unbelievers.

Let the Saints sanctify themselves both in body and spirit, that the Holy Ghost, with all its accompanying powers and gifts, may be more abundantly manifested; for the destroyer is abroad in the earth, and the Saints must live by faith. But, how can we have faith, if we neglect the counsels of wisdom which God has ordained for our preservation?

The time is drawing near when I shall leave you and go to the Valley with my family, according to the request of the First Presidency, as will be seen in their late epistle. But be assured, dear brethren, that the expressions of unbounded confidence, which the Saints have everywhere manifested towards me, will ever be cherished by me with a grateful heart. I shall ever look upon this short period of my life as among the happiest days of my pilgrimage. And if I have been a humble instrument in the hands of God of benefiting any of His Saints, or of advancing His cause in Great Britain, it will afford me great and lasting consolation when far hence in other climes.

The Saints in this land are dear to my heart; I have seen their toils, their hard labors, and oppression, and my heart has mourned over their afflictions. I have loved them because of their strong desire to work righteousness and hearken to the counsels of heaven: I have loved them because of their faith and love to God and His truth; I have loved them because they have loved me: and when I see their poverty and sufferings, my soul yearns over them, and my eyes are filled with tears. In the ful[l]ness of my heart I cry to thee, O my Father and my God. I ask thee, O God, to look upon these, my brethren; behold, how they have sorely toiled these many years, while their children have cried for bread; behold them, O Lord, bowed down in sorrow, under heavy burdens imposed upon them by their cruel taskmasters, and when thou lookest, O Lord, upon these great afflictions of thine own children, let thy bowels be moved with compassion towards them; let salvation and deliverance come speedily: defer not, lest thy people fall under the heavy yoke and perish. O Lord, thy people in this land have become a great people, but this is not their resting place—their eyes and their whole hearts are towards the mountains of Zion—the land which thou hast ordained for the habitations of the righteous in the days of trouble. Glorify thy name, O Father, in working out a speedy deliverance for this great people, that they may rest during the remainder of their days from the hard bondage, wherein they have been made to serve. Gather this people together, that they and their children may learn thy ways more perfectly, and walk in thy paths, and no more be led astray by the vain and foolish traditions of the Gentiles: yea, O Lord, save thy people for evermore.

I shall probably leave England the latter part of next winter, or early in spring, and perhaps sooner; but I rejoice exceedingly that I can leave you under the presidency and watch-care of one of the Twelve, namely, Franklin D. Richards, whose former labors in this country are well known and highly appreciated by the Saints. His unwearied diligence in the cause of truth—his godlike dignity of deportment, combined with a mild and amiable disposition—his sterling virtue and integrity, united with a superior intellect, enriched with the wisdom and knowledge of heaven—have eminently qualified him for the dignified and highly responsible station of presiding over the numerous churches which will soon be entrusted to his charge. Brother Richards will act in conjunction with me as my counsellor while I remain in this country; and it is to be hoped that through our united exertions we may be humble instruments in advancing the great cause of truth in this part of the Lord's vineyard.

Some of the presiding elders have been rather negligent in teaching the law of Tithing according to the counsel which we have heretofore given. Every president of a conference should see that every member of the church of whom tithing is required, is correctly instructed in regard to his duty upon this subject; urge upon them the necessity of strict obedience to this requirement of heaven; it is as essential as any other requirement; no person will prosper who undertakes to cheat the Lord, and slip off to America with his property and money, without paying in this land the tenth thereof. The Lord has commanded and man must obey; for justice and judgment is the penalty of disobedience; therefore we exhort the Saints to obey the law of tithing; obey it strictly with cheerful hearts; obey it without delay. I have already borrowed upwards of £200 over above the tithing I had on hand, to forward nails, glass, and other temple property to the Valley: this was necessary in order that they might be forwarded this season that the great work might not be delayed. The amount borrowed must be within a few weeks refunded, therefore we call upon the presidents of conferences to see that every person who should pay tithing attends to this duty immediately, that there may be funds in the Lord's storehouse to fulfil[l] the purposes specified in the revelations and counsels of heaven. Teach those Saints who have property, and who will not exert themselves to obey this law of heaven, that the Spirit of God shall begin to withdraw from them, and the hand of the Lord shall be against them, and they shall cease to prosper in their business transactions, and a curse shall be upon the labor of their hands, and unless they repent they shall wither away like a branch plucked from the vine.

The perpetual Emigration Fund must also be kept in view; and the Saints should be thoroughly instructed as to the importance of doing all within their power for the enlargement of this fund; it is established especially for the benefit of the poor, to be appropriated according to the instructions which shall from time to time be given by the First Presidency. Let all the arrangements and counsels which have, during my absence, been laid before the Saints by brother Franklin D. Richards, in relation to the collection of this fund, be faithfully complied with. Let the treasurers of the conferences forward to our office immediately the amount of funds which they have on hand, accompanied with a list of the names of the conference in which each resides. After this instruction has been fulfilled, the treasurers will thereafter make quarterly remittances and reports to us, namely, on the 1st of October, 1st January, 1st April, and 1st August. As our office will not be responsible only for the funds which actually reach us, we shall, if necessary, publish from time to time the names of all contributors, with the amount contributed, (with the exception of those who may request us to do otherwise.) This will have a tendency, in some measure, to detect any dishonesty on the part of the treasurers. We hope, however, that among the Saints no dishonesty will be found to exist, and that every man will be faithful and punctual in all things entrusted to his charge. We also say to all the Saints, let none of the Emigration Fund be used for any expenses whatever, but let all expenses incurred in purchasing cheap account books for the treasurers, or in any other way, be settled by the branches, independently of this fund.

Mechanics of every description are greatly needed in the Sale Lake country. Furnaces, forges, glass works, potteries, manufactories of cotton, of linen, of wool, are greatly called for. Let the presidents of conferences seek diligently in every branch under their respective jurisdictions for wise, skilful, and ingenious artizans, mechanics, manufacturers, potters, &c. Counsel those of them that have means, to go immediately to the Valley; and counsel those who have not got means, to use every exertion to obtain means and be in readiness when called for, if funds should be appropriated for their assistance; and remember the maxim, that the Lord will help his Saints who will seek diligently and honestly to help themselves. The presidents of conferences have many duties to perform in relation to the temporal salvation of the Saints as well as spiritual, let them not therefore, become dilatory in relation to this counsel. We urged these things upon you months ago in many of the Stars [Stakes], and we humbly hope that you have not forgotten subjects which we esteem of such vast importance for the welfare of the children of Zion. If you can find men of capital who have never been engaged in the manufacturing business, but who are willing to invest their capital in the establishment of such business, teach them that it is their privilege so to do, and that they shall be blessed with an hundred fold in this life, besides having the satisfaction of seeing hundred of thousands of Saints benefitted by their manufactures. Let the Saints in Great Britain arise with one heart and mind to perform the great and mighty work which is before them, and the Lord their God will bless them, and strengthen their hands, and enable them to perform wonders in his name.

They are called to do great things; let them not, therefore, be faint-hearted nor discouraged, for God is with them.

With feelings of love to all the Saints, and with an anxious, desire for your welfare, I subscribe myself your brother in the kingdom of Christ.

ORSON PRATT.

15, Wilton Street, Liverpool, July 23d, '50.

In vol. 2, no. 19 (October 16, 1850): p. 1, cols. 1–5

Latest News from the Traveling Elders

We have before us a compilation of letters received from Elders, who were sent out last Spring on missions through the States and Canada. To redeem a promise made by us through the Guardian some time since, and to satisfy our friends abroad relative to requested inquires made by them, as to the progress of these Elders, and their different fields of labor, we consider ourselves under obligation to subjoin the following extracts and comments.

The first before us, is a letter from Elder James Wareham, Springfield, Ohio, dated August 10th. Mr. W. says: "I embrace this opportunity to inform you that I am well, and have been ever since I left home. I have nothing of importance to write at present. I have been hunting up some of our brethren, and have found quite a number of them; some in good spirits—others in doubt. I have been preaching in the vicinity of Springfield, and Catawba, but have not baptized any yet; some have expressed a belief in the doctrine, and are on a balance because they possess a considerable amount of property, &c.["]

Elder Royal J. Cutler, writes from Neversink, Sullivan County, New York, under date of the 1st ult.; but does not say anything relative to the progress of the work of God in that region of country.

Elder Isaac Bullock dates one of his letters, September 2d, at Bolton, Warren County, New York; at which place he received quite a number of subscribers for the Guardian: but said nothing relative in the prospects before him, or the progress made in spreading the word of life, or the Gospel of salvation in that section.

Elder James McGaw, writes from Grimes Co., Texas, under date of the 2d ult., and says:

"After being seperated [separated] from you some considerable time, I now write, and state, that I arrived in Texas safely after a month's voyage,—found the Saints in this region generally well; the work appears to be moving slowly, but steadily, and I am still in hopes of performing a good work before I leave this place. I have baptized a few since I returned. I have been preaching principally to the Saints as yet; but expect shortly to start out to different places, where I have been invited and strongly anticipate to find a number of good and virtuous hearers. I have talked to the Saints about gathering, and with but few exceptions they say, that they will be prepared to leave next Spring."

The following is from the pen of Elder John Murray, Lassalle, Monroe County, Michigan, dated Sept. 6th. Mr. M. says:

"I again embrace the opportunity of writing to you a few lines, to inform you of my welfare, and how the work of the Lord is progressing in this locality.

I have been instrumental in the hands of the Lord, of baptizing into the Church RIGHT persons since my last communication to your office, &c., &c."

Elder David James Ross, writes from Yates, Orleans County, New York; his communication is dated Sept. 19th, the purport of which is as follows: "I am well at present. I get full houses; but few receive my testimony in this region."

Elder David Candland, communicates from Halifax, Nova Scotia, where he says, he was warmly received by the Saints. His letter is dated Sept 13th, and contains the following intelligence:

"My labors here have been of the kind peculiar to preachers of the Latter-day Saints. I would have preferred to be the first one here, but I find that some have been before me in years past, and instead of leaving the way open, it is closed, through some unwise course of theirs. Allow me to say, that it is a difficulty of no easy kind, to warm, revive, and Kindle anew the spark of truth, whose gentle and refulgent rays have been beclouded by acts of ill-repaid confidence and esteem reposed in the Elders. A second cause of trial here, is the constant visits of a STRANGITE ELDER, who, as soon as I have any on the eve of baptism, he, by a smooth and oily tongue upsets them; he is like Alexander the Coppersmith, he does me much harm. He solicited an interview privately, which I declined, and gave for my reasons, that as I have replied to him, it would suit me better to have witnesses present, which he accepted. When we met, he promised to renounce the matter if I could show a *single* error; this I did, and more than ONE, but he would not renounce, and so I counted him among the liars, where he, like Judas will have his place, &c."

September the 15th, is the date of a second letter received from Elder Cutler, written at the same place as the former, enclosing a list of additional subscribers for the Guardian, and says: That he expects to return home next Spring.

The spirit and sentiment of this letter shows that he is well, and doing well. Those under his care or tuition, would do well not to despise his counsels because of his youth, for we consider him a very exemplary young man, and earnest in the work of truth, to which he is appointed a minister.

Elder James W. Bay, writes from Cleveland, Ohio, under the same date, and gives cheering accounts of that section of country; he says, that several have been added to the Church there of late.

The last accounts from Elder Isaac Bullock, is dated Sept. 18th, Moira, Franklin County, New York; during his stay at Bolton, Warren County, he says: that he baptized five persons—ordained two Elders, and one Deacon,—organized a Branch numbering twelve members, and left them in good spirits. Furthermore he says; that he visited the old broken down Branches—some that fell off, turned from their evil ways and brought forth fruit meet for repentance; therefore he baptized them over again, and left them enjoying the spirit of God, and the fellowship of their new adopted brethren. He further states, that he finds it very difficult to convince some of the eastern Saints [of] the importance of gathering, and assigns as a reason for their reluctance, "*Prosperity in things pertaining to this life, and their love for the leeks and onions of Egypt.*" QUERY! Have the cares of the world, and the deceitfulness of riches choked the word? We say: "Where your treasure is, there will your heart be also."

Elder A. D. Boynton, when last heard from, was in the State of Massachusetts, performing a good work.

All the comments we have to offer on the foregoing extracts, are simply, that we are always glad to hear of the advancement of truth and righteousness, through the efforts of the servants of the Most High appointed for that purpose. If those heralds of Salvation have their eye single to the performance of that work to which they have been set apart and sent forth; they will retain the spirit of the Lord—honor their Priesthood, and be a blessing to all the honest they may in their travels come in contact with. TRUTH has a charm, an influence, a power, and a virtue that flows from it; although its spirit may not be discerned by the natural eye, nor felt by a polluted heart, yet, that charm—that influence—that power, and that virtue is felt, when an honest and unprejudiced mind comes in contact with the gentle, but powerful words of its possessor.

The Scripture says: "Be ye clean, ye that bear the vessels of the Lord," also, "let your light (not darkness,) so shine before men, that they may see your good works, and glorify your Father which is in Heaven."

Then shall your presence, like suns in their circuit,
Revive and illumine all persons of worth;
And as a reward for the light you exhibit,
The life that's eternal is yours on the earth.

In vol. 3, no. 19 (October 17, 1851): p. 2, cols. 1–2

Letter of Elder Jabez Woodard [Italy, August 1, 1851]

ITALY, August 1st, 1851.

DEAR PRESIDENT SNOW:—A tract of forty-six pages has been issued against us in Switzerland, and a plentiful supply has arrived here; there is the Spaulding story and nothing else, except the common cant of sectarianism, and some quotations from "the Voice of Joseph," and "the only way way [*sic*] to be saved," for which I am very glad. I am happy to say that we now muster thirty-one members; I feel courage in the thought that you have taken the Presidency of the Indian empire; and if there be royal blood within my veins, it will roll with renewed vigor through every fibre [fiber] of my frame, that with stimulated energies I may carry out your counsel; and if I know what honor and friendship, and gratitude require at my hands, you shall be in Italy at the same time you are in India, or elsewhere. I confess that when I found you laid upon me the solemn charge to gather Israel from among these nations, I felt the weight of the office, and at the same time new courage and new patience; my eyes are not closed to the difficulties of the situation, but I know where my strength lies. I feel as though I must fast and pray for every one of these kingdoms seperately [separately], and I see that I must pass through many strange scenes, but by the help of the Lord I hope to overcome.

I strive to acquire a knowledge of languages and customs, laws and regulations, and other things necessary among these nations. If it were possible I could wish to disburden your mind of all future anxieties concerning this mission.

I know by my own experience something of what you must have felt since the moment you were named for the President of such a stupendous undertaking. What thoughts have oft crowded your mind from morning to midnight! What weariness by land and sea! And now a still loftier enterprize [enterprise] engages your attention, or at least one which gives a wider sphere of action. But what can I say that will leave you at rest concerning Italy? Perhaps, now you are absent, it would ill become me to boast of my goodness, still I may hope that I advance a little; and if ever a firm resolve has taken possession of my soul, it is now engraven there and registered in heaven; that by the grace of God; I am determined to tread all things beneath my feet that would militate against the accomplishment of the glorious work in which I am engaged. Yes: I would like to conquer but not for myself alone. I would render unto you that which is due from myself, and make thousands more to feel that which they owe.

The great thought which now occupies my mind is to put the *leaven to work*, as you say; but I do not yet see things open extensively, and I still stick to these vallies [valleys] and mountains; I cast many longing looks and anxious reflections however towards other localities. Turin does not present any opening, but towards the Mediterranean it seems that amid the goings and comings of commerce, some of the seeds might travel far.

Elder Toronto joins with myself in love to you and all the Saints.

Yours affectionately,

JABEZ WOODWARD.

In vol. 3, no. 21 (November 14, 1851): p. 3, col. 3

Letter of Elder George P. Dykes [Hamburg, Germany, October 14, 1851]

Persecution of the Saints in Aalborg—Great increase of the Church in Denmark, upwards of sixty baptized in two months—Conversions in Schleswig—Visit to England and departure for Hamburgh.

HAMBURGH [HAMBURG], COMMERCIAL HOTEL,

October 14th, 1851.

Dear Brother Richards:—Desiring to keep you informed of the history of the times with me, I write you again. In my last, written you from Schleswig, on the 4th of May, I stated I had just began there when I received a letter from brother Snow, directing me to come immediately to Copenhagen, and accompany him to the London conference in June last, which I did; but my stay in England was very short, as I felt deeply pressed in spirit to return to the field of my labors in Denmark; accordingly I left London for Lowestoff, including to sail from the thence to Hjerting, but the steamer after being delayed a few days, over her appointed time, came in at last in a crippled state, and had to go [to the] London Docks before she could return, so I was under the necessity of returning to London again to get a passage. From thence I sailed on the 24th of June from Hamburgh [Hamburg], where I landed on the morning of the 27th, and proceeded immeeiately [immediately] on my journey over land, and by traveling day and night, I was enabled to reach the City of Aalborg, my former field of labor, but, indeed, too late to save the little flock from a very heavy blow; for a spirit of persecution had arisen, and the mob had assembled and broken the windows of the Saints' meeting house, and demolished all the furniture within; and from thence proceeded from house to house, they broke the windows of nearly all the dwelling houses of the Saints in the City, while the civil authorities looked on with seeming indifference.

In a few days after these things occurred, I entered the city, and had not heard a word of them till I stood by the side of the house where I had so often met with the Saints, and where I had preached the word to sinners; but I leave you to judge of my feelings, when, instead of meeting the joyful smiles of beloved Saints, I saw the windows and furniture of the house broken to pieces, and no Saints to welcome me there, for they were not now privileged to appear in the streets without being grossly insulted and sometimes shamefully beaten.

While I was thus deeply pondering over these things, an officer approached and requested me to come immediately to the Mayor's office, which I did, and he peremptorily told me I had better leave the City forthwith, as he would not promise me protection from the mob for one hour. And as there was a steamer then at the wharf to sail that afternoon for Copenhagen, I went on board, but the mob hearing that I was in the city, began to gather, and some went to the Mayor's office to find me, but he told them he had me in prison. Others went to the ship, but the captain told them I had left and gone up into the city, and thus were they ranging about for me till the appointed hour for sailing, when I think there was more than a thousand people assembled on the beach. I was down in the cabin till we were fairly out of reach, when I came up on deck to see the sight, and being thus delivered I gave God the glory, and proceeded on our way, we touched at Hals [Hul], where we took on brother Jenson, the Presiding Elder, he having been obliged to flee from home to save his life, and the next day, the 1st of July, we landed in Copenhagen, to the great joy of the Saints as well as ourselves.

But now came the most arduous part of our duty; to guide the "Old Ship Zion" in such a storm, and sailing in *strange* waters required more than the wisdom of mortals; we therefore gave ourselves to much fasting and prayer, to obtain the Spirit to guide our councils under these dark and gloomy circumstances. Suffice it to say that our prayers were heard and our desires granted, and I must ever remember with pleasure the zeal and diligence of brother Forssgren [Forsgreen] on this occasion, as indeed on all others, and the strict obedience and prompt attention with which brother Hanson travelled [traveled] from place to carry out the measures adopted in our councils; and thus by our united effort, the spirit of the mob was turned from the Saints, and divisions arose among themselves, so that on one occasion the soldiers had to be called ont [out] to still the tumult.

And now let me say, to the glory of God our Heavenly Father, that I here saw what I never saw befose [before], that in so great a persecution every soul was saved alive, both temporally and spiritually, so that *not one* denied the faith in this difficulty.

The enemy not being satisfied with this effort to overthrow the Truth, raised opposition in another way, by sending in priests and other professors of religion to make disturbance in the midst of the congregations, while our Elders were holding forth, by asking questions on points of doctrine, &c. However, this did not last long, for on one occasion, when there was many people assembled, I was speaking on the first principles of the Gospel, and atonement for original sin by the suffering of our Savior, the Spirit was upon me and I spoke in power, not sparing the Lutherian doctrine of "iafant [infant] baptism;" and when I closed I gave the privilege for remark if any one had any thing to say for or against what had been said, as I felt myself fully able to answer every question pertaining to the doctrine of the Saints, and to prove it by scripture, &c.; but every tongue was still, except of those who came forward and publicly acknowledged the truth of what they had heard that day, and desired to be united with us by baptism. The work continued to spread on the right and left, so that on brother Snow's return from England in August, he called a conference, in which the Church was fully organized, and the Elders and priests appointed to their several fields of labor.

I left for Schleswig on the 2nd September, after spending two months and two days in Denmark during which time there was added to the Church about sixty souls, thirty of whom in Copenhagen, and the others in different parts of the kingdom by the native Elders' preaching. The whole Church in Denmark numbers, I think, over three hundred members. (The definite number I do not rightly recollect, as I have not the records with me.)

In Schleswig I found a great military excitement prevailing as the Austrians had stationed a very heavy army at Holstein, and even extending to the very frontier, leaving only a narrow bridge of about thirty yards between their outposts, and the sentinels of the Danish army. The towns and cities here being placed under martial law, I found it impossible to call a meeting of the people, indeed the citizens themselves were not allowed to be out at night after a certain hour without a passport, signed by the commanding general. But not being discouraged by a sight of the military, I determined to do what little I could, as my feelings are very warm towards the German people; yet another difficulty arose; the city was so closely guarded, and all having to be in-doors at the appointed time, that it was next to impossible to find an opportunity to baptize those that should believe. However, I succeeded, and on the evening of the 15th September, 1851, and in the same waters where the first Christians were baptized, when the people were converted from Paganism, were the first Saints baptized in Germany into the new and everlasting covenant; and although there were but two baptized, yet it is laying the foundation of a good work, as there are many more there who who are believing our doctrine.

Finding it difficult to proceed in Shchleswig [Schleswig] at present, and as the Danish government was in daily expectation of the Austrian troops being removed, I thought I would leave for a short time and go to England to see brother Taylor with reference to his intended mission to Hamburgh [Hamburg], which I did, and found him deeply engaged with his capacious soul for the good of England, France, and Germany; and while thus laboring for the spiritual salvation of nations he was not forgetting to bless the Saints *temporally* in Zion. According to his directions I have now come to this city to labor for a season under his wise counsels for the good of this people, hoping as I do that the day of my deliverance is soon at hand, when I shall be enabled to return to the bosom of my family, to remove them from the borders of Babylon (the Council Bluffs) to the vallies [valleys] of the mountains, where they can rest in peace from the tumults of the world, and may it be according to the will of God in the name of Jesus. Amen.

Thus you have a *sketch* of the history of this to me, interesting summer, and the kind dealing and protecting hand of God that have been extended to me, his weak and unworthy servant; and while kind heaven shall give me common intellect must I remember it with the deepest gratitude to Him. And now I close by desiring the blessings of the everlasting God to rest upon all those who wish well to you and the cause of Zion generally.

Your humble and obedient servant.

G. PARKER DYKES.

In vol. 3, no. 24 (December 26, 1851): p. 1, col. 6–p. 2, col. 1

8

News from the California Gold Fields

The Gold Region and Gold Fever

The mountains and valleys of California appear to be glittering with the precious ore. This wonderful discovery was first made by Mormons, if we are correctly informed. Indeed, the gentleman is now here that claims this honor, and to whom, we believe, it is justly due. Gold certainly has a great attractive power, and a charm that few can resist. Not a danger but that has been encountered for its sake. Not a sea or an ocean that has not been navigated, and scarcely a country that has not been explored in search of the god of this world. Had the true God of heaven been sought with half the zeal and perseverance, one might reasonably conclude that the whole human family, like an Enoch, would have been translated to heaven, and left the earth to be inhabited by inferior tribes.

The vast numbers of persons that are going to the golden mountains of California, from the Eastern, Western, Middle, and Southern States, from Europe, from Oregon and from the Sandwich Islands, and also from various other parts by sea and by land, must cause pestilence, famine and war among them. Who will keep order among the miners? None, unless they can be paid for it much as they can make by digging gold; and what company or government will pay that price to soldiers? We do not believe that any will. All classes appear to be neglecting agricultural pursuits in that region, and if sights are not seen there before one year, we shall be ready to believe that the love of money is hardly the root of all evil. They will be on the plains, in the valleys, and on the mountains like the locust of Egypt, sweeping every green thing before them. What a scene can be imagined! Famishing for a little bread while wading in gold dust. Stealing it from one another, fighting, dirking, shooting, &c., &c. Black eyes and bloody noses will be more common there than bread, at times, in our opinion. It in not that class of men, generally, that are of the most quiet and peaceable dispositions that will be draw[n] there.

We are frequently asked: "Is it best to go to the gold regions of California?" We will answer this question by asking another. "What will it profit a man if he gain the whole world and lose his own soul?"

In vol. 1, no. 1 (February 7, 1849): p. 2 col. 3

Outfitting for the Valley and Gold Region

This place is probably the most eligible point on the Missouri river for emigrants from Iowa and Illinois, residing no father south than Quincy, to rendezvous at, preparatory to launching forth upon the great Western Plains. The old Mormon trail by Pisgah and Indian town is a notable thoroughfare, and is settled all along through the State to this place. Travelers need not camp out, or away from inhabitants more than one or two nights, if the roads should be good, between the Mississippi river and this place. Emigrants may start from the Mississippi as early as they please. They will be able to obtain corn on the way for their teams, if they will use a little precaution, and at some places, lay in enough to last them two or three days.

We have no hesitancy in assuring our readers that every article needed in the Gold Mines, from a crowbar to a sieve, from a barrel or sack of flour to the broad-side of a baconed porker, can all be had here at equally as low rates as can be purchased on the Mississippi. We have a goodly number of most enterprising merchants who have anticipated all your wants, and have laid in heavy stocks of all sorts of goods. And being connected with heavy firms in New York, Philadelphia and in St. Louis, they are determined to sell at rates so low that no reasonable man will haul goods or provisions through to this place; and even if he comes by water, it is our candid opinion that he can purchase his goods and entire outfit in the little town of Kanesville at a better rate than he can purchase them in St. Louis or in any of the Eastern cities, considering the trouble, expense of transportation, and risk. We are personally acquainted with the Eastern market, and also with the St. Louis market; we likewise have the price current, weekly, from all these places; and it is our honest sentiment that this is the place for outfitting.

Many think that we have got nothing out here in the *State* of Pottawatamie, but a few simpletons that voted for Gen. Taylor. But if they would just come here, and step into some of our Dry Goods, Grocery, and Hardware stores, and find stocks of $50,000, they might begin to think Pottawatamie worthy of some favorable consideration in the halls of legislation.

Should it so happen that every thing that the most fastidious caterer would require, could not be had at this place; why, just run down to St. Josephs in Missouri where they have every thing, and no mistake—while your teams are resting a few days and treat yourselves to the pleasure of a little more than a hundred miles' trip, through a rich and fertile country, and there your every want can be supplied. Just get a copy of the Guardian before you leave, and run over its advertising column, and most likely you will discover the advertisements of the cheapest houses in St. Josephs. Those you would do well to patronize.

In vol. 1, no. 2 (February 21, 1849): p. 2 col. 4

California

Late intelligence from California represents the supply of gold to be still undiminished. But miners were suffering from sickness and want of provisions.

In vol. 1, no. 3 (March 7, 1849): p. 3, col. 4

Late From California

We learn that general Persifer F. Smith, Governor of California, has issued a proclamation prohibiting foreigners from digging gold on the public domain.

In vol. 1, no. 4 (March 21, 1849): p. 3, col. 1

Gold Diggers, Gold Speculators and Gold Adventurers, California Bound

are pouring into St. Joseph, by the steamboat load, as we learn. This is golden age indeed! Gold is being found on the Platte river, and in various parts of the States. The riches and treasures of the earth are being discovered. Intelligence is being conveyed by the lightning's speed, aerial voyages are contemplated; and in fact, every thing seems to be tending to some important event. "As it was in the days of Noah, so also shall it be in the days of the coming of the Son of Man.' Blinded by worldly enjoyment and prosperity, they were swept away by a wave of God's displeasure. "What shall it profit a man if he gain the whole world and lose his own soul? Or what shall a man give in exchange for his soul?" All the mines of California will not redeem it. Something whispers to us that this golden age, so rapidly running into new projects, new discoveries, &c., &c., will be like the train, which, propelled with too great velocity, runs off the track—like the steam when raised to a very high pitch, it endangers the boilers and passengers. We say then, while you ride on a golden car, look out for rocks on the track.

In vol. 1, no. 5 (April 4, 1849): p. 2, col. 3

Later from California—More Gold— "Diamonds as Big as Hen's Eggs"

A dispatch dated New York. 30th., has the following:

Mr. Parrot, U. S. consul, left Mazatlan on the 10th of April, and arrived in this city yesterday. He brought with him $40,000 in gold dust. He estimates that at least $30,000,000 in gold dust will be taken from the different placers during the present year. Three or four new quicksilver and two silver mines have been discovered. Platinum does not exist in considerable quantity. Diamonds nearly the size of hen's eggs have been found in the Valley. The finder of one demands $180,000 for it.

A New York Volunteer has built himself a small frame house, which was offered for rent to Gen. Smith at $18,000 a year; he gave him a day to consider the proposal.

The crews of the Oregon and California receive $100 per month, and the cooks $150.

In vol. 1, no. 12 (July 11, 1849): p. 3, col. 5

News from California
[New York, July 28, 1849]

NEW YORK, July 28, 5 P. M.

The steamer Crescent City arrived last night, bringing one month's later news from California. The steamer Panama, from San Francisco, arrived at Panama on the 11th of June, with $500,000 in gold. Gold is still found in California in great quantities but such persons only, as are accustomed to hard work, can stand the fatigue of digging it. The number of persons at the mines is estimated at twenty or thirty thousand, of whom about half are foreigners. Business at San Francisco was very dull; dry goods and provisions were selling below the original cost: lumber was still in great demand and selling for $350 per thousand.

Our Consul at Panama would not assume the responsibility of sending the California mails by the Crescent City.

The British frigate Constance was at San Blas, bound to Mazatlan, with $2,000,000 of specie.

The greatest efforts are making in California to organize a state government and demand admittance into the Union. A mass meeting for the purpose of considering the propriety of electing delegates to a convention for the formation of a government for California, took place on the 12th of June. The object of the meeting having been briefly stated by the President, Peter H. Burnett, Esq., addressed the people assembled and concluded by introducing the Hon. Thomas Butler King, of Georgia, who responded to the call with his accustomed eloquence and ability.

The Crescent City has over $200,000 in specie on board.

In vol. 1, no. 15 (August 22, 1849): p. 3, col. 5

From California
[New York, November 12, 1849]

NEW YORK, NOV. 12—P. M.

The Empire City from Chagres, arrived yesterday, bringing half a million of gold dust, and one months later dates from San Francisco. Among the deaths is that of Col. Henry Helm, Late of Cincinnati. Feather river has been nearly drained of the precious metal, places on Yuba river are most productive, where there are about 5 000 persons, mostly Americans, much sickness had prevailed, but was disappearing. Dr. Boynton's company, consisting of six persons, had gathered $8 000 in 7 days. The aggregate number of Americans at present in the gold region, is probably 30,000, and they are incapable of exhausting the treasures. Many are returning from the mines in consequence of the extreme heat.

One hundred and twenty-two females arrived at San Francisco during September, *worth their weight in gold.*

Thomas Butler King was recovering, and expected to reach Washington before the opening of Congress[.]

The French have seized Honolulu, in consequence of the natives refusing to reduce the rates on French brandies; they likewise took Hawaian [Hawaiian] Fort, lowered the flag, and destroyed all the ammunition, &c.; they occupied the Fort for three days, then abandoned it and left the Islands.

The Convention for framing a Constitution for California, had been in session for three weeks, and was expected to adjourn the first week of October. The question of suffrage caused considerable debate; it was finally agreed to admit all male citizens who had six months residence in California, of twenty-one years of age, to the privilege of electors. The legislature to consist of two branches—banking corporations and lotteries prohibited. State officers elected in the usual manner of the U. S. The slave question caused considerable discussion but is now finally settled. A number of vessels from New York, Boston, Philadelphia and Baltimore, had arrived at San Francisco. American flour $10 per bbl; American beef $6; pork $22; many articles are cheaper than in the United States.

The steamship Falcon had arrived at New Orleans from Chagres.

In vol. 1, no. 23 (December 12, 1849): p. 3, cols. 3–4

Gold Seekers

There are great numbers of very enterprising men passing the frontier at this point, and destined for the gold mines of California. They are much earlier this year than last[.] But the season is so very backward that hay and corn are high and scarce. The weather begins to soften a little; yet on Saturday morning last snow and rain fell together in limited quantities.

There are some unprincipled men among the emigrants. They will take corn from the cribs in the night, and faith, chickens from their roosts too; money from the shelf of a washerwoman; and a few nights ago Mr. Ezra Pa[r]rish, living within two miles of this town, had a very valuable horse stolen from his stable, and supposed to be crossed the river in the night, and driven on over the plains, or taken back by some one who had backed out. We do not wish to cast this odium upon the great body of Californians, yet there are some *scaly ones* among them.

We have taken every precaution not to have any emigrant or his property disturbed or molested by the citizens here; and so far, we believe we are spotless in this respect; and we hope that examples of too plain and pointed theft will not be set before the citizens here, lest some wreckless [reckless], ungovernable, hair-brained chap, may be induced to break over the rules of honesty, and follow the bad example[s] that are set before him. This would be most mortifying to us. Let the thief go and perish in the mines if he will not reform, and let the sufferers bear with patience their loss and disappointment, knowing that the thief shall not be released from his prison until he has paid the utmost farthing. Justice will not relinquish his demands upon the offender though he leave the world: neither will the sufferer go unrequited, though he die before it happen; and the longer it be delayed, the longer will the amount accumulate interest in favor of the sufferer. Remember this!

Horses and cattle are being daily sold here at auction; the presumption is that they are the "*bona fide*" property of the persons offering them; still we have reason to believe that stolen horses have been sold here. Our citizens would do well to be on their guard; for although they may sell corn at a dollar seventy-five cents per bushel, and buy a stolen horse for fifty dollars, and the owner soon come along and prove property; then you would not make an everlasting fortune by selling corn at these high prices. We have no objection to your buying property here at auction; but be sure that the vender is the legitimate owner of the property.

In vol. 2, no. 7 (May 1, 1850): p. 2, col. 2

California Items

Official returns show that the total amount of gold dust and bullion exported from San Francisco from the 1st of January to August 14, 1851, was $56,638,204; imported during the same period, $2,892,124—excess of exports, $53,746,080.

San Francisco is once more rising rapidly from the ashes of her misfortunes. Every thing like trade is in a flourishing condition. The mining interests have never been in better condition; and the agricultural resources of the State are being de-veloped.

The fire at Sacramento city commenced in the Tehama theatre, and extended to other large buildings. Total damage, as heretofore stated, $30,000.

A case of Lynch law has occurred at Greenwood Valley. The sufferer was a man named Graham, who was hanged two hours after his capture, on a charge of robbery and attempted murder.

The "Vigilance Committee," of San Francisco, continue their labors, at a monthly expence [expense] to the members of three thousand five hundred dollars. A letter of the 15th ultimo, says that they had recently handed over to the court of sessions various offenders who had fallen into their custody.

T. B. McManus, the Irish patriot, is doing a thriving commission business in San Francisco.

The southern papers are advocating a political severance of the lower from upper portion of the State.

Journals from various sections teem with marvels in the way of gold discoveries. We take the richest as samples.

At Mormon Island the company realized in a week over $5,000. On the 9th August, in three hours, $1,250 were washed out. The succeeding day four shares were sold for $10,000. The river about the island is rich almost beyond comparison in California.

A company of seven miners, working in the bed of the river three miles below Coloma, took out $6,000 last week, and they have as much ground to work as will keep them engaged all summer.

The South Fork Mining Company, No. 1. near Mormon Island, took out forty pounds of gold on the 13th. The company numbers thirty members. They have three weeks to work only, having agreed to tear the dam down after that period, in order to permit the company above them to work their claim, upon which the water is locked up by the dam below. The expectation is that $40,000 will be taken out in the time agreed upon.

Thee persons went up on Bear river early in July, a short distance below Steep Hollow, where they turned the river and worked twenty one days. Upon dividing their money they had a little over $2,200 each. In the aggregate, $7,607 30.

A very rich stratum of decomposed quartz, of the same kind as that taken from Gold Tunnel, in Nevada, has been found on Beuna [Buena] Vista Hill, immediately in rear of Judge Walsh's house, at Grass Valley. A panful of this quartz washed out for a prospect, yielded over forty dollars.

One of the richest cayote [coyote] holes ever discovered in Nevada is that owned and worked by Messrs. Huzzey & Co., west of Cryotteville and near the Lawson Tunnel. The gentleman having taken out as high as two hundred and eighteen dollars in a single panfull [panful] of earth; and a few days ago washed out seven hundred dollars in seven consecutive pansfull [panfuls] of earth, they having yielded an average of one hundred dollars to each pan. The hole is kept dry by a large tube, which is hauled up and down upon a windlass worked by a mule. The gold bearing earth is also hauled up by the same means, there being a great scarcity of water, the party consisting of eight men, are unable to use either tom or sluice. They keep, however, two rockers at work with the water drawn from the hole, each cradle yielding an average of one hundred dollars a day. It is impossible, with the two rockers, to wash per diem one quarter of the earth hauled each day, and it has thus become necessary to pile up the extra earth for washing when the rainy season comes on.

The record had its dark features, however, prominent among which we notice an account of the great ravages of the cholera in Mazatlan.

Emigrants report that a severe shock of an earthquake was felt on the 3d July in the vicinity of the Soda Springs and along Bear River, some two hundred miles west of Salt Lake—a highty [highly] volcanic section of the country.

In vol. 3, no. 20 (October 31, 1851): p. 3, col. 3

Later from California [New York, November 16, 1851]

Arrival of the Steamer Daniel Webster

Eleven Days Later from California.

Favorable accounts from the Mines—Agricultural Prospects—Steamboat Disasters and Loss of Life—Movement for a Division of the State—Alarming Progress of Crime—Flattering Commercial Advices—Increasing Receipts of Gold—Later from Oregon, China, and Sandwich Islands—Deaths, Shipping Intelligence, Markets, &c.

New York, Nov. 16—11 p. m.

The steamer Daniel Webster arrived at her wharf here to night at 11 o'clock. She brings four hundred passengers and one hundred and seventeen thousand dollars worth of gold on freight, and about a half million dollars in the hands of the passengers[.]

The Daniel Webster has come via San Juan. She brings California dates to the 15th of October, being eleven days later than what has heretofore been received. She experienced terrible gales for several days, in which her paddle-boxes were carried away. She, however, weathered the storm nobly, to the praise of all on board.

The steamer Central America, at last accounts had made twenty-five miles up the San Juan River[.]

The steamer Director had capsized on the San Juan river, and seven persons were unfortunately drowned.

The general news from California is now very important. Business generally was dull, and purchasers were holding back for a future reduction in the prices of goods.

Flour was steady. Bricks dull. Provisions drooping. Lumber firm. Dry goods active. Seamen's wages very low.

The money market was variably at three to six per cent, per month. Gold dust $17 per ounce. Sight drafts on the Atlantic cities two per cent.

Agriculture was in a flourishing condition, and the mining news was favorable. New discoveries of gold were daily being made. Quartz mining attracts great attention.

The steamer California, from San Francisco, took out $1,000,000 in gold dust. Two other steamers took large amounts.

The receipts into the treasury for fine taxes, and licenses, were $60,000.

Crime was increasing, and many criminals were returning from the interior.

Five of the Fort Oxford exploring expedition had been killed by the Indians.

The steamer Mora had been destroyed by fire, and several lives lost. The boat was a total loss.

The yield of gold for the present year will exceed that of any previous one.

Steam communication between San Francisco and the Sandwich Islands was about being accomplished.

Movements were on foot for a railroad to Sacramento.

Real estate was active and advancing.

The sloop-of-war Vincennes left San Francisco for a cruise southward.

The Alto California thinks that the movements for a division of the State amount to but little.

Wells & Co.'s liabilities are stated at $200,000.

The project of supplying San Francisco with water seems to be falling through.

The steamer Republic, on her voyage from Panama, struck a rock twenty miles from San Francisco, and the water rushed in rapidly as to extinguish the fires. The passengers were rescued and the steamer subsequently gotten off, but it is feared she is seriously damaged.

Effort[s] are on foot to revive the Chamber of Commerce, which had been broken up since the May fire.

The papers of the 9th are filled with duels, murders, and outrages, and there is strong talk of reviving the Vigilance Committee.

Major Reading, the Whig candidate for Governor, was badly wounded by the accidental discharge of his pistol while out hunting.

The Methodists had started a new paper called the California Christian Advocate.

Lynching was still practised [practiced] at the mines.

The Mormons have purchased Rancho del San Bernardino for $100,000, and intend to build a large city there, to connect the Great Salt Lake City with it by railroad and secure a port in San Diego for their marintine [maritime] intercourse with the world.

News from Southern California was of the utmost importance. The southern counties are coming out strongly for a convention to divide the State. Santa Barbara is the place fixed on for holding it. The various counties were engaged in selecting delegates. An address will be prepared for circulation, and a petition presented to the Legislature at an early day in favor of the division.

News from the mines at Carson's Valley are very discouraging. A company of sixty were taking but two ounces daily. Miners at Middle Fork were doing exceedingly well. Several new discoveries had been made at Cold Spring.

The Calamo Damming Company had proved a failure.

The steamer North America had arrived from Panama in thirteen days, being the quickest trip on record.

The rainy season was about commencing. Financial affairs in California was highly flattering.

A letter from San Francisco says the mines are yielding good returns and the miners are daily increasing in numbers, and confidently anticipate a larger yield of gold than upon any previous season. The commencement of another year it is believed, will find our obligations much reduced, and a large proportion of the receipts of the mines will remain invested with us.

Much more confidence being felt, City and State securities have improved.

Our city has recovered in a great measure from the disastrous fires, and merchants are on their feet with renewed vigor. Many foreign house[s] have been permanently established here, and a large amount of capital is seeking investment.

The California Courier says a gentleman called on us yesterday, and exhibited a letter from a friend at the mines, dated Sandy Bar, or Yankee Slide, giving glowing accounts of the success of the miners in that region; some $30,000 per week was being taken from the Slide, and it was not uncommon for a claim of fifteen feet to yield $1,000 to $2,500 per day. From every region is heard the most cheering accounts.

The Marysville Herald thinks the possibility of navigating the Feather and Yuba rivers is no longer problematical.

The El Dorado News is offered for sale, the proprietors desiring to return to the States.

The rapid run of the Baltic had excited great rejoicing.

In vol. 3, no. 24 (December 26, 1851): p. 4, cols. 1–2

9

Westward-Bound Emigrants

Salt Lake Emigrants

It is intended for companies to start from this point, to immigrate to the Great Valley of the Salt Lake so soon as grass is sufficiently grown to sustain cattle and teams. Whenever a company of fifty wagons have assembled at the camping ground on this side of the river near this place, (the precise place will be designated in due time,) they will forthwith be organized and start on their journey. Thia [This] number can travel with much more ease, comfort and speed than any greater number. Our experience has proven this to us. The men and boys that will naturally go wtth [with] fifty wagons, will be quite sufficient to profect [protect] themselves on the journey against the Indians. Every man and boy capable of using a rifle or a musket, should, by all means, have one, and a good one. If any are deficient in this respect, we will furnish every company with what they may lack, provided the captain and principal men of each company will become responsible for the arms and deliver them safely to the High Council in the Valley. As there is quite a lot of arms here that belong there, and we wish to forward them on. The organization of companies will be strictly military, and every man should be amply provided with arms and ammunition adequate to any and every exigence [exigency]. Our experience last year on the Elk Horn River with the Omaha Indians abundantly shows the importance of a rigid observance of the above.

The bill of particulars, embracing provisions, and other articles to be taken, will appear in the Guardian in due time. Every wagon, before starting, will be examined to see if it contains the requisite amount of provisions, utensils and means of defence. If they are deficient in these, they will not be allowed to cross the river to proceed with our companies. The severity of the winter here, awakens some fears that they have had a severe winter in the Valley, and it will be, most likely, thought better to take a greater amount of provisions than was at first anticipated. A few extra barrels of flour will do no harm.

In vol. 1, no. 2 (February 21, 1849): p. 2 col. 3

Salt Lake Emigrants

Having recently heard from Santa Fe that the winter has been very severe there, and that they are losing many of their cattle in consequence of the deep snow; and this place being much south of the Salt Lake, and approximating near to the same Longitude west, we have reason to fear, that they have had a severer winter in the latter place than they anticipated when they wrote their last Epistle, saying to the emigrants to come with only provisions enough to last them through the journey. They will probably have to feed all their surplus grain to their stock to winter them through, and they may lose many of their cattle despite of all their exertions. If they should, it would greatly retard their farming operations for the coming season; and we therefore think it more safe and prudent for all emigrants to the above place to take at least two hundred pounds of good breadstuffs to every soul above two years old; and those under two years old need not be reckoned at all. All other provisions and niceties, according to the taste and ability of the respective families, in like proportion, if possible.

Milch [Milk] cows should be taken by all means, as many of them as possible. For bread, milk, butter, and honey constitute the usual food of the Saints. Animal food costs cruelty and blood, and should be used sparingly by those who fear God and respect the works of his hands. Let the shedding of blood, be the result of actual need; for the Lord hath said unto us: "Woe unto him that sheddeth blood when he hath no need!"

Whenever God has had a people on the earth whom he thought well enough of to speak to from Heaven, he has suffered offences to come upon them; and has even said that they *must needs come*. Why must they needs come? Martyrs' blood must flow to sanctify the people; for "without the shedding of blood there is no remission." Offences are borne by an enemy's hand, and by it, dealt out to the Saints. Jehovah looks upon a sacrifice of this kind for his sake, and sends pardon and forgiveness to his people. From the days of Abel to the days of Joseph Smith, this has been the case. In view of this, Jesus Christ hath said: "Except a man lay down his life for my sake, he is not worthy of me, neither can he be my disciple. The souls of them who were beheaded for the word of God and for the testimony of Jesus, are crying from beneath the altar, and waiting for their exaltation and for their blood to be avenged upon the earth.

The forgiveness of sins costs richer blood than that of beasts—therefore spare the brute as much as possible—but seek not to save your own life; for if you should effect it, you would stay the action of Jehovah in the forgiveness of sins, and consequently lose your life at last. Remember that the blood of your martyred brethren is a blessing in disguise. It is, indeed, "the seed of the church." It is the token of pardon and forgiveness to you; and the seal of condemnation and woe upon those by whom these offences come. "Rejoice ever more. Pray Without ceasing, and in all things give thanks."

In vol. 1, no. 3 (March 7, 1849): p. 2, col. 2

Gold Hunters and Emigrants, Remember

That you who emigrate to the Salt Lake, must either take provisions enough with you to last you until you can raise your own there another year, or take money or goods to buy with after you get there. We have advised you to take useful articles of goods—plough irons, iron, steel, glass, nails, leather of all kinds, and good and substantial dry goods—such as every family really wants, in preference to taking money. Among other things to take there to sell, every family would do well to take a few entire copies of the Guardian from the beginning. They will sell there as readily as anything, and will be very joyfully received in our opinion, because they contain a regular series of our operations here; and our friends in the Valley will thus get much information that cannot be sent them by letter. It will also help to sustain and support our office here, and it is hoped that every friend of the cause will supply himself liberally with the Guardian before he leaves for the West.

Indeed! the attraction of repulsion may be sufficiently powerful in them to keep the Indians away from your camps, that they will not steal your horses and mules, nor trouble you at all. The attraction of cohesion may also be sufficiently powerful in them to draw you right forward to some rich lead or placer of pure gold. Gold hunters, just think of this idea once, and then leave for those *enchanted* regions without a regular file of Mormon papers if you dare risk it. We tell you the Mormons found the gold there; and now don't call us superstitious if we ask you to supply yourselves with plenty of our papers as an essential part of your out-fit.

Should you leave without this pre-requisite, and after you have got well out on the plains, should there discover, off in the distance, a war party of Indians, following you up—then think that you neglected to take the Guardian.

It is our intention to make the Guardian so useful and so efficient that it will even draw out gold where there is no mine at all. Our circumstances are such that we cannot go to the gold regions ourselves, but we would like to have a little gold, notwithstanding, and we know not how to get it, except we say to you, subscribe for the Guardian.

In vol. 1, no. 7 (May 2, 1849): p. 2, col. 4

The Wisconsin and Iowa Union Company

The Wisconsin and Iowa Union Company of Emigrants, organized at Winter Quarters, near Council Bluffs, on the 23d of May, 1849, adopted the following Constitution:

We the undersigned emigrants to California, in view of the dangers attending the expedition, and for the security of our lives and property, and for our safe advancement on the journey, adopt the following rates of government.

ART. 1. This company shall be called the Wisconsin and Iowa Union Company.

ART. 2. This company shall be commanded by a Colonel and two subordinate officers to be called Lieutenant Colonel and Adjutant.

ART. 3. It shall be the duty of the Colonel to take full control of the company, both judicial and military; to determine upon camping grounds, order halts, and make all other orders necessary to the advancement of the company.

ART. 5. It shall be the duty of the Lieutenant Colonel to assist the Colonel in carrying into effect his orders, and in case of disability of the Colonel by sickness or other cause, he shall take command and exercise all powers conferred on that office.

ART. 5. It shall be the duty of the Adjutant to assist the Lieutenant Colonel in all his duties, and to perform the writing of this company.

ART. 6. The Colonel, Lieutenant Colonel, and Adjutant shall be elected by ballot, and the person having a majority of votes shall be declared duly elected and shall hold their office for the term of the journey except removed by a vote of a majority of the company. And in case of vacancy of either of the above named officers by removal, resignation or death, the commanding officer shall order an election to fill such vacancy within twenty-four hours from the time of such vacancy.

ART. 7. Each primary company of which this brigade is composed shall elect one of their number as Captain whose name shall be given to the Lieutenant Colonel, whose duty shall be to see that his company promptly obey orders of commanding officers, and in case of disobedience to report the person or persons to the Lieutenant Colonel or other general officers.

ART. 8. The Captain of the primary companies shall constitute a legislative body to enact By-Laws under this Constitution, to be approved by the Colonel and his assistants.

ART. 9. All teams entering this company single shall form themselves in companies of five teams and shall then be considered as a primary company, and shall elect their captain as required in Art. 7th[.]

ART. 10. All teams and members of this company that have been received, in case of misfortune in loosing teams, or sickness or any other accidental cause, shall be taken by the company as far as the same shall go under this organization—except they shall choose sooner to stop.

ART. 11. An election for the removal of any of the three first named officers may be called at any time by written notices signed by a majority of the Captains of the primary companies, which shall be publicly read to the company by the Lieutenant Colonel, twenty-four hours before the election.

ART. 12. All mock war-whooping and unnecessary firing of guns or pistols after sunset shall be strictly prohibited by the commanding officers.

ART. 13. The members of this company shall observe the Sabbath while upon the journey, so far as to abstain from traveling and secular labor unless under circumstances rendering it absolutely necessary.

ART. 14. The members of this company shall abstain from the use of intoxicating drinks as a beverage, and gaming shall not be tolerated in any form.

ART. 15. Each and every one whose names are hereunto subscribed, do solemnly pledge our honor as men, to strictly and promptly obey reasonable orders of the commanding officers and to use our influence in preserving harmony, and discountenancing all rangling in camp or train.

ART. 16. No alteration or addition shall be made to this Constitution unless by a two-thirds vote of the company.

The following persons were chosen officers.

J. S. Kirkpatrick, Colonel; W. W. Ferguson, Lieut. Colonel, A. M. Blackman, Adjutant.

[*Editors note: A list of eighty-four names follows. See the name index on the* DVD-ROM.]

In vol. 1, no. 9 (May 30, 1849): p. 3, col. 4

Salt Lake Emigrants

Will not forget that we have counselled them to take three hundred pounds of best breadstuff to a person, old or young, when they start from here. They will find this advice in the 10th number of the Guardian.

Some have said, take only enough to last on the journey; others have said, take 150 or 200 pounds to a person: But we have not said it, neither shall we say it to accommodate any man's condition or circumstances: Yet if any man is disposed to venture without the full amount of 300 pounds to the person, let not that person complain of us, nor of the authorities in Valley, but let him take the entire responsibility of suffering or starving on his own hook, and murmur not in pinching times. If you have not the requisite amount of provisions, nor cannot procure it, neither team sufficient to haul it, you can stay in Pottawatamie County till you can go with a proper outfit. Men and Angel's shall know that we have spoken plainly, and warned faithfully; and our garments, in this respect, are clean.

In vol. 1, no. 12 (July 11, 1849): p. 2, col. 1

Emigrants, Be Not Hoaxed

Emigrants for this place from St. Louis and from other parts should remember that they had better land at Saint Joseph than to land at any place above, unless they come all the way to the Bluffs by water. There are facilities at St. Joseph for coming here by land that are not to be found in the woods a little above that place. Steamers will promise to land emigrants within thirty miles of this place, and then leave them in some lonely desolate wilderness a hundred miles distant from this, where, perhaps, unprotected females are subject to the insults of beings whose form and features would disgrace the dignity of the ourang outang [orangutan].

We would say to our friends: be particular and ship for the Bluffs, or only to St. Joseph, so that when you land, you may be in a civilized community.

In vol. 1, no. 16 (September 5, 1849): p. 2, col. 5

To Emigrants

Salt Lake and California Emigrants may depend upon finding heavy stocks of goods in the Kanesville market. Our merchants, having had two years' experience in ascertaining the natural wants of emigrants to the above places, are preparing themselves to meet the demand of this coming Spring's emigration; and our farmers are preparing their wheat for Flouring. The mildness of the winter will leave a large surplus of produce in the country, most likely; and it will be remembered that those emigrants that went on last year through this place, had very little cholera or any other kind of sickness, in comparison with those who took a more southern route. Pass along this extreme northern route, and but few graves will be found along the line, but the graves on the more southern routes are not few nor far between. This should be remembered, and every emigrant should keep as far to the north as possible; for this is a fact that cannot be contradicted in truth, and if emigrants pay that regard to their health which they ought, they will keep up in as high a northern latitude as they possibly can, particularly at the point where they cross the Missouri river.

In vol. 1, no. 26 (January 23, 1850): p. 2, col. 3

Important Little Item

Every emigrant to the Valley should be particular to carry a quantity of small change, such as five, ten, and twenty-five cent pieces, in order to increase the facilities for trade which is often very convenient in that section. A person, however, sitting by our side, who is acquainted with the golden prices in that country, has just remarked; that it is of no use to take five or ten cent pieces to that place, for there is nothing sold so low there as five or ten cents. Such small stuff will buy nothing at all in that country. But we say, take the small change,—dimes and half dimes; and you will soon learn that they will be a great accommodation to yourself and to others. American quarters should be taken, as Spanish quarters are only worth 20 cents, while the former are worth twenty-five cents.

In vol. 2, no. 2 (February 20, 1850): p. 2, col. 4

Nearest, Best and Healthiest Route to the Salt Lake and California

THE OLD ORIGINAL MORMON CROSSING
AT KANESVILLE,
Council Bluffs, Missouri River,
Twenty-five miles above the Mouth of the
PLATTE RIVER.

It has been proven beyond question that the NORTHERN ROUTE, crossing the Missouri river at Kanesville, 25 miles above the mouth of the Platte river, is the

NEAREST, BEST, & HEALTHIEST ROAD TO SALT LAKE AND CALIFORNIA.

The difficulties of crossing the Horn and Loup Fork of the Platte, have been entirely removed by the subscribers placing upon each of those streams large and substantial flat boats.

Heretofore emigrants have had to lose several days in constructing rafts which at last made it rather a a hazardous undertaking. Besides these considerations it is an undeniable fact that hundreds of persons who went up on the South side of the Platte fell victims to the dreadful pestilence while nearly all those who took the north side escaped unharmed. This is the Mormon trail and it is a subject of remark that so few of those people have suffered from disease while on the route. Another thing the emigrant must have in view, and that is their feed and camping places; the routes from Independence, Kansas, Weston, St. Joseph, and all other places below the Platte before going one hundred and fifty miles emerge into one road consequently when there is such an immense amount of travel, grass and wood become scarce. This too is the very end of the road where it is most needed, because emigrants expect to leave early and it is necessary that both "man and beast" should fare well in the beginning. The above is a very important advantage to those who take the north side and is a consideration compared with which all others sink into insignificance for grass is the only subsistence for stock on the plains.

In addition to these facts emigrants will avoid crossing the dangerous streams of the Saline, the South Fork of the Great Platte, and the Great Platte itself.

To sum up the whole in a very few words, the subscribers would respectfully say to the public generally, and all those who contemplate taking this route, particularly, that at the Kanesville Ferry on the Missouri river, they will find two good boats, each capable of crossing one wagon and team.

At the Ferry on the Horn they have one large and substantial boat capable of crossing a wagon and team every five minutes.

At the Ferry on the Loup Fork of the Platte we will have one excellent boat, which, with *the men* we will have in charge will ensure to all a safe and speedy crossing.

Emigrants who wish plenty of grass for their stock, and camping places for themselves, besides the best chance of escaping all epidemics will find this route far preferable over all others.

Our boats with competent hands will be at their places on the 1st of April; and all may rest assured that what we have said may be relied on with the utmost confidence.

In the Kanesville Market, Emigrants will find every thing necessary for their outfits at as reasonable rates as can be procured in the Western country[.]

SARPY, MARTIN & GINGRY.
Kanesville, Feb. 20, 1850.

In vol. 2, no. 4 (March 20, 1850): p. 3, col. 4

Emigration [June 12, 1850]

We have attended the organization of 350 wagons of Salt Lake. Emigrants up to Saturday 8th inst. Capt. Milo Andrews is ahead with fifty wagons. Next follows, Capt. Benjamin Hawkins with one hundred; Thos. S. Johnson, Capt. of 1st division, and—Capt. of Second Division. We left them at Council Grove 12 miles from Bethlehem west of the Missouri river on the morning of 7th inst. Next in succession is Bishop Aaron Johnson with a train of one hundred wagons. Elisha Everett, Captain of 1st Division, and Mathew Caldwell, Captain of the 2d Division. Next in order is Capt. James Pace with one hundred. Richard Session, Captain of 1st Division, and David Bennett, Captain of Second Division. The Emigrants are generally well fitted out with wagons and teams, provisions &c., &c.

There are some wagons quite too heavy. Those brought from St. Louis are good, but too heavy. A ready wagon with a stiff tongue is unsuitable for the journey. Let no person hereafter buy a wagon for this trip unless its tongue has a joint in the [illegible] forward or the axel true. Light wagons that will bear from sixteen to twenty hundred pounds, are the most suitable for this service. These heavy number concerns should be left here, and not used by our people neither by anybody else unless they choose.

The number of California wagons that have [illegible], [illegible] about 4,500 averaging [illegible] to the wagon, making 13,500 men, and about 22,000 head of horses, mules, oxen and cows.

Our own Emigration to Salt Lake Valley will amount to about 700 wagons as nearly as we, at present, can determine. They take two new carding machines in addition to one sent last year, besides which other valuable machinery. They also take about 4000 sheep and 5000 head of cattle, horses and mules.

With the facilities for improvement that are already in the Valley, and those that are now going, we may expect to see that hitherto, desolate region, growing rapidly into importance, and consideration. Success to the West, and to Western enterprise, to Western men and measures! "Let the Wilderness and the solitary place be glad for them, and the desert rejoice and blossom as the rose."

In vol. 2, no. 10 (June 12, 1850): p. 2, col. 1

Emigration

We feel highly gratified to see our emigrants so well fitted out as they are. They generally have two good yoke of oxen, and from one to three yoke of cows to each wagon. The average freight of each wagon is 1850 pounds. The average amount of bread stuffs to the person, old or young, is one hundred and twenty-five pounds—bacon, sugar, coffee, tea, rice, dried fruit, and other little necessaries in proportion.

To see a people who, three or four years ago, had to sell their all to get bread to last till they could raise it; and now see them with from one to four wagons each, with plenty of good team, thousands of sheep and loose cattle, horses, mules, and machinery of various kinds; wagons all new, and stock all young and thrifty, is gratifying in the extreme.

This people are naturally industrious; necessity has forced them to acquire this habit. Public frown upon a poor miserable lounger in our streets is so severe, that he is compelled to go to work or clear out. This is just as it should be. A lounger should be served as drones are served in the hive, or the vagrant law put in force against them.

It has been our aim continually to encourage industry, and inspire every able person to labor steadily and faithfully, in the most advantageous way, pointing out a field for every man to labor in. And it affords us unbounded satisfaction to behold the result in part. Between seven and eight hundred wagons well fitted out for the mountains, are gone from this point this year. May the Guardian ever continue to encourage industry and economy—to suppress vice and promote virtue—to exalt the honest and industrious,—and to scourge and abase the viscious [vicious], the idle, and such as are too short of good and redeeming qualities! And may those who love this stand which the Guardian has taken, subscribe for it themselves, and influence as many others to follow their example as they can. It is true that some have found fault with the strictness of our course, and pronounced us overbearing and tyrannical. But we have this consolation that such as find fault with us, are either idle and wish to live at the expense of others, that are always borrowing, begging, lounging, and never producing anything useful by their own industry and economy. They can sell whisky, and by it, corrupt the morals of society. They can gather pecuniary strength enough by this foul traffic to become very insolent and saucy, as [at] least some of them; they can see every thing but the hook they are swallowing, which, one day, will pull them out of the water, and hold them up in the sun's rays to dry in the sight of all. All men living are now on the stage and are acting their part. Happy is he that chooses that part that will secure to himself the applauses of wise and competent judges!

In vol. 2, no. 11 (June 26, 1850): p. 2, col. 3

The Emigrants to California Commenced Arriving in the Valley

The emigrants to California commenced arriving in the Valley on the 20th of May, and there has been a continual rush. We observe that Mr. Craw's company, was among the first. Thos. S. Williams who left here on the 6th of May with the mail and a company of California emigrants, arrived at Salt Lake in 32 days, their horses and mules in good condition.

In vol. 2, no. 17 extra (September 14, 1850): p. 1, col. 3

North Side of the Platte!

Our Emigrants, by the advice and counsel of the Presidency of the Church in the Valley, corroborated by our own personal observation on both routes, will be turned on the North side of the Platte, the entire distance; not even crossing it at Laramie. This route is, at least, one hundred miles shorter, having less sand, an abundance of grass, plenty of fuel and water; besides much more free from gravel and rocks, so injurious to cattle's feet. Particulars given from time to time; and a guide will be published in due season that will conduct the emigrant by the way that he knew not[.] It will be furnished and ready at this office.

In vol. 2, no. 23 (December 11, 1850): p. 2, col. 2

Early! Early!! Early!!!

Emigrants to the Salt Lake Country should leave this frontier as early as possible in the Spring—go before the heavy rains fall—before the streams and sloughs become swollen,—as soon as grass will possibly sustain your teams—before hot weather, musketoes [mosquitoes] and cholera come, and even before June comes. The awful scenes of cholera and death on the South side of the Platte last year, should be a warning to those concerned, louder than thunder, to avoid a late start, and to avoid the South side of the River. [There are] More than five hundred fresh graves on the South side of the Platte between the Missouri and Fort Laramie, while from the thousands who traveled on the North side, only three graves can be found that were made this last season.

In vol. 2, no. 23 (December 11, 1850): p. 2, col. 2

Emigrants' Guide to Salt Lake and California

Mr. Clayton, the original publisher of this Guide, is justly entitled to much credit and great praise for his diligence, care, perseverance and untiring industry in measuring the distances from point to point on this route, in describing the country, in pointing out the streams and springs of water, showing the distances, in English miles, from one camp ground to another, so that the traveler may always know, when he starts in the morning, how far he has to go before he finds another suitable stopping place. His statements are to be relied on, as thousands of emigrants can testify. We heard a returning emigrant declare, but a short time since, that every person, crossing the Plains, and who was fortunate enough to obtain Clayton's Guide ought to make him a handsome present when he arrives at the Salt Lake City. This declaration met our approval so cordially that we could not withhold our most favorable response. He published a large edition at first; but other men speculated upon them, and he, a poor man, is left unrewarded for his toil.

This Guide takes the emigrant by the hand at Kanesville, Iowa, and safely conducts him over the Missouri River, and gently leads him out westward on the North Side of the Great Platte river,—that route being decidedly the best, shortest and most healthy. We speak from personal knowledge and experience, having traveled both routes last season. Fuel, grass, and water, are the three staples that constitute the emigrant's inn while crossing the plains. These he will find more plentiful and convenient along the route North of the Platte, than he will on the route South of that river.

This route intersects, at Fort Laramie, all others leaving this Western Frontier; and they continue together to the "Pacific Springs," and a little beyond, being a distance of about three hundred miles. All the Alkali or poisonous springs, marshes, ponds and lakes on the entire routes, may be found within these three hundred miles, and they are so accurately describe[d] and pointed out that no person need be mistaken. Every emigrant, therefore, ought to have this Guide, let him start from whatever point he may on the frontier; for by its aid, he can prevent his teams and stock from drinking of those waters that prove almost certain death to them, if they are suffered to drink.

It is satisfactorily ascertained that there is a safe and practicable route on the North of Platte from Laramie Westward; and those who start on the North Side, may continue on, and not cross at Laramie at all, and thus save twice ferrying that stream at a cost of from five to eight dollars a wagon. We have traveled this route the entire distance from the Sweet Water, with the exception of about fifteen miles in the immediate vicinity of Laramie, and found the road for better than on the South side on every account. The Black Hills are avoided, and also much gravel, flint-rock and pebbles, so ruinous to cattles' feet. There were two or three trains that took this route last year, and they pronounced it a good route, with the exception of about five miles through a Bluff Kanyon North, or North-West of Laramie about 12 miles; and even these five miles, they do not consider so bad as many miles on the other route. A little labor will make it quite passable. The outlines of this route will be given in the next paper.

In some places where Mr. Clayton reprosents [represents] plenty of grass, there is little or none at all. Emigrants have all rushed to these places, until their stock have eaten, tramped, and killed it out; though [illegible line] at the time he made the statements: Yet there is generally plenty of grass a little off the road on the hills, or on the high bench land. This applies to the route west of Laramie: East of that Fort, there is plenty of grass on both sides of the Platte.

As to sandy roads, they are just about the same on both routes—the streams and water courses are also about equal. Though the extreme Northern route has the following advantages over any other. It is about one hundred miles nearer—it affords more grass and timber; and water is more convenient and oftener found. There are fewer hills, rocks, stones and pebbles in the road, and while hundreds upon hundreds died of cholera on the Southern routes,—of all the thousands that traveled up this north route last year, only three persons died. One accidentally killed, one drowned, and one died of cholera.

Kanesville, then, is the safe and sure starting point for Salt Lake, California and Oregon Emigrants; keeping on the north side of the Platte, the entire distance. Claytons' Guide for sale at this office.

In vol. 3, no. 1 (February 7, 1851): p. 2, col. 2

Emigration

We notice in some of our exchanges, statements respecting the Oregon emigration this season, which we consider our duty to qualify; because we are on the Frontier, and know the facts relative to this matter. Some of the papers have copiously diffused through their columns, that the Oregon emigration would be but small this year; but we can assure all such, that their statements are not altogether correct. We have had our eye on all these matters, knowing that the facts would be of interest to the public at a future period; therefore we now give them.

The Oregon emigration by this place has been considerable, and they have taken with them the elements of prosperity, and a sure passport to success; their deportment while passing through here, has been orderly and circumspect,—their appearance healthy and indicating the inculcation of frugal and industrious habits, while their manner seemed to be prepossessing and free; they had their families with them. Their wagons and teams were in excellent condition for the plains, and their stock of cows, sheep, &c., looked remarkably well.

We are glad to see people like these, pioneering their way to a new country, for they are certain to make the Wilderness bud, and blossom as the rose, and the solitary place glad. They carry with them a good and savory influence, which cannot fail to benefit society there, and add considerable to Uncle Sam's revenue, also; what is more cheering than to see a class of healthy and robust men, women and children, leaving the halls of refinement, luxury and ease, in exchange for a life of industry and improvement? we leave the public to answer. The very bone and sinew of society, and national prosperity, are dependant upon its agricultural and commercial resources, and enterprise; therefore, the tillers of the soil are at the foundation of national glory, and should be esteemed as the noblemen of the land; we wish them much success. "*Westward the Star of Empire wends its way.*" The Eastern hemisphere is getting dark and cloudy, and the political atmosphere *South* is charged with explosive matter, and is felt by a goodly number of the citizens there; and under a consciousness of doing better *West*, they are leaving their friends and acquaintances,—the field of political warfare and strife, in pursuit of a more agreeable element, and peaceable homes, on the quiet shores of the Pacific. In consequence of the recent heavy rains, the smaller streams, sloughs and rivers, have been unusually high; and the progress of emigration considerably retarded thereby; but now, the weather is clear and cool, grass good—roads improving every day, and every prospect bids fair for emigrants to proceed on their journey without any further trouble or delay.

In vol. 3, no. 10 (June 13, 1851): p. 2, col. 2

Emigration

Of late we are in receipt of letters from almost every State in the Union; these letters are from various persons belonging the Church, and others who do not; asking information relative to the best course for them to pursue, so as to be able to leave this Frontier next Spring, for the Valley of the Great Salt Lake, California, and Oregon.

Our President here, and much respected SENIOR, (Elder Hyde,) being absent, we are to a certain extent at a loss, what to advance relative to the multifarious interrogations these letters contain. Mr. Hyde will soon be here himself, and give such counsel and instruction through the columns of the Guardian, as will no doubt suit the case of every one that has heretofore applied. His object for leaving this place last Spring, and prosecuting a journey across the plains, was with the view of ascertaining from the combined wisdom of the authorities of the Church at Salt Lake, the best possible manner to regulate Church matters in the States, and facilitate the progress of emigration to that place; in other words, to sit in council with the First Presidency of the

Church in the Valley, and be the honored instrument of bearing the result of their united deliberations to the Saints in Pottawatamie—throughout the States, Canada, &c., &c.

In the meantime the Saints would do well, to be up and doing while it is called to-day, and prepare beforehand articles necessary for the trip. A little forethought or pre-meditation has often proved a bulwark against many inconveniences and trouble incidental to a journey across the western prairies and plains: therefore, it becomes the duty of the Saints to be wise as children of the light, and not encumber themselves with goods and chattels which perhaps will not either benefit themselves, or any other person, who may perchance buy them. We have reference more particularly to our brethren abroad, who intend emigrating by this place! Last season, several very good brethren to all external appearance, were detained in Pottawatamie that might have gone to the Valley, were it not for this growing evil; its origin must arise from ignorance, or covetousness; when the latter predominates, gain is the object, more than anything else; therefore, we caution the Saints against this practice, because it leads to loss, trouble, vexation, disappointment, and sometime apostacy [apostasy].

We have been informed from a reliable source that Major Wharton Commandant at Fort Kearney, with a number of the troops stationed at the Fort, recovered all the property stolen by the Pawnee Indians, from Elder Hyde and Company, in the Sand Hills. We are glad to see the timely interference of the Government Officer in this affair, and we understand that the Major had to bring his Cannon in sight, before these Red Skins would consent to surrender any of the stolen property; but it is said, that before he get through with them, that they had to hand over even t[w]o pocket handkerchiefs that were taken by them from the above named company. Success to good men and their measures!

Major J. E. Barrow, Indian Agent, at Bellevue, Nebraska Territory, has been taking very decided and energetic steps lately, to crush the unlawful traffic of trading liquor to the Indians; and also, to recover any stolen property found in their possession. This is also praiseworthy, and we hope that these isolated cases, are only the precursors of a favorable change, and better times for the citizens on this Frontier, and the westward-bound emigrants.

A united effort by the Government Agents, and Officers, with a sufficient number of troops at their command, we think cannot fail to suppress the Sons of the Forest, from perpetrating such high-handed and outrageous acts, as they of late years have done; and for the benefit of emigrants intending to move westward the coming Spring, and all others concerned we would candidly say: that the old Mormon route via Kanesville, Pottawatamie County, Iowa, has been proven beyond doubt to be the safest, healthiest, and best overland route to either Salt Lake, California, or Oregon.

In vol. 3, no. 18 (October 3, 1851): p. 2, col. 2

Immigration

We understand from a reliable source that a number of immigrants are on their way from the Mississippi side of the State, to this place, and likely to winter here. Their real object we have not yet ascertained, but presume that they are either to settle in this and the surrounding counties, or to leave for the West in the Spring.

Much corn, hay, and other articles of provender will be wanted by them no doubt; therefore our friends in the country need not fear, for they will find a ready market for their surplus produce.

We anticipate a large emigration to leave this point next Spring consisting of settlers here, and also a goodly number from abroad. Wisdom is justified of her children.

In vol. 3, no. 20 (October 31, 1851): p. 2, col. 3

10

Marriages

Married

In this town on Monday evening, the 26th ult., by the Editor, Capt. GEORGE D. W. ROBINSON, of Pottawatamie county. to Miss JANE SUTCH, of this place, late from England.

In vol. 1, no. 3 (March 7, 1849): p. 2, col. 5

Married

In this town on the 11th inst., by the Editor, Mr. ARTEMUS MILLET, of Council Point to Mrs. NANCY LEEMASTER, of Silver Creek.

At Carterville, on Sunday, the 11th inst., by the Editor, Mr. WILLIAM H. LEE to Miss HARRIET A. CARTER, both of that place.

The beautiful bride presented us with a fine loaf, and like herself, it was adorned with white, composed of the best material. In short, the genuine article. Long life to the happy pair!

In this town, by the Editor, on the 13th inst., Mr. GILBERT BICKMORE to Miss KATHARINE J. HUNTSMAN.

In this town on Sunday evening last, by the Editor Mr. LEONARD RICE to Miss ELIZABETH BABBITT, both of this place.

In vol. 1, no. 4 (March 21, 1849): p. 2, col. 6

Married

At Rochester, Noble county, Feb. 18th, by the Rev. Mr, Wolf, Mr. Silas Lion to Miss Edith Lamb.

"Our [printer's] devil calls this a beastly affair, but it remind[s] us of the millen[n]ial era spoken of in Holy writ:" "The Lion and the Lamb shall lie down together, and a little child———" our Bible is lost, and we forgot the remainder of the quotation.—[Exchange. [*sic*]

In vol. 1, no. 14 (August 8, 1849): p. 4, col. 4

Married

In this town by Abel Lamb, on the 26th day of October, Mr. ELISHA PETTINGALE to Miss JANE C. MARSH, both of Indian Town.

In Allreds Branch by Abel Lamb, on the 8th day of November, Mr. ALFRED BRIM to Miss MARY ANN MERRILL, both of Allreds Branch.

With the above notices, we received two fine loaves of cake, all covered with a beautiful white frost, and it was sweet too. We thought this quite emblematical of the fair sex. If they do nip with a little frost sometimes, we cannot but confess it is sweet. Long life and good days to the happy pairs who have just appeared on the stage in new characters.

In vol. 1, no. 21 (November 14, 1849): p. 2, col. 5

Married

Near this town, on Thursday, the 26th ult., by our Senior, Mr. WILLIS K. JOHNSON, son of Bishop Aaron Johnson, to Miss LAURA CRANDAL, both of this county and precinct.

The cake and wine were excellent, both of home manufacture. Our [printer's] devil says that if all newly married folks were as mindful of the printer as this graceful couple, their consciences would never be smitten with the unpleasant appearance of his dark visage in their night visions.

In this town, Jan. 21, by Abel Lamb, Mr. HORACE MARBLE, to Miss MARTHA ANN DA[V]ENPORT, both of Poney Creek.

In vol. 1, no. 25 (January 9, 1850): p. 2, col. 5

Married

In this town by the Editor, on Tuesday, the 29th ult., Mr. STEPHEN WIGHT to Miss LUCY WATERBURY.

In vol. 2, no. 1 (February 6, 1850): p. 2, col. 6

Married

By the Editor, at the Indian Mill Branch, on Thursday, 7th ult Mr. Dunford Atwood, to Miss Elizabeth Jane Garner, both of this County.

On the 2d inst., by the Editor, Mr. Oliver G. Workman, to Miss Susan A. Brown, both if this town.

In vol. 2, no. 3 (March 6, 1850): p. 2, col. 6

Married

At Pleasant Valley by the editor on Sunday, the 5th, Inst., Mr. LEWIS WHITESIDES to Miss SUSANNAH PERKINS both of this County.

On Saturday evening last in this town by the Editor, Mr. WILLIAM G. HOWARD, formerly of Kentucky, to Mrs. MARY CATHARINE SHERRATT, both of this place.

Youth and beauty never fade,
Where the lamp of virtue shines,
Where affection feels no shade,
There the ivy wreath entwines.

At Pisga on Wednesday 17th ult., by Elder Cyprian Marsh, Mr. Levi O. A. Colvin to Miss Mary Ann Davis, both of this County.

We wish this newly married couple length of days, and the enjoyments of this world.

In Coonville Precinct, on May 9th, by Elder Joseph W. Coolidge, Mr. Henry O'Neil to Miss Eunice Ellen Thomas all of Coonville.

In vol. 2, no. 8 (May 15, 1850): p. 2, col. 6

Married

At Garden Grove on Sunday 19th ult., by Elder John Bear, Mr. William H. Hales, to Miss Eliza Ann Ewing, both of Decatar, Co. Iowa.

At Garden Grove of Sunday, 19th ult., by Elder John Bear, Mr. Thomas Ewing, to Miss Mary Ann Carson, both of Decatar Co. Iowa.

In this town by Lyman Stoddard, May 26th, Mr. Jacob Baum, to Mrs. Elizabeth Sperry, both near Carterville. Also June 2d, Samuel T. Burgess to Miss Marinda Hartwell, both of Springville.

In vol. 2, no. 10 (June 12, 1850): p. 2, col. 4

Married

On Sunday, October 27, 1850, by Elder David Candland, Mr. Abraham Chadwick, to Miss Mary Foxhall, both of this place,

The cake and wine were truly excellent.

Smile on this union most propitious,
May the cupid god sustain them;
Heavenly joys and not fictitious,
Crown them in the path of hymen,

On Sunday October 20th, 1850, by Elder D. Candland, Mr. George Norvill to Miss Tiresha Cragan, both of this county.

With the above notice we received wine, but from a rather unexpected source, and Elder Candland has our thanks for the favor.

In vol. 2, no. 20 (October 30, 1850): p. 2, col. 6

Married

At St. Louis, Mo., on Tuesday Evening, Oct. 22, by Elder Alexander Robbins, Mr. John T. Caine, to Miss Margaret Nightengale, both of that city.

With the foregoing notice we received something handsome from the *Night-in-gale,* for the benefit of the printersin the shape of a gold dollar, and our "devil" says:

Long may the laurels of virtue enshrine you,
And twine their sweet wreaths, around your abode;
While peace and prosperity send forth their dew,
To freshen the flowers of beauty and love.

On Saturday, Nov. 9th, 1850, by Elder David Candland, Mr. James Procter, to Mrs. Mary Ann Edwards, both of this place.

The Printers forgotten in this *case.*

In vol. 2, no. 21 (November 13, 1850): p. 2, col. 5

Married

In this town by Elder John Gooch, Jr., on the 16th inst., Mr. James Maycock, to Mrs. Ann Leslie, both of this county.

Success and long life to the now happy couple[.]

In this town, by Elder David Candland, Mr. Andrew H. Scott, to Miss Sarah Ann Humphreys, both of this county.

In Garden Grove, Decatur county, Iowa, by Elder Wm. Critchlowe, Mr. John Zimmerman, to Miss Harriet L. Lamb, on the 23d of October, 1850.

In Garden Grove, Decatur county, Iowa, by Elder Wm. Critchlowe, Mr. Levi H. Callaway, to Miss Mary Van Buren, on the 17th of November, 1850.

In vol. 2, no. 26 (January 22, 1851): p. 2, col. 5

Married

In the Carterville Branch, on Tuesday evening, March 27th, by the Editor, Mr. Davis Bartholomew to Miss Ruth J Jones.

Good cake and wine, they too us sent,
We wish them bliss to great extent;

And may their joys increasing flow,
To perfect happiness below.

In this town, on Tuesday, April 1st, by the same, Doctor F. R. KINSMAN to Mrs. DRUZILLA SEYMOUR, both of this town.

If this couple only knew how many good wishes were expressed towards them over the cake and wine sent to the Printers, they might draw consolation therefrom through life. Only keep on good terms with the ladies, and we'll get plenty of cake and wine, and if they will only keep on comfortable terms with the Printer, they will be sure to get good husbands. When the ladies and the Press form an alliance, woe be to the balance that have to come under the lash of their tongues. The ladies and the Press: They govern the world, God bless them.

At Union Branch, by Elder Joseph W. Coolidge, on the 9th March, Mr. JOHN LISTON to Miss SARAH R. NOYES, all of Union Branch, Iowa.

At Union Branch, by Elder Joseph W. Coolidge, on the 16th March, Mr. REUBEN N HOWELL to Miss MARTHA BUCHANNAN, all of Union Branch.

In vol. 3, no. 5 (April 4, 1851): p. 2, col. 6

Married

At Pleasant Valley, by Elder D. Candland, Mr STEPHEN MAHONY to Mrs. MARTHA BEAVER, all of this county.

At Gravois in St. Louis Couuty, Mo., Feb. 21, 1851, by Elder John Sutton, Mr. BENJAMIN WALKER to Miss JANE MCMICHAEL.

At the above place, March 8th, 1851, by John Sutton, HENRY MOORE, to Miss ALICE JAMES, both of the same place.

In vol. 3, no. 6 (April 18, 1851): p. 2, col. 5

Married

In St Joseph, Mo., on the 21 July, 1851, by Esquire Tracy, Mr. WILLIAM JENNINGS of St. Joseph, to Miss JANE WALKER, late from England.

This newly married couple will please accept the thanks of the printer for kind remembrances.

In vol. 3, no. 13 (July 25, 1851): p. 2, col. 5

Married

In this town Sept. 3d, by E. M. Greene, at his residence Mr. Abram Noe, to Mrs. Mary Jane Brown, both formerly of Cincinnati, O.

We stop the Press to announce the receipt of a large bridal loaf; prosperity attend the happy couple.

In vol. 3, no. 16 (September 5, 1851): p. 2, col. 5

Married

At Pleasant Valley, Oct., 19th, by Elder John Gooch, Jr., Mr. Francis R. Stine, to Miss Harriet Stageman, both of this county.

The *oysters*came in, and also the cake,
The red *wine*sparkling, and not bad to take;
Revived the boys, the "devil" not excepted;
STINE did the clean thing, as we expected.

Success to this pair, in hymen's laws blended;
The printers declare the Union defended;
Long may they reap, the reward of this union,
And find in each other a bosom companion.

At North Pigeon Branch, on Sunday, Oct 26th by Joshua C. Hall, Esq., Geo. W. Thorp (late from Indiana,) to Miss Elizabeth C. Allen. Terre Haute Journal please copy.

The printers received a cake, for which the happy couple have their sincere thanks, and wish them many joyous days together, in their new sphere.

At Gravois, St, Louis County, Mo., August 11th, 1851, by Elder John Sutton, Mr. Robert Graves, to Grace Woodcock.

Also Sept. 22d, Henry Wade to Elizabeth Louis.

Also Sept. 22d, Micheal [Michael] Holding to Ellen J. Sherwood.

Also Oct. 3d, Walter Nichol, to Isabela Dean.

In vol. 3, no. 20 (October 31, 1851): p. 2, col. 6

Married

At Oregon, Holt County, Mo., Oct. 9, 1851., by Elder S. P. Comfort, Mr. John Palmer, to Miss Susannah A. Southworth, of McOlney's Camp, Pottawatamie county, Iowa.

May the sunbeams of bliss and happiness hold sway.
And dull care and sorrow, be banished away.

In vol. 3, no. 21 (November 14, 1851): p. 3, col. 5

Married

In this town by the Editor, an the 5th inst., Mr. William D. Turner, Merchant, to Miss Amanda M. Gee, both of Kanesville (Omitted in our last.)

In vol. 3, no. 22 (November 28, 1851): p. 2, col. 6

Married

Near this town, by the Editor, on the 15th ult., Mr. Norman Jarvis to Miss Sarah Ann Shepperson.

Young and pretty was the bride,
Not unlike the opening flower;
May no evils them betide,
In a dark or trying hour.

In vol. 3, no. 25 (January 9, 1852): p. 2, col. 6

Married

At St. Louis, Mo., Dec. 22d, by Elder Thomas Wrigley, Mr. Daniel Field to Mrs. Mary Hardman, both of that City.

With the above the Printers received the cash, for which they wish the happy pair, many years of joy and peace together, in their new relationship.

May their *ship* ever bouyant and strong to the breeze,
Unfurl her broad canvas and swell;

And ride o'er the waves of life's troubl'd seas,
To the Haven of real for us all.

In Little Pigeon Branch, Pottawatamie Co., Iowa, on Thursday 8th inst., by Elder Thomas C. D. Howell, Mr. James Clemons to Miss Sarah Wilson, all of this County.

Cheerful and merry they'll pass down the stream of time without sorrow invading,

With plenty of friends, no foes to condemn, and virtue enshrine them unfading.

In vol. 3, no. 26 (January 23, 1852): p. 3, col. 4

Married

In Coonville, Jan. 12, by Elder Joseph W. Coolidge, Mr. Jacob J. Crocket, to Miss Eliza A. Anson, all of Mills, Co., Iowa.

In vol. 4, no. 1 (February 6, 1852): p. 2, col. 6

Married

At North Pigeon, by Elder Joshua Hall, on the 25th ult., Mr. William Beal to Mrs. Eliza Janes Hardy, both of this County.

Mr. Thomas Winn to Miss Phebe Orton, Jan. 17th.

Mr. Eli B. Hamilton, to Miss Sarah Orton, Feb. 1st.

Mr. Hiram Vanleuven to Miss Nancy E. Bennett, Feb. 5th, 1852, by Elder G. C. Snow, all of Carterville.

In vol. 4, no. 2 (February 20, 1852): p. 3, col. 4

11

Deaths

Died

In this town on the 13th of June last, of consumption, Miss LOLY A., daughter of Moses and Cornelia Clawson, aged 16 years 4 months and 1 day.

Also, in this place of consumption on the 22nd ult. Mr. WALLACE son of Moses and Cornelia Clawson. Aged 19 year, 6 months and 4 days.

Thus has a good and excellent citizen, a worthy and faithful member of the church, been bereft of two members of his family by the withering touch of the icy hand of death. Peace to the memory of the departed, while a hope full of immortality measurably consoles the heart-stricken parents, till again they meet, where the King of terrors has no dominion.

In vol. 1, no. 5 (April 4, 1849): p. 2, col. 5

Died

In this town, on Monday the 16th inst., at 11 o'clock, A. M., at the residence of Mr. John Needham, Miss HANNAH, daughter of ROBERT and ANN BOOTHE, recently from St. Louis. Aged 18 years.

The deceased was a member of the Church and was firm in the faith to the last. She has left behind a character unspotted; a name on which her kindred and friends will ever dwell with delight. She has several brothers and sisters; but at the time of her death they were all absent, except one sister: nevertheless many warm hearted and sympathetic friends crowded round her sick-bed, and every kindness which friendship and affection could bestow, was brought to her aid and comfort. Her sickness was but short—so short that it scarcely seems a reality; and we involuntarily ask ourselves: is it indeed so? Has she passed away from us, no more, on earth, to be seen or heard in the friendly and social circle of society? Yes, sister Hannah, you have left this vale of tears. You have gone from the evil to come, to associate with beings of a purer and higher order. Peace to your ashes. If we are faithful to the end, as you were faithful, we shall soon meet with yon to mingle in the beattitude of Heaven.

In vol. 1, no. 6 (April 18, 1849): p. 2, col. 6

Died

At Lake Branch, August 14th, ALBERT, son of Albert and Susannah Lutz, aged 5 months and 20 days, of disease of the head.

On the 29th ult., SUSANNAH, daughter of Albert and Susannah Lutz, aged 5 months and 3 days of canker.

On Tuesday the 11th inst., JOHN E. only son of JOSEPH E. and HARRIET JOHNSON, aged one year and five months. After a short illness of six days.

"The fairest flowers are soonest called,
The brightest dew-drop falls."

In vol. 1, no. 17 (September 19, 1849): p. 2, col. 6

Died

Near Pigeon Tabernacle, on the 12th, inst. of Diarrhoea, JOSEPH son of Lucius N. and Alice Scovil, aged 13 months and 20 days.

So fades the lovely blooming flower
Sweet smiling solace of an hour.

In vol. 1, no. 19 (October 17, 1849): p. 2, col. 6

Died

In this town, on Friday the 25th inst., PHEBEE B., wife of C. C. Pendleton, Esq., aged 29 years.

In vol. 1, no. 20 (October 31, 1849): p. 2, col. 6

Died

In this town on the 7th inst., of Quick Consumption, Mr. WILLIAM SHERRATT, aged 28 years, late from England.

In vol. 2, no. 4 (March 20, 1850): p. 2, col. 5

Died

We are informed that Oliver Cowdry, [*sic*] Esq., died, at Richmond, Ray County, Missouri, on the 3d day of March last, of Consumption.

In vol. 2, no. 5 (April 3, 1850): p. 2, col. 4

Died

On board the steamer Sacramento on her way to Council Bluffs on the 5th instant. IRVIN H., only son of Wm. H. and Emily C. Branch, from Connecticut, aged 2 years, 6 months and 20 days.

At Bullock's Grove, on the 23d inst., of Small Pox. AMOS GARDNER, son of Moses J. and Polly Gardner, aged 13 years, 2 months and 19 days.

On board the steamer St. Louis, on her upward trip from New Orleans to St. Louis on the 30th ult., of general debility, MARY, wife of James Needham, and mother of John Needham of this place, (from Lancashire England,) aged 61 years.

Mrs. Needham, accompanied by her husband and a part of the family, were on their way from England to join their son (John Needham and family,) at this place; having been seperated for eight years. Although now they have an extensive circle of friends and acquaintances on this, and the other side of the Atlantic to mourn over the loss of an affectionate wife and mother. Yet they feel confident that her merit will be rewarded, and her acts benevolence and kindness remembered in the day of retribution.

In vol. 2, no. 9 (May 29, 1850): p. 2, col. 6

Died

On Monday July 20th, at 1 o'clock, P. M., Mrs. ELIZABETH P. CROMBIE, formerly of Boston, Mass, aged 38 years.

Farewell dear mother, repose in peace,
From worldly care, y've received release,
The sons will meet thee, in a better clime,
Where no death prevail, nor health decline.

Where life, eternal life, sustains,
The vast assemblage on there domains,
Repose in peace, unto you will come,
When God may call us to gather home.

At Council Point, on the 17th inst., John F. L. ALLRED, of cholera, aged 23 years.

In Indian Mill Branch, of the small pox, Wm. B. Coffin, on the 9th of June; aged forty-one years.

Also, on the 4th of August, Lusetta Levens; aged two years and six months.

In vol. 2, no. 14 (August 7, 1850): p. 2, col. 6

Died

In this town on the 21st of August, MARY, wife of Elder Thomas McKenzie, aged 34 years, formerly from virginia [Virginia].

Mary sleep on, and now take your rest,
May your spirit find ease with the rest of the blest,
Your troubles were great and your labors too,
In serving the Lord since you left Nauvoo.

You left us bereaved, dear partner and friend,
But still we take comfort, and cheer up our mind,
With the sweet consolation that you shall arise
In the first resurrection to claim you own prize.

At the residence of Mr. Wm. Goosby, Andrew county, Mo., on Saturday, 12th of July, Mr. CURTIS BLACK, of this county, of some unknown cause.

Mrs. Black is requested to call at our office as soon as convenient, we have a letter for her.

In vol. 2, no. 16 (September 4, 1850): p. 2, col. 5

Died

In Keg Creek Branch, October 16th, 1850, of Conjestive Chills and Inflamation, LOREN DUNN, aged 23 years 6 months and 6 days.

In Child-bed, at St. Louis Mo., on Sunday Sept. 9th at 10 o'clock P. M. CAROLINE the beloved wife of ALVA M. MONTEARTH, formerly of Bradford, Essex County, Massachusetts.

Her saint-like deporment [deportment], coupled with an amiable disposition and truly benevolent heart, won for her while living the affection of her relatives and friends, and now leaves an indelible impression on their minds; all who had the pleasure of her acquaintance loved her most tenderly, and mourn to be bereft of her society thus early in life. Yet they feel comforted and supported, by the unquestionable evidence she manifested to all, that she possessed the same spirit that was in Christ, and having entered into the new and everlasting Covenant, and kept the commandments of God, according to the requirements of the Gospel: she is therefore one of the children of God, and an heiress to eternal life, and as such will have a part in the first resurrection, and will come forth on that glorious morn, to live and reign with Christ upon the earth a thousand years.

Also on 12th Sept. CAROLINE AUGUSTA, infant daughter of the above, aged 12 days.

In this town on Tuesday the 22d inst., of Billious Fever, LETTIS, wife of James Procter of this place, aged 48 years.

In vol. 2, no. 20 (October 30, 1850): p. 2, col. 6

Died

In Linden Mo., on Sunday, Nov. 3d, of the Flux, Maj. G. C. MATTLACK, late Indian Sub, Agent at Council Bluffs.

In vol. 2, no. 21 (November 13, 1850): p. 2, col. 5

Died

West of the Missouri river, and 8 miles east of Salt Creek, June 26th, 1850, SARAH ATLANTA, daughter of George W and Elizabeth M. Catlin, of cholera, aged 3 years and 8 months.

On Platte river, July 5th, 1850, of cholera, ELIZABETH M. CATLIN; wife of George W. Catlin, aged 23 years.

In Harris Grove, May, 25th, 1850, ORMUN, son of John and Angelina Nay, age 1 month.

In vol. 2, no. 23 (December 11, 1850): p. 2, col. 5

Died

In Andrew County, Mo., on the 25th August, of *HEZEKIAH PECK, aged 68 years.

Br. Peck had been a member of the Church of Jesus Christ of Latter-Day Saints, since the year 1830, and ever possessed firm and unshaken faith in the Gospel. M. L. P.

* His death was published in the 22d number, but from an error which occur[r]ed we again publish it.

In vol. 2, no. 26 (January 22, 1851): p. 2, col. 5)

Died

Of palsy, at Pleasant Grove Branch, May 23d, JEREMIAH HATCH, Sen., aged 84 years and 8 months. He was a solder of the Revolution.

On Tuesday, July 2nd, GEORGE SPAIN, from Kent, England, of Congestive Fever, aged 25 years.

In recording the decease of this young saint, we would notice shortly, that in October 1850 he came among us a stranger, and soon manifested a desire to know something of the principles of the Latter-day Saints; to use his own words, he knew not what had brought him thus far west, he knew nothing of the Mormons till he approached near their settlements but so many things were said against them, that as he came nearer to this place, he slept with his knife under his head, but finding that they had been basely and maliciously misrepresented, he mingled freely among them; and during the winter, when others were engaged in the joyous dance, he would sit till past midnight with some who had suffered much among the people; in short, he heard the truth and obeyed the gospel, he was a consistent, faithful, and obedient member, charitable to the poor, oft hauling wood to warm the widow and orphan, over industrious in his out-door labor beloved by many and respected by all, and without even one enemy as far as we know: we can truly testify of him. Blessed is he—he rests from his labors, he died in Christ, and awaits an early resurrection,—when once the vials of God's wrath are poured out upon the wicked and disobedient. His latter end was peace.

In vol. 3, no. 12 (July 11, 1851): p. 2, col. 6

Died

On the way to this place in Monroe Co., on the 22d of June, of Snake Bite, THOMAS, son of John and Elizabeth Mills, formerly of the Isle of Man, Europe.

Millenial Star, will please copy.

At Keg Creek, Upper Crossing, August 8th, 1851, MARY, Daughter of William and Eliza Sommerville, aged 1 year and 10 months, lacking 1 day, of an inflam[m]ation of the lungs, attended with fits.

In vol. 3, no. 15 (August 22, 1851): p. 3, col. 3

Died

At St. Joseph, Mo., on the 25th of June, of consumption, Miss ESTHER SOPER, daughter of Mr. Samuel Soper formerly of Hempstead, Long Island, N. Y.

At St. Louis, Aug. 5th, JOHN HARDMAN, aged about 35 years.

At Oregon, Holt County, Missouri, August 3d, 1851, Mr. THOMAS EDWARDS, of Kanesville, Iowa, late from South Wales.

The deceased was one of the unfortunate inmates of the Bar Room, of F. A. Pollock, that was destroyed by lightning, on the night of the 17th July, as stated by Mr. Jackson's letter. He was at the time of the calamity, a day laborer for Mr. Pollock, employed in mowing and saving Hay, and was consequently sitting in the Bar Room at the time the barrels were burst, and the room filled with burning liquor, which has proven the death of seven of the eight men that were present.

There is no evidence to prove, nor any reason to believe that the deceased had been drinking, or playing cards, or engaged in any unhallowed practice during the day or evening, or even while he was in our County; but after he escaped from the room his burning fragments of cloths were torn off him, his wounds immediately dressed, and from that time until his death, the citizens generally spared no money or pains, that they thought would alleviate his sufferings, and restore his health.

The praiseworthy conduct of Sheriff Beeler, Dr's. G. B. Thorp and A. S. Holladay, deserves particular mention, notwithstanding the deceased was a foreigner, a stranger, a poor man, and a Mormon; these gentlemen provided a room, and hired two brethren to attend to him, and nurse him day and night—furnished board for the nurses, and diet for the sufferer, and dressed his sores once and twice a day as long as he lived, and when he died they furnished him a good coffin and burial clothes, and saw that he was decently buried, at their own expense.

The deceased bore his afflictions and sufferings with almost unexampled fortitude, and patience, and died in the full assurance of a resurrection with the just, and an exaltation in the Kingdom of our Father: he died very willingly, and he even expressed himself anxious to die for five or six days, before the messenger came to his relief. The deceased had ten dollars and forty cents in his pockets at the time of the calamity, which was used to help defray the expences of his sickness. And the County Court at its late cession, refunded the gentlemen above named, their money, and paid all bills presented, growing out of the late disaster, out of the County Treasury.

The deceased said he had two cousins, living at, or near Kanesville, and he wished them informed of his death, and burial; it is to gratify this his last, and very reasonable request, and to try to do justice to, or say a word in behalf of the citizens of this place for their magnanimity and kindness to a stranger, that I make this communication.

Very Respectfully Yours,
In the Covenant of Peace,
S. J. COMFORT.
Oregon, Mo., Sept. 5th, 1851.

In vol. 3, no. 16 (September 5, 1851): p. 2, col. 5

Died

At Council Point, on Wednesday the 8th inst of Congestive fever, Dr. George Coulson, aged 50 years and 18 days.

Br. Coulson occupied a conspicuous place among the Saints in Pottawattamie,—he was a member of the High Council,—and President of that portion of the High Priests Quorum remaining here. He was a kind father, a good husband, and a faithful brother in the Kingdom of God, and left a wife and family to lament his loss, in connection with many warm friends. We saw him while he lay in his coffin, open to the view of his numerous friends who had gathered from different sections of the country to perform that ceremony that man owes to his fellow-man, and while gazing upon the mortal remains of the departed, our inward thoughts suggested:

That he lay like a warrior taking his rest,
With his martial cloak around him.

In this town on the 2d of October, Miza Lyonia Pratt, infant son of William D. and Losana Pratt, aged one year five months and thirteen days.

At Council Bluffs, on the 28th September, 1851, Hannah Ford, in the 50th year of her age, formerly of Oneida Co., N. Y.

She died, leaving six children to mourn her loss, and in the faith of Latter Day Saints. Her death leaves a blank hard to be filled in the place where she resided. Peace to her ashes.

In vol. 3, no. 19 (October 17, 1851): p. 2, col. 5

Died

In Kanesville, on Friday, 21st inst., of Typus Fever, Elder William Howell, late from Abardare, Wales. Aged 36 years.

Brother Howell has left behind him a name immortalized,—not engraven on monuments of wood and stone, the devices of men's hands; but gloriously inscribed with the sprit of the Highest on the tablet of a pure, and honest heart which he has been instrumental in turning from darkness to light, and from the power of sin unto the service of the living God.

DEATH, like the *hour frost*does often pass by,
The stalwart and strong of the Earth;
While the pure and lovely violet lies,
Benumbed beneath his cold breath.

At Plumb Hollow Branch, October 12th, Mary Scrogge, wife of Archibald Scrogge, a native of Scotland.

In Kanesville, on Thursday, the 20th inst., of Typhus Fever, PATIENCE D. NAOMA, daughter of Abraham and Patience D. Palmer, aged 7 years.

In vol. 3, no. 22 (November 28, 1851): p. 2, col. 6

Died

At Platte City, Piatte Co., Mo., on the 20th of October, JANE, wife of John J. Allred, aged 24 years. She left 3 children, (the youngest ten days old) to lament her loss.

Deseret News please copy.

In vol. 3, no. 24 (December 26, 1851): p. 3, col. 4

Died

At Honey Creek, Oct. 10, 1851, ELIZABETH AVEYARD, of black canker Aged 60 years.

November 14th, '51, of black canker, SARAH AVEYARD. Aged 32 years.

Also, Dec. 7th, '51, her husband, BENJAMIN AVEYARD, of consumption. Aged 35 years.

They were natives of Stockport, England, came from Fall River, Mass., last spring, and were bound for Salt Lake Valley.

In vol. 3, no. 25 (January 9, 1852): p. 2, col. 6

Died

At Council Point, on the 8th ult., ORLIVA, daughter of Orrin D. and Flavilla Farlin, aged 19 months.

In St. Joseph, Mo., on the 16th day of December, 1851, MARY GREENALGH. Aged 37 years.

She has left a family of small children to mourn a mother's loss. She was formerly from England having joined the Church there, and passed through all the persecutions in Illinois, is now gone to reap the reward of the righteous in a world with out end.

In vol. 4, no. 2 (February 20, 1852): p. 3, col. 4

12

Words of Wisdom

A Promise

A promise should be given with caution, and kept with care. A promise should be the result of mature reflections. A promise and its performance should like the scales of a true balance present a mutual adjustment. A promise delayed is justice deferred. A promise neglected is an untruth told. A promise attended to is a debt settled.

In vol. 1, no. 2 (February 21, 1849): p. 4, col. 6

A Short Sermon for Parents

It is said that when the mother of Washington was asked how she had formed the character of her son, she replied that she had endeavored early to teach him three things, obedience, diligence and truth. No better advice can be given by any parent.

In vol. 1, no. 3 (March 7, 1849): p. 4, col. 6

Keep a Close Mouth

Keep a close mouth in the presence of him that is curious to know all the particulars of your affairs.

In vol. 1, no. 7 (May 2, 1849): p. 3, col. 1

True and Beautiful

Some one has remarked, with equal truth and beauty, that education does not commence with the alphabet. It begins with a mother's look, with a father's nod of approbation or sign of reproof, with a sister's gentle pressure of the hand or a brother's noble forbearance. With hands-full of flowers in green daisy meadows, with birds admired, but not touched, with creeping and almost imperceptible emmets, with humming bees, and glass bee hives, with pleasant walks in shady lanes with thought directed, in sweet and kindly tones and words, to nature and acts of benevolence, to deeds of virtue and to the source of all good, to God himself.

In vol. 1, no. 14 (August 8, 1849): p. 4, col. 5

Best Shield

The best shield against slanderers is to live so that nobody will believe them.

In vol. 1, no. 14 (August 8, 1849): p. 4, col. 5

Youth and Old Age

Youth indulges in hope—old age in remembrance.

In vol. 1, no. 26 (January 23, 1850): p. 4, col. 2

Real Excellence

Those who possess any real excellence, think and say the least about it.

In vol. 2, no. 1 (February 6, 1850): p. 3, col. 4

The Contented Man

The contented man is the richest man, and also the happiest man. In earthly things he wishes no more than nature; he can frame his thoughts to his estates, that when be hath heart he cannot want, because he is as free from desire as superfluity. He has seasonably broken the headstrong restiveness of prosperity, and can manage it at pleasure.

In vol. 2, no. 4 (March 20, 1850): p. 1, col. 4

Patience is a Power

Patience is a power in man, warning him to reign his spirit.

In vol. 2, no. 6 (April 17, 1850): p. 1, col. 6

An Investment in Knowledge

Dr. Franklin, speaking of Education, says: "If a man empties his purse into his head, no man can take it away from him. An investment in knowledge always pays the best interest.["]

In vol. 2, no. 9 (May 29, 1850): p. 1, col. 3

Concealing Sacrifices

Some persons are capable of making sacrifices, but few are capable of concealing how much the effort has cost them; and it is this concealment that constitutes their value.

In vol. 2, no. 10 (June 12, 1850): p. 4, col. 4

Say Little

Say but little, think much, and do more.

In vol. 2, no. 19 (October 16, 1850): p. 1, col. 5

Omission

Omitting to do good, is to commit evil.

In vol. 3, no. 6 (April 18, 1851): p. 1, col. 2

Property

Property left to a child may soon be lost; but the inheritance of virtue—a good name, an unblemished reputation—will abide for ever. If those who are toiling for wealth to leave their children, would take half the pains to secure for them virtuous habits, how much more serviceable would they be. The largest property may be wrested from a child, but virtue will stand by him to the last.

In vol. 3, no. 18 (October 3, 1851): p. 1, col. 4

Worry

To enjoy to-day, stop worrying about tomorrow. Next week will be just as capable of taking care of itself as this one. And why shouldn't it? It will have seven days more experience.

In vol. 3, no. 25 (January 9, 1852): p. 1, col. 5

Wounded Feelings

Have any wounded you with injuries, meet them with patience; hasty words rankle the wound—soft language dresses it, forgiveness cures it, and oblivion takes away the scar.

In vol. 3, no. 26 (January 23, 1852): p. 1, col. 4

13

Humor

Modern Dictionary

MARRIAGE—The gate through which the happy lover leaves his enchanted regions and returns to earth.

DEATH—An ill-bred fellow who visits people at all seasons, and insists on their immediately returning the call.

AUTHOR—A dealer in words, who gets paid in his own coin.

BARGAINS—A ludicrous transaction in which each party thinks that he has cheated the other.

CRITIC—A large dog that goes unchained and barks at every thing that he does not comprehend.

IMPOSSIBILITIES—Dinner at a hotel without mince pies or bread pudding, and breakfast on a steamboat without sausages.

JURY—Twelve prisoners in a box to try one or more at the bar.

GRAVE—An ugly hole in the ground, which lovers and poets wish they were in but take uncommon pains to keep out of it.

LAWYER—A learned gentleman who rescues your estate from your enemy and keeps it himself.

POLICEMAN—A man employed in the corporation to sleep in the open air.

TONGUE—A little horse which is continually running away.
HONESTY—An excellent joke.

In vol. 1, no. 2 (February 21, 1849): p. 4 col. 6

Going Off Well

A person who had been listening to a very dull address, remarked that every thing went of[f] well, especially the audience!

In vol. 1, no. 3 (March 7, 1849): p. 4, col. 6

Gentlemen

"Men are made in the image of God." Gentlemen are manufactured by barbers, tailors, and boot blacks.

In vol. 1, no. 14 (August 8, 1849): p. 1, col. 4

Hot Water

Men are frequently like tea;—the real strength and goodness is not properly drawn out of them till they have been a short time in hot water.

In vol. 1, no. 14 (August 8, 1849): p. 4, col. 5

Lady's Hair

Why is a lady's hair like a bee-hive ? It holds the comb.

In vol. 2, no. 9 (May 29, 1850): p. 3, col. 4

Mrs. Partington's Last

"I verily believe," exclaimed the old lady, "that all those bills they talk about in Congress, are counterfeit they are so hard to pass."

In vol. 2, no. 10 (June 12, 1850): p. 4, col. 4

Lawyer

I, think now I see a new *fee*-ture in this case, as the lawyer said, when his client informed him that he had plenty of money.

In vol. 2, no. 11 (June 26, 1850): p. 4, col. 3

Phonography

A lazy boy out in Indiana spells Andrew Jackson thus:—&ru Jaxn.

In vol. 2, no. 13 (July 24, 1850): p. 4, col. 3

Graveyard

A little girl, walking one day with her mother in a grave-yard, reading one after another the praises of those who sleep beneath, said: "I wonder where they bury the sinners?"

In vol. 2, no. 15 (August 21, 1850): p. 4, col. 3

Lazy

Constitutionally tired is now the polite way of expressing the fact that a man is naturally lazy.

In vol. 2, no. 19 (October 16, 1850): p. 4, col. 3

Butter

We heard a good joke once of a party of young fellows who found fault with the butter on the boarding-house table.

"What is the matter with it?" said the mistress.

"Just you ask it." said one, "it is old enough to speak for itself."

In vol. 3, no. 3 (March 7, 1851): p. 4, col. 1

Married Man

Why is a married man like a medical student? Ans.— He must listen to lectures.

In vol. 3, no. 8 (May 16, 1851): p. 1, col. 3

Father's Asses

Three students at college met an aged countryman, and wishing to have a little sport with him, thus accosted him. The first said—"Good morning father Abraham," the second, "Good morning, father Isaac," and the third, "Good morning father Jacob," the old gentleman replied, "I am neither Abraham, Isaac, nor Jacob; but I am Saul the son of Kish, who went to seek his father's asses, and lo! I have found three of them."

In vol. 3, no. 9 (May 30, 1851): p. 4, col. 2

What a Pity

An exchange paper says the girls in some parts of Pennsylvania, are so hard up for *husbands*, that they sometimes take up with Printers and Lawyers. *Poor souls!*

In vol. 3, no. 19 (October 17, 1851): p. 4, col. 3